NACONDA

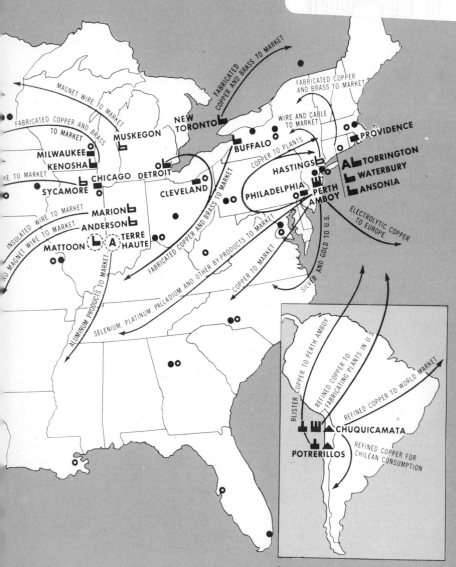

FABRICATED COPPER AND BRASS TO MARKET

FABRICATED COPPER AND BRASS TO MARKET

FABRICATED COPPER AND BRASS TO MARKET

MAGNET WIRE TO MARKET

FABRICATED COPPER AND BRASS TO MARKET

WIRE AND CABLE TO MARKET

RE TO MARKET

NEW TORONTO

MUSKEGON

MILWAUKEE
KENOSHA

PROVIDENCE

BUFFALO

COPPER TO PLANTS

HASTINGS

TORRINGTON
WATERBURY

CHICAGO DETROIT

PERTH AMBOY

ANSONIA

SYCAMORE

CLEVELAND

PHILADELPHIA

INSULATED WIRE TO MARKET

MARION

ELECTROLYTIC COPPER TO EUROPE

U MAGNET WIRE TO MARKET

ANDERSON

FABRICATED COPPER AND BRASS TO MARKET

MATTOON

A TERRE HAUTE

COPPER TO MARKET

ALUMINUM PRODUCTS TO MARKET.

FABRICATED COPPER AND BRASS AND OTHER BY-PRODUCTS TO MARKET

COPPER TO MARKET

SILVER AND GOLD TO U.S.

SELENIUM, PLATINUM, PALLADIUM AND OTHER BY-PRODUCTS TO MARKET

BLISTER COPPER TO PERTH AMBOY

REFINED COPPER TO 7 FABRICATING PLANTS IN U.S.

REFINED COPPER TO WORLD MARKET

REFINED COPPER TO FABRICATING PLANTS IN U.S.

CHUQUICAMATA

POTRERILLOS

REFINED COPPER FOR CHILEAN CONSUMPTION

ANACONDA

The American Brass Company
Anaconda Wire & Cable Company
Andes Copper Mining Company
Chile Copper Company
Greene Cananea Copper Company
Anaconda Aluminum Company
Anaconda Sales Company
International Smelting and Refining Company

Anaconda

ANACONDA

By ISAAC F. MARCOSSON

Illustrated

DODD, MEAD & COMPANY · NEW YORK

HD
9539
.C72
A6

LIBRARY OF CONGRESS CATALOG CARD NUMBER: 57–9380
PRINTED IN THE UNITED STATES OF AMERICA
BY KINGSPORT PRESS, INC., KINGSPORT, TENNESSEE

TO

THE MEMORY OF

MARCUS DALY

FOUNDER OF ANACONDA

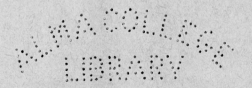

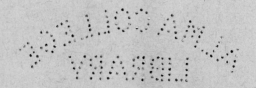

ACKNOWLEDGMENTS

One of the compensations that the author has derived in writing this book has been the spirit of generous cooperation shown by the men associated with the Company. From Cornelius F. Kelley to the managers of plants and mines from Montana to Chile, they have manifested pride in the fact that the story of their great corporation was at last to be authoritatively published. Mr. Kelley's fabulous memory has been matched by his unflagging interest in the undertaking. Mr. Glover, Mr. Weed and Mr. Dwyer have given invaluable assistance.

Of particular aid have been E. O. Sowerwine who has drawn unsparingly upon his long and intimate knowledge of company affairs, Mord Lewis, J. D. Murphy, Thomas E. Conrad and last, but by far not least, my wife Ellen Petts Marcosson, who accompanied me on my visits to every Anaconda installation in the United States and to Chuquicamata.

The author is also deeply indebted to E. G. Leipheimer, for many years the able editor of The Montana Standard, whose admirable manuscript, "Anaconda, A Story of American Enterprise," prepared in 1946, has been of inestimable value. The material assembled by Claude Rice was likewise useful.

Among the books read were "The Brass Industry" by William G. Lathrop, "You and the Atom" by Gerald Wendt, "Atoms for

Peace" by David O. Woodbury, "The War of the Copper Kings" by C. B. Glasscock, "Copper Camp" by the Writers' Program of the Works Project Administration of the State of Montana, "The Journals of Lewis and Clark" edited by Bernard de Voto, "Apex Controversies at Butte" by Reno H. Sales, "George Hearst, California Pioneer" by Mr. and Mrs. Fremont Older, "The Pulse Beat of Industry," McGraw-Hill, "Romantic Copper" by Ira B. Joralemon, "Montana Wide and Handsome" by Joseph Kinsey Howard, "The Story of Copper" by Watson Davis, "Montana the Magnificent," Montana Power Company, and "The Porphery Coppers" by A. B. Parsons.

The periodicals read included Fortune, December 1936 and 1937; Mining World, July, August and September, 1954; Engineering and Mining Journal, August 1954 and May 1955; Life, August 8; "The Yerington Story" reprinted from Explosives Magazine; "Mining Engineering," December 1952; "Metal Progress," September 1950; reports of the Brookhaven National Laboratory; The Hungry Horse News, and many issues of The Montana Standard.

I. F. M.

CONTENTS

ILLUSTRATIONS

Photographic supplement follows page 82

ANACONDA

♤ 1

THE ANACONDA EMPIRE

O N A crisp October morning in 1875 a former soldier in the Union Army staked out a claim on a hill overlooking what is today the city of Butte. Below him straggled the crude streets of a mining camp bent on gold and silver. Beyond him the snowy peaks of the Rockies gleamed under a bright autumnal sun. All around stretched the dusty Montana plain. The prospector was Michael Hickey; the claim to which he had registered ownership was the Anaconda mine, destined to become a fabulous copper producer that made its site and the adjacent area the richest hill on earth. From that hole in the ground on Butte Hill, cradle of a copper Golconda, stemmed the Anaconda empire stretching from the Rockies to the Andes with its constructive impress laid on two continents.

The story of the Anaconda Company is more than the history of the birth and farflung expansion of a corporation that has become the largest non-ferrous mining and metal fabricating organization in the world. It is also the biography of an achievement rich in romance and shot through with high industrial adventure that has recorded an epic in mining. Anaconda spans the evolution in mining and metallurgy. It stands as a monument to Free Enterprise as well as an enduring tribute to big-visioned men of the type of Marcus Daly, Cornelius F. Kelley and John D. Ryan whose courage, character and fortitude combined to make mining and industrial history, and likewise vivify the familiar American tradition of self-made success.

The annals of industry project no more inspiring chapters than are written in the careers of the pioneer and the major builders of Anaconda. You have Daly, the penniless Irish immigrant boy who worked as dock laborer in New York, risen to be a copper king; Kelley, whose first pay was as dollar-and-a-half-a-day water boy for a gang of railroad construction huskies, becoming the dominating force in the progress of the company; Ryan, the onetime clerk in a country general store, twin pilot with Kelley in shaping the course of the industrial saga which is Anaconda. Other able men in the company, yesterday and today, have mounted from modest beginnings to important executive posts to make notable contributions to mining research, operation, metallurgy and technology.

The human qualities compounded into the creation and expansion of Anaconda are identical with the elements that were woven into the fabric of American democracy. From Daly through Kelley there have been the projection of rugged individualism and the impetus of dogged initiative that made Anaconda the pioneer of the modern large scale copper mining industry in this country and the pathfinder, as well, in its ramified activities from ore to metal product.

Another element shaped the early course of the company and animated its development. It was the infusion of western capital that made the initial development of the Anaconda mine possible. Sparking this capital was the pioneer, uninhibited spirit of the West which has been a motivating factor ever since.

The West contributed not only the original capital but also the first know-how that made the Butte District the greatest mining area in all metal history. From Nevada came the mining methods so successfully employed later at Butte; from Colorado came the men who built and operated the first successful smelter in Montana; from California and Missouri came the Argonauts who opened the first gold and silver diggings that resulted in Daly's discovery of the rich copper vein on The Hill. Thus the beginnings of Anaconda reflected the pioneer, adventurous temperament which was its heritage from the West.

All the dictates of business prudence should have told Daly to withdraw from what became a treasure trove when, to his momentary dismay, the Anaconda mine changed from silver to copper. In that crucial hour in the history of Anaconda and of Butte, the United States was not a copper consumer. Gold and silver were the objectives of man's desire. Copper was employed only for sheathing ships, roofing churches and public buildings, cooking utensils, wash boilers, light cannon, massive doors, bronze bells and brass hardware. Far ahead loomed the era when the red metal would be indispensable, the most useful, save iron and steel, of all the metals. Moreover, Butte was difficult of access; the processes of ore reduction were primitive; Montana was still a frontier.

Imbued with the spirit of the West, Daly persisted. Copper was a challenge to his adventurous makeup and with copper he laid the foundation of an empire. The syndicate that financed him had faith in the ruddy, smiling Irishman. That faith paid off and mining history was written.

Since copper was the foundation on which the structure of Anaconda was reared, it is important to define its genealogy and, what is more important, its influence upon the nation's economy.

No metal, save perhaps gold, has so romantic a background as copper—well termed the metal of destiny. It is bound up in history and legend down the ages unfolding a drama of compelling and dramatic interest. Because it is found in nature in a free metallic state or in ores that are readily reduced, it was the first metal used by the human race preceding the use of iron by about four thousand years. Eight thousand years before the dawn of the Christian era it was employed by the Incas in Peru, the Egyptians, the Chinese, the races of Asia Minor and the Romans and the Greeks. The first source of copper is attributed to the Island of Cyprus. There it received its initial name. The natives called it Cyprium metal. Later the Romans termed it Cyprum. Subsequently it became copper.

Copper is the most important of all non-ferrous metals, both in quantity and value of world output. Copper-bearing bronze was the first alloy to be employed by man. So extensive was its substitution for stone in making weapons, tools and utensils that an early period came to be known as the Bronze Age.

The early quest for gold wrote a serial of conquest by force of arms and ruthless ravishment of nations, as was the case of Mexico when the Aztecs felt the brutal impact of Cortes. So, too, in Peru under the iron hand of Pizarro. With copper there was no conquest by military might. Its discovery was accidental. An ignited oil seepage that came in contact with an outcrop of ore revealed the red metal. Henceforth, its development was along the road of peace and utility.

Copper, which was to contribute so vitally to the structure of American industry, was dug centuries ago by Indians on the Keweenaw Peninsula in Michigan, seat of the first major production in the United States. Because of its malleability, toughness, corrosion resistance, conductivity and capacity to alloy, copper became the indispensable metal.

The average person has never bought a pound of copper yet he uses it in some form every day from the time he enters his bathroom in the morning to switch on the light to the moment when he turns off his bedside lamp and goes to sleep. Moreover, nearly every activity in his house is geared to copper. The utensils and gadgets in his kitchen, the lights that illumine his rooms, the car he drives and the telephone the family uses, all are geared to copper. Whether he is in the home, the office or the factory, whether he travels by railroad, bus, airplane or steamship, man's activity today is linked with copper.

We measure our economy largely in terms of tons of steel, barrels of oil and kilowatts of electricity, but these measures of our progress and production would be well-nigh impotent without the employment of copper. Copper is the keystone in the industrial arch from which the United States has soared to world productive supremacy with its miracle of the assembly line and mass output.

This supremacy stemmed to a large degree from 1882, a year historic in the story of Anaconda because in that year Daly took over the Anaconda mine to make it the cornerstone of a vast domain and launch an era in copper. That year also witnessed another momentous event closely linked with copper because before those twelve months passed into history, the Age of Electricity was born and with it a new World of Light, Power, Communication and Transportation.

In September 1882 Thomas A. Edison started the Pearl Street generating station to light the streets of New York, the first plant for the transmission of electric power in the United States. Edison had produced the first commercial incandescent lamp in 1878, putting into practical use the amazing force discovered nearly a century previous by Galvani. With that history-making achievement the Wizard of Menlo Park was instrumental in opening a field for copper then beyond the vision and dreams of men.

The Pearl Street station supplied the electric power for five thousand lights. Two years later it supplied eleven thousand lights. The pioneer plant used 128,793 pounds of copper for wiring and equipment, an insignificant amount compared with the vast tonnage now employed in the United States for the millions of miles of our telephone and telegraph lines, to say nothing of the miles used for farm, factory and community service. The electrical industry has become an industry of superlative growth, exceeding all others in the use of copper, a major factor in the American way of life with its comforts and conveniences which have wrought the highest standard of living anywhere.

Most people think of Anaconda as solely a copper producer since its name has become synonymous down the years with that of the red metal. As a matter of fact, copper accounts for barely half of its metal production. Anaconda not only operates mines in half a dozen states and in three foreign countries but also concentrates, smelts, refines, fabricates and conducts a host of other operations as the plants at Anaconda; Columbia Falls and Great Falls in Montana; Weed Heights in Nevada; Perth Amboy and a score of places elsewhere throughout its vast domain attest. With the acquisition of The American Brass Company and later the creation of Anaconda Wire & Cable Company, it entered the fabricating field to obtain an outlet for its metals under the aegis "From Mine to Consumer." Anaconda installations are dispersed from the Naugatuck Valley in Connecticut to the western slopes of the Rockies; from a Butte shaft a mile underground to an Andes headframe 11,000 feet above sea level. Such are the types of operation that combine for the world's greatest non-ferrous metals enterprise, both as producer and fabricator. Until the Iron Curtain separated it from alien operation, Anaconda conducted an important lead, coal and zinc operation in Silesia.

Anaconda has more metal in its ore reserves today than ever before in its seventy-five year history. Its Chuquicamata mine in Chile is the world's greatest single copper ore body with more than a billion tons of ore hidden in the massive Andean slopes, while the Greater Butte Project's

Kelley mine, the new Berkeley Pit, Ryan Shaft, the Northwest Project, the Special Development Program and other reserves account for 40,000,000 tons of copper or more than one-fourth of the known world copper reserve. This means 80,000,000,000 pounds of the red metal. Furthermore, the development of old and dormant mines on the famous Hill at Butte and elsewhere is stepping up output and reserves with advanced technology that make for more economic and efficient operation. The Anaconda Geological Department is ceaselessly prospecting in a dozen states, Chile, Canada and Mexico; in fact, wherever there is a possibility of a copper or zinc ore deposit in the Western Hemisphere.

With two products Anaconda is supreme: The company is the largest producer of zinc in the United States, accounting for twenty per cent of the domestic production. With further development of the Butte mining area, Anaconda became the biggest manganese producer in this country, turning out ninety per cent of the total United States production. The production of ore at Butte and its processing at Anaconda, Montana, into nodules have been followed by the development and operation of ferromanganese plants in Anaconda and Great Falls. This project has contributed much to the economy of the United States and to the welfare of the company.

Copper, zinc and manganese comprise only part of Anaconda's twenty mineral products which are all metals save for phosphate rock and sulfur. The rock is employed to make treble superphosphate and phosphoric acid, while the sulfur is used to process copper ore. The company owns the Leviathan sulfur mine in California. Then, too, there are the other ore products, chief of which are gold, silver, lead, cadmium, bismuth, iridium, arsenic, platinum and selenium.

Two comparatively new operations reveal how Anaconda has marched with scientific advance and met an expanding utilitarian need. Near Grants in New Mexico the company's

Jackpile uranium mine, which tops all others in size and output within the confines of this country, is making a significant contribution to the manifold possibilities of atomic power for the pursuits of peace as well as war. In 1955 the company dedicated its aluminum plant at Columbia Falls, Montana.

Anaconda's ownership of nearly 400,000 acres of Montana timber and the sawmill at Bonner contribute an operation typical of the degree of self-sufficiency that has been such a factor in the expansion of the company. Anaconda owns water-supply companies, seven daily newspapers and a weekly, and the forty-mile electrified railroad that hauls the Butte ore to the Anaconda reduction plant. In Chile the company operates railroads, ships and other service facilities.

Anaconda has kept pace with the ever-changing evolution in mining. Methods have changed from the simple hand procedure of highly selective mining to the mass production operation of block-caving and open pit mining which permit the exploitation of comparatively low grade ore bodies. The open pit is the most economical of all mining operations.

Metallurgy, too, has changed. Tools and processes are continually improved. Many of the important developments in this field have been engineered by Anaconda's staff and are in wide use throughout the industry. With the grade of ore now being treated in the United States, averaging less than nine-tenths of one per cent copper, the importance of work in this field is evident. Improved methods of ore treatment, together with intensive development, account for the fact, already indicated, that Anaconda now has a greater tonnage of ore reserves in its properties in the United States and Latin America than at any other time in its history.

Developments in brass and wire mills have continued apace with Anaconda to the fore. Today 3,000 pound copper cakes are rolled into continuous coils of strip metal for the automotive industry. Discovery of new uses for copper occur daily in electronics and other fresh fields. All these advances are the traditional far cry from the brass buttons and copper kettles that were the mainstay of the brass industry when it began in the Naugatuck Valley of Connecticut a century and a half ago.

Over the years Anaconda's financial structure has grown tremendously. In 1895 it was incorporated at $30,000,000. Total assets at the end of 1955 exceeded $911,000,000 and shareholders' equity was $701,000,000. Book value of lands and mining claims was $263,000,000 and of plants, $655,-000,000 before depreciation. Working capital amounted to $183,000,000.

Since 1895, including production of subsidiary companies from date of acquisition, the company has produced 36,-900,000,000 pounds of copper, 10,500,000,000 pounds of zinc, 4,100,000,000 pounds of lead, 742,000,000 ounces of silver and 5,800,000 ounces of gold. The company's fabricators have marketed 27,400,000,000 pounds of copper and brass products since 1922. Reckoned in dollars, the sales of metals, products and services have totalled $10,500,000,000, which, together with the $130,000,000 owned on notes at December 31, 1955, after the payment of taxes, direct and indirect labor, supplies and power, have provided $764,-000,000 for distribution to stockholders who today number 115,555.

The years since the end of World War II have been especially productive of capital funds. The company emerged from the war period with working capital totalling $171,000,000, of which $129,000,000 was in cash and Government securities. Gross income has remained at favorable levels throughout most of the postwar years, averaging $437,000,000 per year, or more than double prewar levels.

From January 1, 1946 to the end of 1955, construction

expenditures amounted to $387,000,000. Of that total, more than $100,000,000 has been devoted to items that broadened the base of the company's operations. Planned program for future expansion during the subsequent five-year period will probably entail expenditures in the neighborhood of $250,000,000.

Such is a bird's-eye view of Anaconda operations comprising a structure reared for permanence and rich in the American tradition of progress through constructive change. In the three quarters of a century since that first fabulous mine on the Hill started Butte on the way to become the Copper Capital, practically every year has witnessed enlargements, all geared to the last word in technology and research. From the original Anaconda Mining Company through Amalgamated and The Anaconda Copper Mining Company to The Anaconda Company, the name necessitated by diverse activities, the company has registered an epoch of advance. Whole communities have sprung up under the stimulus of company activities; onetime deserts and forests have been transformed to yield to the steady progress of Anaconda enterprise.

♦ 2

PLACER GOLD TO COPPER GLANCE

PIONEER-born on the Last Frontier, Butte provided a fit setting for the beginnings of the Anaconda domain. Here nature contrived with man's age-old lust for precious and non-precious metals. Through her mysterious alchemy she had deposited on a spur of the Main Range of the Rocky Mountains, close by the western flanks of the Continental Divide and at the northeasternmost headwaters of the Columbia River, the greatest deposit of mineral wealth ever discovered on this earth. Kelley best described this treasure trove when he wrote:

"There it rises—a tiny particle of granite measured by the expanse of this earth's crust, yet nowhere else has there been a spot known to man in which the hidden forces of nature contrived to concentrate the wealth of mineral that it contained and that its fissured mass still embraces.

"To the geologist, the engineer, the metallurgist and the industrialist, its successive stages of development have written pages that have made chapters in the book of mining endeavor. That book began when primitive man first saw nuggets shining in the beds of streams or particles of native copper that had dropped as molten metal from the campfire he had learned to ignite. Down through the ages the ceaseless struggle has continued, the concluding chapter still remaining to be unfolded in that long to-morrow which is to come."

For ages that "tiny particle of granite" stood aloof and almost forbidding, a mere elevation on a well nigh trackless, tree-dotted plain. It remained for men of vision, faith and determination to adapt those rich gifts of nature to the needs of mankind.

Long before pick and shovel broke into the grim escarpment which is Butte Hill, the area which is now Montana, played its part in the sequence of events that helped to shape the destiny of the nation. In the early dawn of the nineteenth century President Thomas Jefferson completed the Louisiana Purchase. With that transaction our manifest national destiny was established. From that moment the path to our future marched westward across the then unknown thousands of miles.

Jefferson read the signs of the times and dispatched Lewis and Clark on their historic expedition of exploration and discovery. With that epic journey the Great West, with its immense potentialities for colonization and development, and its fabulous store of mineral wealth, was brought into the ken of the United States.

For nearly six decades the West beyond the Mississippi languished, habitat of trappers, hunters and tribes of warlike Indians. The fur trade was the only beneficiary.

The discovery of gold in California precipitated the greatest gold rush the world has ever known. The rush had major significance for the Butte area. Once the California diggings became exhausted, the Argonauts, ever athirst for treasure, cast their eyes elsewhere. Nevada and Utah were the first regions to feel the impact of the migratory prospectors. In Nevada, Marcus Daly learned the mining technique which he was to capitalize to such rich advantage on Butte Hill.

Some of the early stragglers from the California mining camps found their way to the Idaho country of which

Montana was then a part, forerunners of the horde that was to put Butte on the mining map and contribute a picturesque chapter to the saga of Anaconda. Most of the pioneer prospectors engaged only in placer mining, that is, the washing of the sands in the stream beds and digging down to bedrock below those sands where the tiny gold particles came to rest in the perpetual processes of erosion from the veins or fissures in the mountains above. The dredging operations came later.

Gold, and later silver, were the objectives that the prospectors' hearts were set upon. In those early days the mining industry in the West was haphazard, every man on his own. The great strike that uncovered the Comstock Lode and the glittering, now vanished, glories of Tombstone, Leadville and all the other gilded landmarks in mining annals, were all to develop, to become, in time, the tombs of hopes and dreams.

When the mining industry in the West was born, there was no thought and little knowledge of copper. The first locations on what came to be known as the Butte District, were all made on the basis of silver-bearing ores after the gold placers were exhausted. The fabled Anaconda mine was first staked out as a silver claim. For years Butte was a gold and silver camp.

From 1850 until Butte began to produce a slight amount of copper in the Seventies, the Lake Superior region in Michigan supplied the scant copper requirements of the country. The existence of the Michigan deposits of native copper had been known since 1636. The red metal was used extensively by the Indians for weapons and ornaments. Copper had also been found in Maryland, New Jersey, Tennessee, Vermont and Pennsylvania, but none of these discoveries was commercially significant. It is interesting to note that Paul Revere, who founded the copper rolling industry in this country, obtained some of his copper from the brief Maryland deposits.

The first real development of the American copper industry began in 1844 when white men started to exploit the Lake Superior deposits. Copper mining, however, did not expand on a broad scale until the dawn of the electrical era which brought to the ageless metal a new and miraculous youth.

The early settlement of Montana, successively part of the Missouri, Nebraska, Idaho, Dakota and Oregon Territories, where Anaconda was to record its historic narrative of productive achievement, was retarded by two handicaps. One was its remoteness from the routes of travel. Up to the 1860's there were three ways of getting into Montana. One was from the south by wagon road from Corinne, Utah, terminus of the railroad; another was from the east over the Bozeman Trail; while the third was by steamboat up the 2,500 miles of the Missouri River connecting St. Louis and Fort Benton. Just about this time the Mullan military road was constructed from Walla Walla, head of navigation on the Columbia River, to Fort Benton, highest point for river boats on the Missouri. At this time only twenty white men lived in the Montana region.

The second handicap that delayed the early settlement of Montana and the unfolding of its riches, was the grip exercised by the Hudson's Bay Company which held a monopoly of trade in the entire Northwest Territory, then known as the Oregon Country. The company feared that settlement of the region would interfere with its fur trading and fought to keep, what later became Montana, an Indian country. It was not until the Hudson's Bay Company's last post—the posts were called forts—in the United States was eliminated in 1872 that the opposition to settlement prospecting was removed. Adventurous spirits, however, in search of gold ignored the Hudson's Bay Company's efforts to keep them out and pioneered the way for the era of mining that made Montana the Treasure State.

Once-hidden underground riches projected a considerable part of the Great West into Statehood. California was made a state by her gold resources that attracted settlers to engage in agriculture and merchants to supply the miners; Nevada, Utah, Idaho and Colorado, by their lead and silver assets; Montana added a star to the nation's flag because of her mineral wealth, the most diversified of any of her sister states. The Great Seal of the Commonwealth bears the words, *Oro y Plata*, the Spanish for gold and silver. If copper had been developed when the seal was devised it would surely have included the word *cobre*, the Spanish word for the red metal.

The approach to Butte, which means the approach to what became the beginning of the Anaconda domain, recorded a stirring serial of mining adventure. Men of grit and courage, frustrated by the exhaustion of mines in California and Nevada, survived the hardships of cold, hunger, and the menace of warlike Indians to reach what loomed ahead as a new El Dorado. The news that gold had been discovered in what was then the Montana Territory was like the smoke of battle to a war horse.

Yet, the hardships endured by the men who opened up the original Montana diggings were less arduous than those that beset the Argonauts who sought the golden fleece in California in 1849. They were obliged to cross the Indian-ridden plains, risk the fever-ridden jungles of the Isthmus of Panama, or make the long hazardous trip around the Horn. The hunger for gold transcended all obstacles to comfort, convenience, even life itself.

The first authentic discoverer of gold in Montana was a Scotch half-breed named François Finlay, commonly known as "Benetsee." In 1852 he found light, float gold on what is now Gold Creek about twenty miles west of Deer Lodge. Later, half a dozen men on their way to Salt Lake City found more gold than had been discovered by "Benetsee." They gave a piece to a Deer Lodge pioneer who proudly displayed it as the first piece of the yellow metal found in that part of the country.

It was not until the spring of 1858 that there arrived at Gold Creek the two men, James and Granville Stuart, credited with the first practical gold development in Montana. They found color that panned out ten cents to the pan. Because their food supplies became exhausted, together with the loss of four of their horses, they abandoned the site. When they returned in 1860 they found that Henry Thomas, nicknamed "Gold Tom," had just sunk a shaft thirty feet deep from which he was getting a little gold. Subsequently the Stuarts set up the first sluices to be used in Montana.

The first big gold strike in Montana was on Grasshopper Creek at Bannack, briefly Montana's first capital, in southwestern Montana near the present town of Dillon. John White, a Colorado prospector, and his four companions made this discovery in July 1862. News of a gold strike, like bad news, travels fast. By the following winter a stampede had started for Bannack. Within a few months the place had a population of five hundred. In the midst of the biting cold, many of the miners struck out for new fields. Food supplies ran out. The miners were saved from famine by a group of Minnesota immigrants travelling the Mullan Road to Oregon. When they learned of the gold strike they joined the community. Bannack became, for the moment, the most important gold placer east of the Rockies.

As so often happened in those haphazard days of prospecting, it was not long before Bannack had more prospectors than paying claims. The golden sands were running out in the following winter. Then came the second strike which developed from one of the many freaks of Lady Luck.

A party of miners headed by William Fairweather and Henry Edgar had set out from Bannack to meet a kindred

group led by Granville Stuart. Their objective was the
Yellowstone. The two parties failed to meet. Stuart's group
was gone two months, endured great hardships, had several
skirmishes with the Crow Indians during which two of
their group were killed and a third seriously injured. No
gold was found.

The Fairweather party camped for eight days to await
a junction with Stuart and his party. During this interval
they were beset by Indians who relieved them of their
horses, giving in return some footsore Indian ponies. They
were told to go back to Bannack on pain of death.

The party started to return to Bannack but by a different
route from the Madison River across the mountains. Now
came the chance discovery that led to riches. One day at
noon tired, discouraged, and not knowing exactly where
they were, they camped on a creek bordered by alder
bushes. Their horses were lame; the only food was the game
they shot for fortunately the Indians had not taken their
guns.

Four of the men wandered off and looked for gold. Henry
Edgar stayed by the campfire. Fairweather went across
the creek to tether the miserable ponies. As he was rounding
them up he picked up a piece of rim rock which meant that
this was a good place to prospect. He called to Edgar, who
brought a pick and pan. The two men dug in the grass and
washed out a pan full of dirt. In that one pan they found
$2.40 worth of gold. By evening, they had cleaned up $12.30
worth. The next day all six men together panned $150.
Such was the discovery of Alder Gulch.

Fairweather and his companions were so excited that
they forgot to eat the venison dinner that had been prepared. Exultant, they started again for Bannack, eighty
miles away, to obtain food, clothes and tools. It was agreed
among them that no mention would be made of this discovery. Their beaming faces, however, betrayed the secret.

When they set out on the return journey they were trailed by several hundred eager miners. Within a week more than three hundred men were working in the Gulch.

Alder Gulch was the first bonanza to be unearthed in Montana since it disclosed astounding values. From the placers which the harassed Fairweather party, fleeing from Indians, had discovered, $30,000,000 in gold was taken out in three years.

So many southerners flocked to Alder Gulch that the first town reared on the site was named Varina after the wife of Jefferson Davis, President of the Confederate States. Judge Sidney Edgerton, later a Territorial Governor, refused to hold court until the place was renamed. It then became Virginia City in honor of the community in Nevada made famous by the Comstock Lode. The influx of southerners inspired a contemporary chronicler to write: "In the late Sixties Montana was full of gold, Indians, whiskey and fugitive rebels."

The hardships of life under almost primitive conditions were matched by other difficulties. Indian depredations continued. With the wresting of millions of dollars in gold from the gravels, large numbers of lawless characters were attracted to the territory. They formed bands, preyed on the miners, plotted robberies and committed dozens of murders. The outrages became so numerous that a vigilance committee was organized. The ringleader, Henry Plummer, and scores of his bandit followers were hunted down and hanged. Law and order was established.

Still more gold was now to be turned up in Montana. A year after Alder Gulch revealed its treasure a group of prospectors had prospected as far north as the Dearborn River without finding the yellow metal. After various fruitless searches they started back to Alder Gulch, camping on the Prickly Pear. It was the last chance to retrieve their fortunes. They sank two holes to bedrock and found nuggets which disclosed a rich strike. The gold rush to Last Chance

Gulch followed. This gulch later became the city of Helena.

These three strikes put Montana on the mining map for the first time. Although all petered out with their aftermath of ghost towns, with the exception of what became Helena, the time was at hand when the mineral wealth of the Hill at Butte was to be unearthed and a fabulous chapter of productivity recorded. With it the era of the Anaconda Company began.

In 1858 Caleb E. Irvine camped on what is now Butte with a pack train of goods for trade with the Indians. He found an old pit about five feet deep which had been dug years before. Near the hole, which had been dug at a point where the present Butte post-office stands, were some worn elk horns which had evidently been used as gads and hand-spikes. From all appearances the work had been done many years before but by whom no one ever knew. This old pit was later to be known as the Original Lode around which much Butte mining history was to evolve. Irvine obtained water for his camp from a spring in a gulch just below it. This became known as Town Gulch, later Dublin Gulch, and was the site of the first settlement in the old town of Butte which secured its water supply from the spring.

All the while, a straggling stream, the Silver Bow Creek, skirted the area which was to become Butte. On or near its banks a vast fortune lay imbedded in rock, waiting for the hand of man to uncover it.

The first locators on a Butte vein were William Allison and G. O. Humphreys. Searching for gold and silver they noted the pit that became the Original Lode and sank a shaft in it. This was the initial operation in Butte. The year was 1864; the season, mid-summer. Humphreys and Allison worked the dry gulches, particularly Town Gulch, hauling the gold-bearing earth down to Silver Bow Creek and washing it there. Just about this time other prospectors, finding the diggings at Bannack, Virginia City and Alder Gulch played out, flocked to the Silver Bow. Still other prospectors came in from the Comstock in Nevada. A small-sized rush was on.

A settlement named Silver Bow Town sprang up on the banks of the creek. By the end of 1864 more than a thousand men were washing the gravels there and nearby. In this way the Butte mining district was opened up. As the prospecting area widened, operations began to dwindle at Silver Bow Town. The area around the Original Lode, however, took on life and activity for hundreds of miners flocked in. The miners called the settlement Butte City after the high butte which rises from the valley's western end and a distinguishing mark in the vicinity. Later the population, all miners, saloon keepers and small merchants, dropped the word "City." Thus Butte emerged to become in time the Copper Capital and to be acclaimed as the citadel of Anaconda.

In 1865 Butte was a rip-roaring camp, tough, lawless, with nearly every man carrying a brace of pistols and a bowie knife stuck in one of his boots. Gold and silver were wrested in quantity from the placers. Then mining history began to repeat itself. The placers were worked out. By the early Seventies, Silver Bow was a ghost town.

Meanwhile the Butte area had undergone considerable development. Humphreys and Allison recorded the Original Lode in 1864 and the Missoula in August of the same year. A few weeks later they recorded the Buffalo Claim. Before the end of that year Humphreys and Allison had a shaft eighty feet down on the Original Lode. They were probably the first to find and recognize copper but, since they were seeking gold and silver, they did not try to develop the copper showing.

The Butte mining area was originally divided into two districts. One was the Summit Valley District, the eastern part, and the Independent Mining District on the west. The first laws and regulations for the Summit Valley District of Silver Bow County, which later became Butte, were adopted at a meeting of miners held on August 20, 1864. They were laid down only for placer mining. Little attention was then bestowed on the regulations for lode locations. Since no important lode mining was done until the Seventies, the Federal Mining Law of 1872 ruled when quartz mining became active. Most of the lode claims in the District were staked out under this law.

All the while gold vied with silver as the dominant metal. From 1862 to 1868 the Montana region yielded $90,000,000 in gold, a patch on the wealth copper was to produce in later years. In the beginning of her mining development, what became the State of Montana in 1889, contributed to the stream of wealth that flowed from the west to help heal the financial wounds of the nation sustained in the Civil War.

Joseph Ramsdell is credited with opening up the first body of commercial copper ore in Butte in his Parrot No. 2 in August 1866. Dennis Leary had already discovered and located Parrot No. 1. Other miners worked the black, manganese-stained silver-bearing veins. In 1865 the *Montana Post* of Virginia City reported that a copper-silver brick, exhibited by R. P. Parrot and assaying $1,236.67 to the ton, had been seen by a correspondent of the paper.

In view of the present-day indispensability of copper, it is a striking fact that those Butte miners of the Sixties regarded the red metal as a nuisance. They were eager for gold and silver. A non-precious metal hindered the hunt for the treasure they sought.

There was another difficulty. The miners understood the treatment of some ores for the recovery of silver but the copper ores, now coming up, presented a problem. There was no plant in the west for the treatment of copper ores. In the east there was a small plant in Baltimore. Facilities for treating silver ore existed but they were useless for the now almost despised copper.

In those days Swansea led the world in copper smelting

and refining and had gained the title of "metallurgical capital of Wales." No other community anywhere could vie with its skilled workmen and the number of metal works which employed them. It was natural, therefore, that the few Butte copper producers should send their ore abroad to Swansea. To ship ore across the Atlantic was not only expensive but took toll of time. It was months before the copper plate could reach the market. It was something of a handicap because the uses of copper then, as already indicated, were limited. The first shipment of ore from Butte to Wales was in 1866 and came from William Park's Parrot No. 3.

In view of the time and expense involved in sending ore to Swansea the Butte miners turned to their own devices. In 1867 a smelter was erected to treat the silver and copper ore of one of the Parrot mines. The builder was Dennis Leary, a member of the vanguard of Irish who were to make such an indelible impress upon the fortunes of Butte and of Anaconda as well.

Some evidence of the crudity of this pioneer smelter is gained from the fact that the blast was supplied by a blacksmith's bellows. In the same year a stamp mill was put up by Hendry & Ray as well as additional furnaces for the treatment of copper and lead ores. In 1868 the Davis mill was built and a furnace erected for smelting the ore from one of the Parrot lodes which had been developed to a depth of 155 feet. Inability to flux the ore properly led to the abandonment of the project.

The Butte townsite was laid out in 1867, when the settlement took on a degree of organization. It was to experience rebuffs and hardships until the development of the Anaconda mine brought stability, progress and prosperity.

Despite the sporadic presence of copper, gold and silver were still the great objectives. Placers were being worked but, as the months passed, they began to give out. The difficulty in smelting the copper ore and the obvious exhaustion of both gold and silver, brought disheartenment to the camp. Many of the miners flocked to fresh fields. By 1868 the population of the town had dwindled to not more than one hundred men. Gone was the onetime hurly-burly of a roaring camp; gone the glamor of free spending and riotous living. For the first and only time in its history, Butte took on the desolate appearance of a ghost town. It was not until the early Seventies that the full significance of the oxidized silver ore near the surface in many of the veins was generally understood. With that understanding came the rebirth of Butte, born of the faith of one man.

Among the prospectors who came to Butte in the mid-Sixties was W. L. Farlin. He had worked on the placers with moderate success but had achieved little more than a living. Farlin was a quiet, secretive individual who kept to himself. Soon after his arrival in the Butte area he staked out the Asteroid claim and was the first to work a quartz mine in the district for gold and silver. In his early placer days he had picked up a rock taken from the black ledges in a shallow prospect hole. He held on to that piece of rock which proved to be a lucky stone for him. Like so many of his fellow miners he became discouraged with the look of things in Butte and went to Idaho where he had that piece of rock assayed. It was found to be rich in silver and copper.

Armed with the information that he was soon to capitalize into wealth, Farlin returned to Butte and relocated the Asteroid claim under the new name of Travona. Development of the Travona opened up a treasure trove, justifying Farlin's faith in it.

Just about this time Dennis Leary who, with Henry Porter, had followed wagon tracks to the camp of Humphreys and Allison, located the Parrot No. 1 mine in 1864, naming it after a prominent young lawyer who had practiced before the first court set up in Virginia City. Joseph

Ramsdell located an adjoining claim in the same year, calling it Parrot No. 2. It was also known as the Ramsdell—Parrot.

The success of Travona stimulated interest in silver ores at Butte. Back flocked the miners to the place they had abandoned, this time to stay. Figuratively, silver now lined the clouds that hung over the town on Silver Bow Creek. Silver was king. By the end of 1875, with silver production rising rapidly, Butte had a population of 4,000. Henceforth, the future was bright with high hope that was to be realized in terms of rich production.

Farlin was up and doing. He began the erection of the Dexter Mill and claimed to have produced the first silver bullion by roasting and amalgamation. By 1876 there were four quartz mills and a concentrating works in the Parrot Butte District. The original Parrot mine was 160 feet in depth and shipping fifty per cent copper ore.

Up to the end of the Seventies the Butte mines were famed only for their silver output and their silver possibilities. Every month a new property contributed to the wealth of the camp. Among the richest of the claims was the Acquisition discovered in 1875. Other mines that produced heavily at the peak of the Butte silver era were the Alice, the Moulton, the Lexington, the Bluebird and the Silver Bow. Another mine which was to figure in subsequent Butte history was the St. Lawrence located by Edward Hickey. He had no faith in the claim and gave a half interest to a German named Valentine Kropf for help in assessment work. After Marcus Daly acquired the Anaconda mine he offered to buy the St. Lawrence claim. The two owners were glad to get rid of it. Kropf sold his half for $47 and Hickey his for $75.

The St. Lawrence repeated the history of other mines deemed useless by the original owners and then developed into big producers. It came into the Anaconda fold and under expert operation was rated a valuable addition to the mines on the Hill. Today it is part of the Greater Butte Project which is accelerating output through the Kelley mine and adjacent properties.

Butte was now alive with activity. It had become not only the leading mining town in what was still the Montana Territory, but also the leading silver-producing district in the world.

One by one, the mines that were to live in Butte history were opened up. They included the original Parrot Colusa, Ramsdell's Parrot, Mountain Consolidated and Leonard, many to be bound up in the story of The Anaconda Company. Smelters sprang up. No longer did a blacksmith's bellows supply the blast. The Bell, Dexter and Continental plants were among the first.

By this time Butte had once more become a tumultuous silver camp. Experienced miners from the mother lode mines of California, the hard rock workings of Arizona, Nevada and Colorado, and the pits of Michigan, mingled with softies from the East in the motley crowd that worked, gambled and drank in the fast growing town. Butte was becoming a melting pot for soon the vanguard of the Cornishmen, the Welsh and the Irish arrived. It was not until copper became king, however, that the rip-roaring Butte came into being to give American mining a picturesque tradition of color and drama.

The naming of mines in those boisterous days produced interesting stories. The Never Sweat claim affords one instance. After the claim had been located, the locator went to the Recorder's office to register it. He was so incoherent with excitement that he was speechless. When the clerk urged him for a name he said: "Well, I never sweat upon any of the names I give my claims," whereupon the clerk said: "Why not call it the Never Sweat?" As such it was recorded.

Then, too, there was the naming of the Wake Up Jim claim. It was located by two men. One would work in the shallow shaft in the early daytime and the other, on the afternoon shift. They lived in a cabin nearby. One day the man working on the day shift blasted a round of holes. He went back to see what had developed and then hurried to the bunk house. On arrival he yelled to his partner, "Wake up, Jim, we struck it." This is the way the claim gained its name.

There now arrived on the Butte scene the man who was to shape the destiny of Butte, to become the progenitor, so to speak, of The Anaconda Company, and to be enshrined in the annals of copper. That man was Marcus Daly.

Some rich silver ore had been shipped from the Acquisition to Walker Brothers of Salt Lake City. The Walkers, then one of the leading financiers of mining in Utah, had come to the United States from England. The father died in Mississippi and the widow, with four sons, traveled across the plains to the West. They lost the considerable bunch of cattle they had when they started, arriving in Salt Lake City with only a heifer, one steer and an Indian pony pulling their wagons. The brothers started a small store which developed into the Walker Department Store. In 1857 the Walkers opened the Walker Brothers Bank in Salt Lake City, which still flourishes. From this bank stemmed their many ventures in mining. The Walkers' climb to fame, so far as this narrative is concerned, rests on the fact that they engaged Daly for the operation that marked his entry into Butte and his start as mine manager.

The Walkers retained Daly, a veteran of the Comstock Lode and the fabulous Ontario and Ophir mines, as adviser with regard to their mining investments. They asked him to go to Butte and, if possible, purchase a silver mining claim for them.

Silver, let it be emphasized again, was the major metal in the camp. Copper was still a sort of stepchild, tolerated, and generally regarded as having only a nuisance value.

That stepchild was to become a gilded Cinderella before many years passed.

After a careful survey Daly purchased the Alice mine in the autumn of 1876 for $25,000 and became superintendent of the property. The Alice, which had been discovered and located on January 2, 1875, was one of the most promising silver properties in the district. Under Daly it developed into a heavy producer. Acting for the Walkers he continued as its superintendent, with a stock interest in the property until 1880 when he sold his holding.

Late in December 1881 the people of Butte were startled by the shriek of a locomotive whistle, the first to be heard in the camp from a passenger engine. It was an auspicious and historic day, duly celebrated, because, at long last, Butte was connected by rail with the outside world. That first rail line was the Utah and Northern which connected Butte with Ogden. The road later became part of the Oregon Short Line and still later a unit of the Union Pacific system.

On April 16, 1883, just two years after the iron horse first chugged into Butte, a well set-up man paced up and down the little railroad station at Silver Bow on a dark and dismal evening late in autumn, awaiting the arrival of his family from San Francisco. He was Jeremiah Kelley who had been a resident of Butte since 1881.

Jeremiah was four years old when the family emigrated to America from Ireland. Mrs. Kelley's grandfather had started a boys' school in Fall River, Massachusetts, so there the Kelleys went for their first halt in the New World. Jeremiah then went to the Shenandoah Valley in Virginia and attended the Georgetown High School.

Enthused by the news of the gold discoveries in California, Jeremiah decided to go west. He shipped as a cabin boy on a vessel that sailed around the Horn and arrived in San Francisco. The Grass Valley region in California first attracted him. Now began his career in mining that was to be his passion for the remainder of his life. It was in Grass Valley where Kelley met John W. Mackay and James G. Fair who were to become the silver bonanza kings.

Nevada's silver riches were attracting hundreds of ambitious men eager to make their fortunes. The fabulous Comstock Lode was the magnet that lured them to the state, the name of which was to become synonymous for years with silver. Kelley went to Nevada where he became one of the pioneers in the Mineral Hill camp in Eureka County. Mineral Hill was a small town ten miles from a railroad. Here Kelley became manager of a promising property.

Subsequently, after a brief sojourn in Fall River, Kelley returned to Mineral Hill in 1873. Meanwhile he had married in San Francisco and returned with his bride to Mineral Hill. Mrs. Kelley had crossed the Isthmus of Panama by rail to visit her brother Dennis in San Francisco and it was through him that she met her husband. The Mineral Hill district was so remote that it could not support a Catholic church. A priest came once a year to say mass in the Kelley home.

Kelley's meeting with Mackay in Grass Valley now paid off. Mackay sent word to him about the silver wealth being uncovered at Virginia City. The Comstock Lode was still the mining wonder of the day. Kelley went to Virginia City and made a fortune in mining stocks. Within a year he had lost it. In Virginia City he met Marcus Daly who was then employed in the Comstock Lode. The men became fast friends. Both had mining in their blood and knew the business from underground up.

In 1875 Kelley moved to San Francisco with his family. After the disaster in mining stocks he went back to prospecting, determined to try his luck in Butte which, by this time, was a great silver camp. Transportation was difficult for the railroad had not yet reached Montana. Kelley was obliged to make the trip on horseback. He outfitted at Los Angeles, then a Mexican camp. His friend Marcus Daly was in Butte in charge of the Alice mine and there was a happy reunion.

Kelley's first post at Butte was as operating manager of the Lexington silver mine. It also produced some gold. Kelley, like Daly, was a good miner but knew nothing about copper. He soon learned the ropes however and made good. There were only two smelters in Butte to treat sulphide ore so Kelley built a third one at Bell. Next Kelley undertook the management of the Bell silver mine. Here he was in his element for silver was his first mining love.

Jeremiah Kelley was a man of high character and proven courage. His courage was never more manifest than when he quelled the riot at the Bell mine in June 1885. The firm of William Wallace & Son, brass and copper founders in the Naugatuck Valley of Connecticut, which had financed the Bell property, went broke. When the Bell miners presented their monthly pay checks at the bank they were told "no funds." Infuriated, they marched in a body back to the mine. Massed in front of the office of James King, President of the company, they yelled, "Let's kill him." The moment was tense; bloodshed seemed imminent.

At this critical juncture Kelley, calm and collected, stepped out of his office. Drawing a pistol he dispersed the mob and order was restored. Such was the caliber of the man who waited at the railroad station at Silver Bow to greet his family. Kelley boarded the train and rode with his wife and the four children on to Butte, a few miles away.

In the family group that stepped down from the dingy, wooden passenger coach was a sturdy, blue-eyed boy, already tall for his age, who had just celebrated his eighth birthday. The boy was Cornelius Francis, fated to become the dominant force in the expansion of The Anaconda Company—the future Mr. Copper of mining lore and legend.

♠ 3

THE MAGIC HILL

AMONG the prospectors who flocked to Butte in the mid-Sixties were two brothers, Edward and Michael Hickey by name. They hailed from St. Lawrence County, New York, and were typical of their kind—rough and ready but generous, good natured, with a streak of sentimentality which was part of their Irish heritage. Edward had knocked about the west for some years. Then, inspired by the silver strike in Butte, he drifted to the Montana camp, at that time a rip-roaring community. In time Edward staked out the St. Lawrence mine, named for the Hickeys' home county and later on, the Diamond, Rock Island, Tuolumne and other claims.

It was reserved for Michael Hickey to make the discovery that put Butte indelibly on the mining map and laid the foundation of the Anaconda empire. He had served with General George B. McClellan's Army of the Potomac and saw action before Richmond and Petersburg. Like his brother Edward, he was attracted to Butte by the rich silver output so there he went in 1866 to try his fortune. He first worked on the gold placers a few miles northwest of Butte. In the year of his arrival in Butte he noted the great outcrop on what was to become the famous Hill. One day he picked up a piece of green carbonate of copper. Hotfoot on the hunt for gold and silver he threw the piece away, little dreaming that beneath his feet lay a treasure of copper. The site, however, made an impression on Hickey. Years afterward he stated that in 1867 he had earmarked the claim which became the Anaconda.

It was not until nine years later that Hickey took the historic step that was the prelude to a fabulous era in mining history. On October 19, 1875 he staked out the claim on the great outcrop. With a bundle of three-foot stakes under his arm, the raw-boned prospector climbed Butte Hill. Pacing off his alloted 1,500 feet by 600 feet he staked out a quartz claim and posted his location notice. The stakes were actually driven by his friend John Gillie, then a young mining engineer who had lately arrived in the Butte district. He was later to become manager of mines for all the Anaconda properties in Butte.

Hickey then bestowed the name on his claim, a name destined to have a world-wide significance. In the trenches before Richmond he had read an editorial in the *New York Tribune* written by Horace Greeley. In it the great editor had said: "Grant will encircle Lee's forces and crush them like a giant anaconda."

The word "anaconda" caught Hickey's fancy. He therefore named his claim Anaconda. In this way the name that became a household word in mining was brought into being. It had caught Hickey's eye amid the din of armed conflict and the boom of siege guns and it turned out to be prophetic. In the years to come the mines on the Hill adjacent to the Anaconda mine were to be the battleground of bitter litigation and the clash of embroiled miners.

In the interval between the fateful staking out of the Anaconda claim and the dawn of the following January, Hickey underwent considerable agony of mind. Back in those boisterous Seventies one of the favorite outdoor sports in Butte on New Year's Eve was jumping claims. Those horny-handed miners often had slight respect for location rights. Stakes would be pulled up and claim notices torn from their fastenings. Luck was with Hickey for his assortment of granite boulders was left undisturbed. It meant that he was left in full possession of his property.

By 1880 Hickey had staked out twenty-five claims in the Butte area. The annual assessment work on all of them required an outlay beyond his financial means. He thereupon gave Charles Larabie a half interest in Anaconda to enable him to sink the shaft forty-five feet deeper. Hickey had barely scratched the surface.

At this juncture Marcus Daly stepped into the Anaconda picture. In the previous year, that is, 1880, he had sold his stock interest in the Alice mine, which he had operated for the Walker Brothers, for $30,000 and was looking about for a property in which he could capitalize his rich experience as mine operator. He had been much impressed with the outcrop of the Anaconda claim which he regarded as an extremely promising mineral deposit of great size with a fine silver showing in the vein near the surface.

Rambling over the Hill one day Daly encountered Michael Hickey who said to him:

"I've sunk a forty-five foot shaft on my Anaconda claim and I've sure got silver ore but I've got to go deeper to make it pay. If you'll deepen the shaft, we can make a deal."

The upshot was that Daly acquired a third interest in the Anaconda claim from Hickey and Larabie for $15,000 which he stipulated was to be used for development work. His development work disclosed good silver ore. With the unerring instinct that marked his mining career, he obtained from his partners an option on their interest on the basis of $30,000 for the entire property. He offered the option to Walker Brothers but they could not be induced to go deeply into an operating venture. Daly then went to Salt Lake City to see Robert C. Chambers, a prominent lawyer who was legal adviser for the Haggin—Hearst—

Tevis syndicate for their operations in developing mines in Utah and elsewhere. Daly had become well acquainted with Chambers in Utah.

Henceforth the syndicate and Daly were to loom large in the approach to, and the devlopment of, the Anaconda mine. It may be well therefore to get a close-up of these personalities who financed an epic chapter in the history of American mining.

The Haggin—Hearst—Tevis syndicate developed from a law partnership formed in Sacramento in 1850 by James Ben Ali Haggin and Lloyd Tevis. It continued until the death of Tevis in 1899. Both men had been attracted to California by the gold discoveries. In 1853 the firm moved to San Francisco where the partners met George Hearst who became their associate and piloted them to phenomenal success in mining ventures that rolled up great fortunes for the trio.

Rarely has a group of men represented such a combination of mining acumen, sound business judgment and the courage to venture, as reposed in the syndicate, later to have an invaluable associate in Daly. Each member of the Big Four, as they came to be called, had a distinctive personality, each a flair for enterprise that enlisted special knowledge and experience. Together, they formed a team that had no peer in the annals of the mineral and land development of the West.

Haggin's forbears settled in Kentucky in 1774. His father was a successful lawyer in Louisville. His mother was the daughter of a Christian Turk, who, forced to leave Constantinople because of his religion, went to England where he studied medicine. Later he practiced his profession in Philadelphia. The Turkish strain in Haggin accounted for his name, Ben Ali. From his mother, Haggin inherited his massive build with its forty-five inch chest. To his strong body he owed the physical resistance which enabled him to live until nearly ninety-two.

Haggin studied law in his father's office and then practiced his profession in Natchez, Mississippi and St. Joseph,
Missouri. At twenty-four he married and moved to New
Orleans in the year of the gold strike in California. Within
twelve months he opened a law office in San Francisco.
From this time on, the West was to be the field of operations
that made him a Croesus of California.

When his law office was destroyed by fire Haggin moved
to Sacramento where he became a Deputy Clerk of the
California Supreme Court. Here he renewed an acquaintance with Lloyd Tevis whom he had known in Kentucky.
They formed a partnership, opened a law office in 1850 and
were so successful that they moved to San Francisco.

Haggin and Tevis supplemented each other perfectly.
Haggin, as one of his biographers put it, was "silent, phleg-
matic, cold, uninviting, imperturbable," while Tevis was
"talkative, active, ubiquitous." Each was endowed with
big vision and developed a Midas touch. Success was their
touchstone. Haggin, however, had the more adventurous
spirit as subsequent events proved.

Although highly successful in their law practice with a
considerable amount of money lending on the side, the
partners yearned for more active participation in the great
new western world that was opening up fast around, and
beyond, them. Successively they went into irrigation and
made deserts bloom. They financed telegraph, railroad
and express enterprises. Tevis became President of Wells
Fargo & Co. This famed company was bound up in a dramatic phase of the exploitation of the West. Its pony express
and bullion shipments, carried on stage coaches often held
up by bandits, contributed a chapter of adventure to the
stirring story of those exciting days.

The Haggin—Tevis—Hearst mining syndicate, which
was to make the development of the Anaconda mine possible and, with it, the elevation of Daly to giant mining
stature, was formed in 1870. From the start Haggin was the

dominating personality. Surefire business did not appeal to him. His ambition was to develop a property from the prospect stage. Tevis arranged credits, Haggin was the watchdog of expenditures, while Hearst, with his almost uncanny nose for ore, found the mines. When Daly joined the syndicate he concentrated on the Anaconda mine and the development of the reduction works at Anaconda. Much of the success of the syndicate was due to Haggin's keen appraisal of men as was shown in his unwavering loyalty both to Hearst and Daly.

The development of the Ontario mine into a fabulous producer was typical of the syndicate methods. It bought the property with only a meager outcrop showing. After three years, that is, in 1875, they had about $1,000,000 in silver ore assured. While building a $325,000 stamp mill they rented local mills. They spent more than half a million dollars before they declared a dividend. Eventually the syndicate took $8,000,000 in dividends from the Ontario. Haggin believed in spending money to make money as was also the case with Anaconda, as you will presently see.

At the height of its career the Haggin—Hearst—Tevis—Daly syndicate owned or controlled one hundred gold, silver and copper mines scattered from Alaska to South America. The syndicate registered, among many other achievements, ownership of the greatest silver mine, the Ontario; the greatest gold mine, the Homestake; and the greatest copper mine, the Anaconda.

The syndicate's phenomenal success depended on George Hearst's initial appraisement of a mining opportunity, his willingness, always supported by Haggin, to take a chance, and to pay liberally for a good prospect. Had it not been for Hearst's friendship for, and his confidence in, Daly's judgment the opening of the Anaconda mine might have been considerably delayed. Without the initiative of these two remarkable men its development, too, would probably never have attained the peak it reached.

In many respects the early lives of Hearst and Daly ran in parallel lines. Like Daly, Hearst was born on a farm and, in his boyhood days, he knew the pinch of poverty. Each worked at nearly every phase of mining from mucker up. Hearst's father was a Missouri farmer. Near the family farm were a group of lead mines. The lad visited them often with his father who peddled his farm produce around the countryside. The mines fascinated the boy. The miners liked the eager lad and took him down the shafts. He then got a minor job at one of the properties and learned how operations were carried on. It was here that he developed the interest in mining that he was to capitalize into millions in the later years. So avid was the boy's interest in mines that the Indians called him "Boy That the Earth Talks To." Hearst had earned enough money when he was twenty-two to start a small general merchandise store. He was prospering when his father died, leaving the burden of the farm and several thousands of dollars in debts to the son, with his mother, a sister and an invalid brother to support. He farmed, ran the store and, through a lucky find of lead ore, paid off all the debts.

When Hearst was thirty he heard the news of the gold discovery in California. Like so many thousands of others, he got the gold fever. With a party of Missouri neighbors he started in March 1850 for what loomed ahead as the Promised Golden Land, driving ox teams along the Santa Fe trail. With only a little money left, Hearst finally reached California and went to work at placer mining in El Dorado County in the vicinity of Placerville. Together with two associates he discovered a promising gold-quartz vein and erected one of the first stamp mills to be put up in California. When the ore became too low in grade to yield a profit, the group sold out.

Hearst now went to Nevada City, took a job in a general store and later bought an interest in it. He sold out and moved to Sacramento where he opened a general merchandise store. It is interesting to relate that among his competitors in the store business were Charles Crocker, Collis P. Huntington and Mark Hopkins, who were to become railroad kings.

Running a store was too tame an operation for a man with the vision and virility of George Hearst. Mining was in his veins so he forsook ribbons and calico to go back to his first real love. He went to Nevada City, California where he profitably developed some gold mines. In the midst of these operations he heard of the discovery of rich ore on the Comstock Lode in Nevada. He sold his holdings and went to the area that was fast becoming the Mecca of mining. It was somewhat akin to 1849 all over again. The Comstock Lode which was to create the Bonanza Kings—Mackay, Fair, Flood and O'Brien—had been named by William Thomas Page Comstock, called "Old Pancake" because he would never take time to bake bread. He sold his share in the fabulous Lode for $11,000. Years later, alone and penniless, he killed himself in Butte.

In Nevada Hearst established the reputation that aligned him with the Haggin—Tevis syndicate, as it was first constituted, and made him unique among mining men. Here he met the Bonanza Kings but, more significant for the future, he became acquainted with Marcus Daly. The men clicked from the start and a close friendship developed.

Hearst's first achievement in Nevada was characteristic of the man and his methods. Some dull, bluish material had been found in the places where panning was being done and regarded as a nuisance in the same way that copper was regarded in the early days of Butte. A specimen was sent to Nevada City to be assayed and was found to assay $3,196 to the ton in silver and $1,595 in gold. Hearst learned of the assays, went to the place where the "blue stuff" had been found, realized that the area was rich, and acquired a half interest in what became the Ophir mine for $10,000. To finance the purchase he sold his remaining mine—The

Lecompton—at Nevada City. He now formed a company,
The Washoe Gold and Silver Mining Company No. 1, to
finance the Ophir. This was Hearst's first major plunge into
mining finance and the first mining corporation organized
by him. The name Washoe was used later for the great
smelter at Anaconda. Subsequently Hearst sold his share
in Ophir for $45,000 which was the basis of the fortune
which enabled his son, William Randolph Hearst, to build
a newspaper empire.

Hearst had not only been conspicuous in opening up the
riches of the Comstock area but also pioneered the treatment of the silver ore. He financed the building of the first
pan-amalgamation mill, completed in 1860. This process
became the standard process for treating silver ore.

The year 1870 was epochal in Hearst's career because
it marked the beginning of the association with Haggin and
Tevis. In the decade prior to 1870 Hearst achieved a wide
reputation as successful mining operator. His nose for ore
had given him the title of "Lucky." He was so scrupulous
in his dealings that he was called "Honest George." Haggin
and Tevis visioned the possibilities of western mining with
the completion of the first transcontinental railroad and
needed a qualified mining man to advise them. Hearst
was the logical choice. He became a partner of the two
Californians. The Haggin—Tevis—Hearst syndicate came
into being.

The first venture of the syndicate was the purchase and
successful operation of silver mines at Mineral Hill, Nevada.
This district has particular historic interest. Jeremiah Kelley, as you have seen, was a mill superintendent in the camp
and it was here that Cornelius Francis Kelley was born.

Hearst's first big find for the syndicate was the famous
Ontario. Herman Sudden had discovered the Ontario
outcrop in 1872 at the only place where the ore came to the
surface and had sunk a shallow shaft. Hearst had just looked
at the McHenry mine which was under bond to the syndi-

cate. On his way home he met Daly at Lake Flat. Daly had seen the Ontario project, was impressed with the showing and urged Hearst to buy it. The purchase was made for $33,000. In this way one of the outstanding silver properties in all mining history came into the possession of the syndicate.

Hearst's next big find rivalled the Ontario in richness and historic interest. It was the Homestake, greatest of all gold mines. The claim was located in the Black Hills of South Dakota in 1876. During the following summer Hearst investigated the district and obtained a thirty-day option on the prospect for $70,000. All that Hearst had to go by was a wide outcrop and a fairly productive open cut. The option was exercised and Homestake became a syndicate property to bulwark its wealth in fabulous fashion. Since it was first opened up it has produced $160,000,000 in dividends and is still producing them.

The naming of this famous mine reveals an interesting story. Hearst had led a roving life, moving about from one property to another. When he departed for South Dakota, Mrs. Hearst said to him:

"George, if you find a good mine let us have a homestake."

George found the mine and it became the Homestake.

Hearst was an impressive figure of a man for he measured six feet, was erect, with a large nose, deep-set eyes and a long bushy beard. Though deeply involved in political battles, Daly never sought a public office; Hearst went in for politics and became a United States Senator from California.

Hearst represented a type of mining man peculiar to the period that witnessed the beginning of his career and the two decades that followed. He was self-educated, which meant that he learned the ropes the hard way. World mining practice prior to the Seventies was crude and stereotyped. Technically educated mining engineers, when they did enter the scene were, at the start, looked at askance and often subjected to ridicule. Scientific geology was regarded as newfangled and useless. Hearst shared in this conviction.

An incident in which Hearst figured will illustrate the attitude of the self-educated miner toward what came to be the new generation in mining. While he was operating in Virginia City a young man came into his office and asked for a job. His name was John Hays Hammond, he was twenty-five years old, and hailed from San Francisco.

Hearst asked: "Have you had any practical experience?" whereupon the young man replied:

"No, but I have graduated from the School of Mines at Freiberg, Germany."

Hearst bridled as he retorted:

"You've been to Freiberg and learned a lot of geological theories and big names for rocks. They don't go in this country. I don't want any kid-glove engineers."

Undeterred, the young man came nearer to Hearst and said almost in a whipser:

"If you promise not to tell my father, I did not learn anything of importance at Freiberg."

That settled it for Hearst, who now said:

"Start work tomorrow."

Hammond's job started him on the path that led to fame and fortune. Together with Dr. James Douglas and Dr. Louis D. Ricketts, he became one of the great mining engineers of his time, friend and adviser of Cecil Rhodes, the Guggenheims, and many other notable figures.

When the graduates of mining schools demonstrated their worth and inaugurated the era of scientific mining, Hearst fell in line. Many of the syndicate's big operations stemmed from the investigations of college-bred geologists.

Like Hearst, Daly was a self-taught miner reared in the school of hard knocks. To a greater degree than Hearst, however, he became amenable to scientific geology. The value of this asset in mining was amply demonstrated in the bitter Apex litigation in Butte in the late 1890's and early 1900's. Utilization of mining geology in the operation of properties is one of the many highly important features of mining practice that Anaconda pioneered. Furthermore, Anaconda was the first mining company to keep a staff of geologists studying workings as work progressed.

It remains to complete the story of the quartet that made the opening of the Anaconda mine possible. Marcus Daly's career is one of those inspiring stories of self-made success that kindles faith in the opportunities of democracy. Those opportunities, however, demand a man capable of seizing and capitalizing them. Such a man was Daly.

Nurtured in hardship, Daly was a child of peat and bog for he was born in Ireland on December 5, 1841 near Ballyjamesduff in County Cavan. He was one of seven children. The period of his early boyhood included the bleak and desolate years of the famine of 1846–7. Blight destroyed the potato crop and potatoes were the chief sustenance of the impoverished country. The next two decades witnessed a mighty exodus from Ireland to the United States. Escape was the only recourse of a hungry population living in sod huts and eking out a bare existence. That exodus enriched America for, among those exiles, were men who became outstanding in mining, nowhere to a greater extent than in the ranks of the creators and builders of what became The Anaconda Company.

Before he was in his teens Daly did his full share of work on the family farm, developing the strength that was to stand him in good stead in later years. As the youthful years lengthened the lad became increasingly disheartened with the sordid conditions about him. He had seen scores of his neighbors go off to America, the land of gilded promise, and he made up his mind to join them. It was flight from desperation.

Just how Daly obtained the money for the passage is not

known. It is generally believed that his favorite sister Ann, who had married John O'Farrell and was then living in San Francisco, supplied the major part of it. In any event, Daly embarked for New York in 1856 when he was fifteen. It was a venture that demanded courage but Daly was never lacking in this quality.

Alone and friendless, the youth cast about for a job. His first employment was as errand boy in a commission house. He then worked as hostler in a livery stable and in a leather works in Brooklyn. Finally he went to work on the Brooklyn docks. Here he became acquainted with the captains and crews of ships. He had set California as his goal, not because of the gold discoveries but because sister Ann lived in San Francisco.

Daly somehow managed to wangle passage on a ship, working his way to the Isthmus of Panama, then overland and up the coast to the Golden Gate. When he arrived in San Francisco he found that jobs were scarce. One reason was that the gold rush of 1849 was over. The only work available was on a truck farm near the city. He saved some money and went to the placer mines, to begin his career as miner. Some experience in placer and hydraulic mining accrued during this period. Underground work appealed to him strongly so after a year he went to Grass Valley where he earned his living with single jack and double jack and learned to timber and use explosives. In Grass Valley he met Mackay, Fair and O'Brien, then on the threshold of their spectacular foray into silver on the Comstock Lode in Virginia City, Nevada, which was to make them nabobs.

The year 1862 found Daly in Virginia City where he became foreman for Mackay at the Comstock mine. Mining technique at the Comstock was then the best in the country, an admirable place for Daly to gain experience. During his stay in Virginia City he became well acquainted with

Mark Twain, then a reporter on *The Territorial Enterprise* which he helped to make famous. Daly participated in the fake hold-up of Mark Twain in 1864 which the Comstock miners perpetrated on Twain in retaliation for his criticism of the guests at a party they had given for him. Far more important than the acquaintance with Mark Twain was Daly's meeting with George Hearst which developed into a friendship that shaped his future career.

Daly remained on the Comstock until 1868 when he joined the rush to White Pine. By this time the Comstock had been worked down to 1,000 feet below the surface and was yielding low grade ore. When Daly arrived on the scene White Pine had supplanted the Comstock as a bonanza. The Hidden Treasure and the Eberhardt mines were producing as high as $27,000 silver a ton, while the Defiance had turned out $40,000 silver in one day. Thousands rushed to Treasure City, as it was called, following the news of the rich output. The mines, however, did not last long since they were blanket deposits. Treasure City joined the list of ghost towns.

Daly anticipated the exhaustion of the White Pine properties and now went on to Mineral Hill, Nevada. This move was significant for two reasons. One was that here he met Jeremiah Kelley. The other was that he worked for a time for the Haggin—Tevis syndicate not only at Mineral Hill but at Eureka.

Not content with the future possibilities of Mineral Hill and Eureka, Daly looked about for a new opportunity. By this time he was a skilled miner with a large and varied experience. Already his instinct for ore-finding had manifested itself. Now came the first contact with the Walker Brothers. The year was 1870. It is generally believed that Hearst recommended him to the Walkers who employed him to open up and develop the Emma mine in Utah. Following the linking of the Central and Union Pacific railroads, the Mormon State had blossomed with mining camps. The Emma was the first fully developed mine in Utah.

As Daly opened up the Emma vein, it widened to thirty-five feet and the grade of ore increased from $125 to $250 a ton in silver. In the first eighteen months the mine returned $2,000,000. Daly, with his uncanny instinct, felt that the property would be short-lived. On his suggestion the Walkers sold a half interest in it. Meanwhile Daly had moved to the Ophir and Dry Canyon districts, about fifty miles south of Salt Lake City.

Ophir launched a happy epoch in Daly's life. When he arrived there Z. E. Evans was in charge of the Mountain Tiger property in which he owned an interest with the Walkers. The Mountain Tiger group included the Silver Chief, Zella and Rockwell, all operated as one mine, together with the Silveropolis mine where horn silver was first found in Utah. They were all silver properties.

Evans lived upon Trail Street not far from the house that Daly occupied. Evans had a charming daughter named Margaret. Soon both became conscious of each other. Romance was soon to flower amid the headframes and the hoists.

Margaret was anxious to go underground so Daly invited her and a girl friend to have a trip through the Rockwell. In coming back along an incline Margaret slipped but Daly caught her before she fell. From that time on their friendship ripened into love. They were married in 1872 at the home of Joseph Walker in Salt Lake City. Ophir registered another important event in Daly's life for here, on April 15, 1874, he became an American citizen in the Federal Court of Utah Territory.

At Ophir Daly developed the Midas touch with mines that became one of his chief assets. The mines he managed invariably developed rich output. He had become known and respected in all the Utah and Nevada camps. As events proved, he was only at the beginning of his career.

Daly's development of the Alice mine at Butte had given further evidence of his ability as operator. His purchase of an interest in the Anaconda claim demonstrated his faith in the Butte area. The refusal of the Walker brothers to take over the Anaconda enabled him to proceed on his own. These, then, were the preliminaries to the step that was to enable Daly to fulfill his destiny. We can now return to his momentous trip to see Chambers in Salt Lake City.

Daly desired to offer the Anaconda option to the Haggin—Tevis—Hearst syndicate. The syndicate was fully acquainted with his work and had already made him a tentative offer to join their staff. That, however, was not a sufficient inducement.

When Chambers told Daly that Hearst was in San Francisco his reply was:

"I will write to him."

"No," replied Chambers. "You had better see him personally. I will give you a letter of introduction to Haggin."

Armed with the letter Daly took a train for San Francisco. Haggin and his associates were impressed with his faith in the Anaconda claim which he then believed would equal the Ontario as a silver producer. The net result of the conference was that Hearst was despatched to Butte to examine the prospect. Hearst had bought the Ontario on Daly's recommendation and had implicit faith in his judgment. It followed that he shared Daly's confidence in Anaconda. The syndicate, therefore, purchased the option and then exercised it, paying $70,000. Daly received a free one-quarter interest.

The syndicate gave Daly a free hand and a satisfactory drawing account for developing and equipping the mine. Development showed satisfactory silver ore. When a considerable tonnage had been uncovered, the Dexter mill was

leased from W. A. Clark. After further tests proved satisfactory a large mill was ordered from Chicago for erection
on the property. Now came the strike that made mining
history and projected Daly into the ranks of the great in the
American copper story.

II

Daly took over operations at the Anaconda as General
Manager and set to work with his accustomed vigor. He
located the working shaft at the present location of the
Anaconda and suspended work at the discovery shaft. At
300 feet a cross-cut was driven and the drills encountered
the vein. Daly and his lieutenant, Mike Carroll, stood behind the workmen while the holes were loaded and the
blast exploded. Daly picked up a mass of gleaming rock and
exclaimed: "Mike, we've got it." The rock was chalcocite,
solid copper, in other words, a copper glance. As one biog-
rapher of Daly put it: "That dramatic moment timed the
beginning of the greatness of Marcus Daly." The time was
late in 1882.

The Anaconda developed into a fabulous property. It
was the richest deposit of copper sulphide that had ever
been found. With it, the large scale copper mining industry
in this country was born. Nothing like its output had ever
been turned up before, but it also raised a serious problem.
None of the syndicate of which Daly was now a member had
any experience with copper or metals other than gold and
silver. Here was an entirely new type of ore for which no
treatment plants or facilities had as yet been pioneered on
the North American continent except that small plant at
Baltimore.

There was little reason then to hope that copper, produced from the Anaconda ore, could successfully compete
with the native copper ores of the Lake Superior district.
Furthermore, the limited copper market at that time
scarcely warranted a large production of the metal. In 1882

the annual consumption of copper for the entire world represented about two weeks' supply at the present time.

Daly was undeterred. He had the faith, the hope and the courage to go ahead when all others in the Butte district regarded the production of copper as a hopeless economic undertaking. Only his associates in the syndicate stood behind him. His first step was to cancel the order for the pan-amalgamation mill ordered from Chicago. He now drove below. By May 1883 the mine had been opened to a depth of 600 feet with five leads. It contained rich bodies assaying 55 per cent copper. The width of the vein was from 50 to 100 feet. The next procedure was to reduce the ore. In view of the lack of facilities in this country Daly decided to ship part of the Anaconda output to Swansea where the metallurgy was determined and where it was demonstrated that the smelting of the ores and the recovery of copper could be satisfactorily accomplished. Shipments were first sent by ox team 350 miles to Corinne, Utah, and thence by rail to Atlantic ports. Later they went over the Northern Pacific to Portland and then on to their destination in Pacific sailing vessels. From 1882 to 1884 Daly shipped to Swansea from Butte 37,000 tons of ore averaging a 45 per cent copper content.

The copper men at Swansea were amazed at the richness of the shipments from Butte. They wrote back asking if they were receiving an ore or the product of some new process in which the copper had been reduced. They had never seen or heard of massive chalcocite ore before. All the chalcocite they, and for that matter the entire world, had seen up to that time was in small specimens in mineralogical collections.

With the big vision that led him, and the courage that always animated his ventures, Daly widened his zone of operations. In 1882 when the Anaconda mine had not begun to disgorge its riches and the market for copper seemed remote, he bought in behalf of his partners, the St. Law-

rence, adjoining the Anaconda on the east, from Edward
Hickey. He also purchased the Never Sweat claim, another
filing on the Anaconda vein from the newly formed Chambers syndicate. Both of these properties became, and remain, valuable assets of The Anaconda Company. With
the acquisition of these valuable properties began the accumulation of mineral wealth that made the scarred elevation that brooded over Butte the Magic Hill.

If it were true, as his partners believed, that Daly "could
see farther into the ground than any other mining man," he
certainly saw, with uncanny certainty, that he had the copper ore for a large development. Moreover, he knew that he
could mine and treat this ore to produce copper at a price
to compete in any world market. Reinforcing this was the
conviction that the use of copper would provide an outlet
for his product.

Various historic developments served to substantiate
Daly's faith in the future of copper. The Centennial Exposition at Philadelphia in 1876 had revealed the application of electricity for varied usage. At this exposition, Alexander Graham Bell had first transmitted speech through a
copper wire, heralding the advent of the telephone which
was to use, as the years passed, millions of miles of copper
wire. Equally important was the operation in 1882 of the
first electric generating plant to light the streets of New
York. Coincident had been the invention of hard-drawn
copper wire and the start of cable development. Arc lighting was demonstrated on a street corner in Newark and
interior electric lights were installed in Wanamaker's Store
in Philadelphia. In 1880 Edison had received a patent for
the incandescent lamp and began to experiment with the
trolley car. His experiments with incandescent lamps and
electrically operated transportation were worked out with
the Wallaces who had a brass plant at Ansonia, Connecticut which is now one of the properties of The American
Brass Company, a wholly owned subsidiary of Anaconda.

In an attic of the old Ansonia plant the first electrically operated car was perfected by the Wallaces and Edison.

The potentialities of these inventions and their utilization with the accompanying requirements for copper, must have buoyed Daly's faith in the production of the red metal. There was an additional factor. Copper production in Great Britain had dropped from 16,000 tons in 1860 to 3,800 tons in 1881, Chile's output was reduced from 50,000 tons to 38,000 tons in the same year, while in the United States production had increased to only 44,000 tons in the year when the Anaconda mine was opened up. We were importing copper for our consumer demand. In the realization of these factors Daly had the soundest conception of his time as to the future of copper. Standing alone and without encouragement from his mining colleagues in the then infant industry, he had the courage to invest more than $15,000,-000 in mines and plants. His ability to produce copper and a deep-seated confidence that the gleaming metal would find wide and ready use in the economy of a growing country, were eminently characteristic of the man.

Like the face of industry, the face of the expanding United States was changing. The move from farm to city, which got under way soon after the close of the Civil War, was accelerated. Increased urban population means increased demand for factory products. As frontiers vanished —Montana was the last—under the impact of immigration to the West, a civilization sprang up where once the sage brush flourished. The time was soon to come when the great mining camps that had been bedlams and hunting grounds for the fortune hunter, would be stabilized into orderly productive areas. Mills, smelters and refineries would spring up, metallurgy develop into a science, and industry be organized. In this chain of mining and reduction, Anaconda was to take a commanding place.

Daly anticipated the momentous change and took the first step toward the organization of the American copper industry. With it he achieved independence of Swansea. There were a few crude, almost primitive, smelters at Butte for copper had begun to show increasingly in the district. There was vital need for adequate reduction facilities. Daly set to work to satisfy that need.

Satisfied that the process of smelting and reduction of ores at Swansea could be satisfactorily accomplished, Daly decided to build a smelter. In 1883, under the informal organization of the syndicate, he started the construction of the first copper reduction works three miles below the site of the present town of Anaconda. He also erected a twenty-stamp mill for the reduction of silver ore. This mill was operated for two years under the name of the Anaconda Gold & Silver Company, which was never incorporated.

By this time Daly's expenditures, often in undertakings of an experimental character, had mounted into the millions of dollars with very little corresponding return. Tevis, who was the pinch-penny in the syndicate, expressed doubt as to the wisdom of investing such large sums in Butte and elsewhere. Daly called for a conference of the syndicate and insisted that one or all of the partners come to Butte and appraise the work he had done and pass judgment on his plans.

Haggin made the trip under protest. The rugged, bearded Californian made a careful inspection of all the properties and then said, as Daly reported his remarks:

"You have made me a vast amount of trouble. I am getting old but you drag me out here, race me through your mine workings, and tell me what remains to be done. It was all unnecessary. The property is bigger than you led me to believe; you have shown me where all the money has gone. Indeed, I cannot see how you could do the work with so little money. Hereafter please keep in mind what I told you when we began this enterprise—when you need money draw, and keep on drawing."

When Haggin returned to San Francisco, Tevis suggested

that the Butte project be cut down or modified, or at least that Daly be required to find financing for his own one-fourth interest. Haggin replied simply: "I will see Daly through." After that no question was ever raised with regard to Daly's plans or expenditures. Figuratively, Anaconda and its sister mines became a mint that coined gold for the syndicate.

The first outpost of the Anaconda empire was now set up with a smelter in what became the town of Anaconda. The obvious site would have been Butte but the amount of water required was not available there. It was thought for a while that Daly would select a site on the Madison River and property was purchased there. The final selection, however, was on Warm Springs Creek twenty-six miles west of Butte and it was there that the first smelter was built. Warm Springs Creek was chosen because of the availability of a plentiful supply of water.

Daly and a close friend, Morgan Evans, through whom he bought the land for $20,000, chose the town site. Standing on a hill Daly saw a cow grazing peacefully some distance away. Pointing to the cow he said:

"Do you see that cow grazing? The Main Street of our town will run north and south in a direct line from here to where that cow is standing."

The city plat was completed June 25, 1882. A few merchants bought lots and several stores and a bank opened their doors.

So it came about that Anaconda was born. Daly suggested that it be named Copperopolis. The first postmaster, however, discarded it because there was already a town of that name. He chose Anaconda, already emblazoned on a historic mine, and now to be linked to a famous reduction center.

In the fall of 1883 the concentrator building was completed. A large ditch was constructed from the creek to the site of what came to be known as the Upper Works. A flume for the delivery of cord wood from the Big Hole country was built down the mountain on Mill Creek.

As soon as copper from the smelter reached the market, competition from the Lake Superior copper made itself felt. To meet this competition Daly decided to improve the smelter, increase its size and thus reduce costs. Accordingly he sent Otto Stahlman, his Chief Metallurgist, to Europe to visit the copper smelters and refineries. Stahlman had estimated that he could make the trip for not more than $2,500. Daly handed him a check for $10,000, saying: "If you go to Europe for Anaconda, keep in mind that you go as a gentleman. When this money begins to run low, draw for more."

Upon Stahlman's return the smelter with a capacity of 5,000 tons per month was built. The refinery produced 1,500 tons of refined copper a month and another refinery of equal capacity was now under construction. Around it developed the myriad activities that make Anaconda today one of the major centers of ore reduction with an unchallenged prestige. With the expansion of the Anaconda interests, Anaconda's sister plants rose up from Montana to Chile.

The Anaconda Reduction Works went into full swing in September 1884. The ore sent from the Anaconda mine carried eight to ten per cent copper with a variable quantity of smelting ore that usually contained an average of about twenty-five per cent copper. From the beginning the works at Anaconda also treated custom ores and ores purchased from mining concerns that had no metallurgical plants of their own. Thus, activities by small operators and prospectors were encouraged.

At first Anaconda had no water system. When the west side of Main Street was burned out in the winter of 1885 the residents fought the flames with snow. As the population increased an adequate water system was installed as well as lighting facilities, a hotel, sewers, fire and police protection, street cars and municipal buildings. From a tented community, Anaconda became an organized municipality.

With the operation of the works at Anaconda, Daly faced the major problem of transportation between the mines at Butte and the smelter. The first ores from Butte were delivered in wagon trains. Later the Montana Union Railroad hauled the ore. The freight rate was seventy-five cents a ton which Daly regarded as excessive for a haul of twenty-six miles. In 1892 he refused to enter into a new contract with the road for more than fifty cents a ton. The road turned down the offer whereupon Daly said: "We will build our own road," and build it he did. In planning the road he had the advice and assistance of his friend, empire builder James J. Hill, President of the Great Northern.

In September 1892 the Butte, Anaconda & Pacific Railroad was incorporated. Built by miners from Butte, it went into operation January 1, 1894. Daly's judgment had vindication in the fact that his road brought shipping costs down to about twenty-five cents a ton, or one-third of what the Montana Union had charged.

Daly's activities at Butte instigated the construction of the Great Northern through to Butte in 1887 to haul the ores and copper to the smelter and refinery at Great Falls, which was more favorably situated for power, located as it was near the falls of the Missouri River. The Great Northern was also enabled to carry the copper from the refineries to the markets of the East. With the extension of the railroads began the industrial and agricultural development of Montana.

Daly derived a great satisfaction out of this railroad which so amply proved its worth. With its completion he had a small private car built. When he went to and from Butte the car was attached to the end of an ore train and, as so often happened, he rode in solitary splendor.

Anaconda lay deep in Daly's affection. Except for his family, his ranch and his race horses, it was his pride and joy. To a large extent he regarded it as his home for, in the early years of his operations, he spent as much time as possible there. One aspect of his famous feud with W. A. Clark grew out of his impassioned desire to make Anaconda the capital of Montana. He spent half a million dollars in the contest which ended in a victory for Helena.

Largely in order to provide a habitation for himself in Anaconda he built the Montana Hotel at Main Street and Park Avenue, constructed and equipped in Daly's usual lavish fashion. The bar is a reproduction of the famous bar in the Hoffman House in New York where stage and financial celebrities gathered for years. All woodwork in the bar is mahogany. With huge pier glass mirrors and sparkling chandeliers, it is a show sight for it remains untouched. The Red Room adjoining the bar, equipped and furnished in Victorian style, was the meeting place for many mining and political personages during Daly's day of power.

So great was Daly's affection for his favorite horse, Tammany, that he brought out the artist Newcomb from New York to inlay in fine wood a perfect head of the animal in the center of the floor of the bar. The head is a composite of more than a thousand small squares of hardwood varying in tone to catch the fine sheen, shades and markings of the magnificent animal. Daly never walked over the head on the floor. Moreover, anyone found standing on it was compelled to pay for the drinks of everyone in the room.

The Montana Hotel proved to be an expensive luxury for Daly since it seldom had a guest except the great man himself. Yet he kept it fully staffed. Frequently he was the only guest in the huge dining room which could accommodate a banquet for five hundred people.

As Daly embarked on big scale mining operations it was found that large quantities of heavy timber were required in the mines for supporting the rock of the stopes in the veins. The mines at Butte alone required from 40,000,000 to 50,000,000 board feet a year. While the square-set timbering was expensive because of the heavy lumber needed, as well as the labor involved in framing, many of the ore bodies then, and now, cannot be mined in any other way.

Daly rose to the emergency with his customary foresight. He purchased 6,000,000 board feet of standing timber in northwestern Montana in the late Eighties. This was the nucleus of the present day timber holdings of The Anaconda Company which total 386,137 acres. The original timber acreage, much of it acquired from the Federal government, the Northern Pacific Railroad and in the Bitter Root Valley, was in pine, Douglas fir, western larch, spruce and hemlock.

Daly had the standing timber. He now started in on his mill program by setting up mills at Hamilton and St. Regis in Montana and Hope in Idaho. Thus Anaconda brought the timber from virgin forest down into the mines. It was the beginning of the self-sufficiency which has marked so many Anaconda operations.

Large areas from which the timber had been cut were found to be suitable for agricultural purposes. Daly now organized the Blackfoot Land & Development Company for the purpose of employing logged-off land for farming. In this way the areas, together with subsequently acquired timber districts, became substantial factors in the agricultural expansion of Montana.

The question of an adequate fuel supply for the Anaconda works rose up to pose another problem for Daly. As with timber, he was quick to act. He purchased coal lands at Belt in Cascade County, Montana. Later he bought mines at Diamondville, Wyoming. Montana mines were acquired at Carbonado and Washoe in Carbon County, Storrs in Gallatin County, Cokedale in Park County, Sand Coulee and Spring Creek in Cascade County.

A period of temporary discouragement began in 1888

when the newly completed Anaconda works burned. They were rebuilt with all metal construction the following year. In less than a decade the entire plant, that is, the Upper and Lower Works, were found to be inadequate. The Washoe Copper Company, capitalized at $20,000,000, was then formed by Daly and his partners to construct the new reduction works at Anaconda. It borrowed $7,200,000 from The Amalgamated Company which H. H. Rogers had been instrumental in forming, for constructing the works which came to be known as the largest reduction operation in the world.

The Washoe Company developed into a large enterprise. It owned the Moonlight, Clear Grit, Cambers, Washoe, Pacific, Odin and Gold Hill claims and operated three of them. It also owned real estate in Butte, 1,900 acres of coal lands in Carbon County, Montana, a coking coal property in Gallatin County and one hundred coke ovens.

Meanwhile hard times were prevalent in Butte. The drop in the price of silver had seriously affected silver mining. As a result, silver production was limited to that which came from the copper ores. Seven smelters which had been erected in Butte, ceased operations. The price of copper dropped to nine cents a pound.

Daly again exhibited his faith in the future of the copper industry. In 1892 he achieved an output of 100,000,000 pounds of the metal. With this, his enterprise became the greatest copper producer in the world.

The interests of Daly and his associates continued to expand. In 1891 the Butte City Water Company, originally the Silver Bow Water Company, owned by W. A. Clark, was reorganized and acquired. Seven years later the company was again reorganized as the Butte Water Company. A further supply of water was developed from Big Hole River on the Atlantic side of the Continental Divide. Butte's water needs have been abundantly supplied ever since.

III

Up to the beginning of the last decade of the nineteenth century the four men comprising the syndicate had operated as partners without corporate organization. On January 19, 1891 they incorporated The Anaconda Mining Company for a term of twenty years with a capital of 500,000 shares of a par value of $25. Eleven months after the incorporation, the capital stock was increased to $25,000,000. Haggin, who had acted as trustee throughout the syndicate period, transferred all the property owned by the group in exchange for its capital stock. All this stock, except for qualifying shares, was issued to Haggin. The properties were operated through this company until 1895 when it ceased to function.

The properties taken over by The Anaconda Mining Company were:

I. The Anaconda group made up of the Anaconda, St. Lawrence and Never Sweat claims and a number of adjoining claims.

II. The Mountain Consolidated group, consisting of a series of thirty-eight claims totalling 283 acres upon a wide vein system parallel with the Anaconda vein about half a mile to the north. The principal claims were the Diamond, Modoc, High Ore, Green Mountain and Mat. Mountain Consolidated comprised what had formerly been called the Diamond group and the Syndicate group.

III. The Union Consolidated group composed of a number of silver mining claims located three-quarters of a mile northwest of the west end of the Syndicate group.

IV. The Anglo-Saxon group which became the Orphan Girl Mine, contained two full claims and two fractional claims on a vein of low grade silver ore. It later developed into an important zinc property.

A summary of the operations of the mines owned by The Anaconda Mining Company from November 1874 to June 1895 when The Anaconda Copper Mining Company was incorporated, reveals the following production: copper, 707,402,130 pounds; silver, 18,567,628 ounces; gold, 83,349 ounces. Vast significance attached to these figures. From the Seventies silver had reigned as king, for Butte had become the greatest of all silver camps after Comstock's glory had departed. By the end of 1884 the Butte mines had produced 14,599,700 ounces of silver. Silver was still being produced but a change was now under way. The temporary collapse in the price of silver was not the only factor. Many of the mines which showed silver values near the surface developed into copper deposits at depth. The time was at hand when the silver star would fade and, figuratively, the reflection of the once-spurned red metal would illumine the sky over Butte. The copper era dawned.

Up to this time Daly and his partners had been engaged in building their enterprise for fifteen years. No dividend had been declared and no profits divided. All money derived from operations had been put back into the business to strengthen its structure by the acquisition of additional ground on the great veins in Butte, the construction of the smelter in Anaconda, the purchase of timber lands and coal mines, and the construction of the Butte, Anaconda & Pacific Railroad.

Behind, and animating this period of expansion which witnessed the birth and the first historic epoch in the large scale American copper mining industry, stood the steadfast figure of Daly. Physically short of stature, yet he towered over his contemporaries like a Colossus. His courage and vision, which were to project Anaconda on the march to its place in the sun, were never more manifest than in the years following the organization of The Anaconda Mining Company. A close-up of the man, his personality and his characteristics, will reveal how he became a giant in copper.

Daly's life was as colorful as his achievements. You have already seen how the fifteen-year old immigrant lad, a fugitive from a poverty-haunted farm in Ireland, landed alone and friendless in New York and earned his way to California. He was short and ruddy with blue eyes and a winning Irish smile. His moustache seemed to bristle at times, seldom in anger, but he could build up a strong state of mind and express himself with a degree of profanity not surpassed in a community of strong speech. His anger was quick to cool for he was the most generous of men in word and deed. Daly was an exceptionally modest man, keenly aware of his cultural deficiencies, which was one reason why he never consented to become a candidate for public office. Few people knew the inner workings of his mind but he was quick to detect the mental processes of others.

Although he amassed millions he remained simple in personal tastes and habits. He rose at 6:30 and generally ate a beefsteak for breakfast. In Butte he usually lived in a small room over the mess hall at the Anaconda mine. To be sure, he built a luxurious home, had a showplace ranch and a stable of the fastest race horses in America, but there was always an inherent simplicity that was one of his outstanding qualities.

Linked with this simplicity was a truly democratic spirit. Daly chewed tobacco and it was no infrequent sight to behold him sitting on the edge of a wooden sidewalk in Butte expectorating into the street. If he needed a fresh chew, he would stop a miner and ask him for one. This leads to the relation with his men. He hired most of them himself and knew the great majority by name. He also knew many of their families.

Despite this close kinship with his employees, Daly could be firm but always just. The story of the great strike that threatened the Butte mines is typical. A committee of employees waited on him demanding higher wages. Their wages were already the highest in the nation. Daly told the committee that he could not accede to their demands, whereupon the men said they would strike. Daly replied:

"That is your privilege in this country but remember that if you do, it will not be long until there is much suffering among the men who have saved no money. When that time arrives don't hesitate to call on me. I will see that none of your wives or children suffer until the men get work again. I have been a working man all my life and know how hard their lot can be sometimes. I cannot grant your demands because it would be an injustice to my company and to the men who have invested millions of dollars here. Besides, I am boss and do not propose to divide my duties with you. Personally I will do all I can for those dependent upon your work."

When Daly's remarks were reported back to the men they decided not to strike. They remembered the innumerable kindnesses he had shown them when sickness, disability or some trouble in the family left them short of funds. His philanthropy, which extended in many directions, was personal.

It was during the years of his early career in Butte that the traits in his character, which had hitherto lacked opportunities for their unfolding, came into full play. With them developed forcefulness, often even to aggressiveness, and the quick-wittedness that marked him ever afterward. Back of these traits was the sound judgment so evident in all his undertakings.

Daly inspired loyalty. With his Irish streak of sentiment he had a particular devotion for the men associated with the beginning of the Anaconda mine which launched him on his career. The personnel in charge of the early operations at Butte included Michael Carroll who stood with Daly when the copper glance in the Anaconda mine was disclosed and later became General Superintendent. His assistant was John O'Farrell, Daly's favorite nephew, son of his devoted sister, Ann. When John died his brother, Michael

O'Farrell, became Assistant Superintendent. Others in the group in at the start of the Anaconda enterprise were John Gillie, who had planted the stakes for Michael Hickey on that memorable October morning in 1882; August Christian, chief engineer of the Anaconda group; John P. O'Neill, who became Superintendent of the Anaconda, Never Sweat and St. Lawrence mines; Joseph Laird, who was placed in charge of the Mountain Consolidated and Green Mountain; William Skyrme, Superintendent of High Ore and Moonlight mines; and James Higgins, Superintendent of the Bell and Diamond mines.

The reference to the O'Farrells brings to mind the fact that even before Daly became affluent he brought all his sisters and brothers over to America and saw that they were comfortably and successfully settled. Here was another manifestation of the Irish character, this time its clanishness.

To a considerable extent Daly was his own geologist. That uncanny nose for ore seldom failed him. He described the structure to the east of the Anaconda mine to an eminent engineer as follows: "You have here at the base the heavy, thick Anaconda, and then as you go east it breaks up and slivers off in many fine veins just like a horse's tail." This is how the Horsetail area got its name.

Unlike Hearst's early frowning attitude toward college-trained geologists, Daly was quick to evaluate their worth and to appreciate the virtues of technology. He laid the foundation for the staff of scientific men who have not only been a tremendous factor in the development of Anaconda but have made invaluable contributions to the science of mining.

In another respect Daly pointed the way for the future. When the price of copper was depressed with mines shutting down and stockpiles high, he never wavered in his determination to expand. He was ever willing to take a chance and the chance paid off. So it has been down the decades with The Anaconda Company. When the business sky was dismal the men who charted the course of the organization found the money and bought properties. It was in a dark period that the company embarked on fabrication and made it a bulwark in the creation of the largest non-ferrous mining and fabrication organization in the world.

Daly, mindful perhaps of the limitations that hedged in his early boyhood, was keen on sports. He organized and trained football teams from among college stars and sent them out to play throughout the country. This, however, was incidental to his abiding passion which was horses. Haggin, with his innate Kentucky flair for fine horseflesh, probably inspired Daly to go in for racing. Haggin, however, concentrated on breeding thoroughbreds. Daly went in for both breeding and racing, building up one of the great stables of the country. The sport of kings drew him irresistably.

Daly developed a 22,000 acre ranch in the Bitter Root Valley. Here were his breeding, training and racing stables. The mansion, the miles of parked roads, the stables, the two exercise tracks, one open in summer and the other covered for winter, all combined to constitute a showplace for the nation. Here, in later years, he made his home. His ambition was to transplant the best stock of England, Kentucky and California to the high altitude of the Bitter Root Mountains, contending that horses trained in high altitudes could outrun those trained in lower altitudes. So it came to pass.

At the Bitter Root ranch Daly developed some of the greatest horses in the history of the American turf. His favorite, and the star of the stable, was Tammany which he bought as a colt at the Belle Mead sale. Tammany won the Suburban, the Great Eclipse Stakes, the Withers, the Jerome Handicap, the Lorrilard and many other races. One of his notable victories was in a match race at Gutenberg track with Lamplighter, owned by J. R. Keene, for $40,000 a side. Daly was credited with winning a quarter of a million dollars on the race. So great was Daly's affection for his favorite thoroughbred, one of the greatest winners of all time, that he named the largest stable at Bitter Root Tammany Castle. Other noted racing horses that bore the Daly colors were the unbeaten Colin, Hamburg, Hamburg Belle, Scottish Chief, Lady Reel, Killarney, Bathampton, Montana and Ogden, winner of the Futurity. Sales of the Daly horses at Madison Square Garden after his death netted more than two million dollars.

There was one episode associated with Daly's racing that caused him to be twitted by his friends for years afterward. He had a ticket worth $40,000 on Tammany in a race at Gutenberg. Tammany won. Daly was so enthused over his victory that he forgot to cash the ticket. A few days later his chief trainer asked him what he had done with the ticket. Daly looked abashed and then said: "I left it in the pocket of a shirt and sent it to the laundry."

A characteristic Daly story relates to the founding of *The Anaconda Standard*. There are two versions of this story. In the early Nineties John H. Dursten came out to Montana to make a fortune in mining. He had been editor of *The Syracuse Standard* and was a capable newspaperman. Like so many others he failed to make his pile. Daly met him, was impressed with his agreeable personality and hired him to be a sort of purchasing agent and general factotum.

One day Daly and Dursten were having lunch in the dining room of the Montana Hotel. Save for the waiter who served them, they were the only occupants. Dursten had a Helena newspaper in his hand. To Daly he said:

"I have just read in this paper that you have bought an untried yearling for $7,000."

Handing the paper to Daly and pointing to the paragraph, he continued: "Is this true?" Daly replied, "Yes."

Dursten then said:

"If you can afford to pay $7,000 for an untried yearling, you can afford to lose $100,000 on a newspaper."

To this Daly answered: "I am on."

Dursten went to New York, bought complete newspaper equipment and set up a plant at Anaconda. Competent newspapermen were engaged and *The Anaconda Standard* was born. At one time it was said that the *Standard* had more Linotype machines in operation than in any New York City newspaper plant. On the printing press was a brass plate with the words "Marcus Daly." At the start the *Standard* was sent down in a hand-car to Butte where it rolled up a circulation of twenty thousand.

The second version is that Daly, determined to found a newspaper, went to New York to consult journalists as to how he should go about it. One editor suggested Dursten. Daly then asked him to take over the job, purchase the equipment, go to Anaconda and start the paper. The first version is more probable.

The Anaconda Standard and *The Butte Miner* were merged in 1929 into *The Montana Standard* as a morning daily, published in Butte. A six-day morning edition of *The Anaconda Standard*, devoted entirely to local news and advertising in Anaconda is published there and inserted in *The Montana Standard* for Anaconda circulation only.

While Daly and the Anaconda group mounted to power, Butte took on a new look but it was anything but serene. Gone was the haphazard gold and silver era of the roaring Seventies when the miners lived in tents and shacks, with the straggling streets and rough highways deep in mud and snow in winter and blowing with dust in the summer. Now, in the Eighties, Butte was in process of change from disorganized mining camp into some semblance of a town with hotels and homes. Only the physical aspect, however, was altered. The majority of the residents, mainly miners, continued to be rough and boisterous with more red lights than white lights, more saloons and gambling houses than stores.

No productive era in the annals of American mining

presented such a colorful picture as the Butte of those roistering days, and no other famous mining district matched its history. Famous camps had their day of glory but exhaustion of ore bodies took its ruthless toll. Fabled Virginia City in Nevada, Comstock, Tombstone, Central City, Leadville and all the rest passed into the limbo of ghost towns to become mausoleums of vanished hopes. Not so with Butte. She survived a fabulous strike and went on to enhance her rich heritage, with the guarantee of many future decades of productivity ahead.

Moreover, no other American community has undergone such a kaleidoscopic change as Butte, cradle of Anaconda. Those hectic Eighties witnessed life in the raw. Around the Magic Hill swirled lust, passion, riot, strikes, and, in later years, bitter litigation that embroiled the copper kings.

For ten years after Daly opened the Anaconda mine, Butte was almost a continuous brawl. A black eye was a badge of honor. Holiday celebrations began a week in advance with hangovers lasting for a week afterward. Money was hard earned but easy spent. Most of the miners were unmarried so there were no house ties to bind. There were baptisms in mines, weddings in saloons, revival meetings with beer signs cluttering the walls. Rags and riches, wealth and squalor, vice and virtue, all mingled in the myriad, fantastic contrasts that never saw a dull moment. Art blossomed spasmodically amid the turmoil. Sarah Bernhardt, Mrs. Fiske, Harry Lauder, lent their presence before brawny miners decked out in gold nugget watch chains and their Sunday, but uncomfortable, best clothes.

So it went. Butte was a town of dash and variety, with two communities, one above ground and the other below. Amid all the disorder the miners on the Hill continued to delve deeper into its mineral wealth. Pleasure, variegated as it was, was incidental to the task that made it possible.

No phase of the Butte picture was more picturesque than the polyglot population. Daly had brought in furnace men and metallurgists from Wales, miners and superintendents from the gold and silver mines of the Southwest and mill men from the Michigan mines. They constituted only part of the motley array of race. With the development of the Anaconda and adjacent mines came the influx of Cornishmen, so many Finns that a populous district was called Finlandia, Germans, Poles, even Turks and Chinese. Butte became a racial cross-section of the United States.

From the beginning, the Irish were so prominent that people began to call Butte Shamrock City. Dennis Leary was the first to stake out the veins. Michael Hickey found Anaconda. His brother Edward located the St. Lawrence and other mines. Daly contributed a rich tradition. Then, too, there was Jeremiah Kelley whose son, Cornelius Francis, was to guide Anaconda to power and prestige.

In this connection it is interesting to note the large part played by the Irish in the development of mining in the West. Mackay, Fair, Flood and O'Brien became the bonanza kings of the Comstock, which was discovered by two other Irishmen, Peter O'Riley and Pat McLaughlin. An Irish general, Patrick E. Connor, staked out the first claim at Bingham, thus opening up a legendary copper area.

Butte's day of riot and revelry lived out the nineteenth century. With the turn of the twentieth came stabilization, fostered by the expansion of the Anaconda interests which were to become the dominant force both in the development of the community and its prosperity as well. The town grew up and the people quieted down. The population increase from 4,000 in 1882 to 10,783 in 1890, while Silver Bow County, which is really Butte, now had 23,714 persons. Ahead lay the fruitful years that made Butte the Copper Capital.

♠ 4

ENTER MR. COPPER

WHEN the eight-year old Cornelius Francis Kelley stepped down from that dingy wooden passenger coach in the Butte depot in 1883, he entered a new world. Behind him lay the calm of San Francisco with its orderly streets and an equally orderly population bent on conventional pursuits. In Butte he found himself in a community still alive with the boisterous frontier spirit, with brawny, shirtsleeved miners dominating the streets and the clang of hoist machinery filling the air. It was a swift transition, calculated to appeal to the boy's imagination and he soon adapted himself to the environment in which his destiny lay.

Jeremiah Kelley took his family to the Superintendent's house at the Bell Mine where they remained for some years. They then installed themselves in a house in Corra Terrace which was located about a mile east of Main and Daly Streets in Walkerville. Cornelius finished his grade school classes in a small Walkerville school. On Saturdays after school hours he returned home and hitched up the family horse to a buggy. The horse was named Centennial although he was not that old. Cornelius then drove his mother down to Dennis Driscoll's grocery, a mile from the Kelley residence. While Mrs. Kelley made her purchases, the boy roamed about the store enjoying the odor of pickles, cheese and apples. He was handsome, keen-eyed and affable and soon became a favorite of the shopkeeper who plied him with fruit which he invariably took home. There was a reason for this temporary abstinence.

After Mrs. Kelley finished her purchases Cornelius drove her to the Sullivan boarding house where she visited with Mrs. Margaret Sullivan who conducted the establishment with her grown daughters, Nora, Margaret and Julia. While the women chatted the boy revelled in the pastries for which Mrs. Sullivan was famous in the town. The love of sweets never forsook him.

Marcus Daly was a frequent visitor in the Kelley home. The men were old friends, the contact having begun at Mineral Hill. Often in the evening Daly and Kelley spun stories of their experiences with the eager-eyed Cornelius, who literally sat at their feet, an absorbed listener. It was then that the lure and romance of mining first stirred the boy, particularly the legend of the Anaconda, with which his name in later years was to be indelibly linked. Into his youthful ears were also poured tales of the stirring days when the Comstock Lode, Ophir and Ontario held the eye and interest of the mining world. It was a fascinating experience never to be forgotten.

Cornelius then entered the Butte High School. Although strong and of athletic build, he never went in for school sports except baseball. As he advanced in his teens he gained his full height of over six feet. Then, as in the succeeding period of his life, he stood out in any group, a commanding figure.

Whether in or out of school, Cornelius capitalized every waking hour. On the day before his first High School summer vacation started, he was walking home when he saw a group of huskies laying ties for the Montana Union Railroad which ran from Ogden to Butte. The foreman of the

gang was Fred Malone. As the boy came up to him he said:
"Sonny, go down to that spring and get a bucket of
water."

"What will you give me?" demanded the youth.

"I'll give you a dime," said Malone.

Cornelius brought up the bucket of water and received a
dime. It was the first money he ever earned.

The second money earned by Cornelius was as a $1.50 a
day water boy for the Butte, Anaconda & Pacific Railroad
while it was being constructed, and later for surface gangs
at the Diamond mine. Now came his first real contact with
mining. During the last High School summer vacations he
carried ore samples on mule back to be assayed, cleaned
lamps and became a nipper, that is, the boy who takes dull
tools up to the surface to be sharpened. All these activities
were at the Anaconda mine.

Cornelius graduated from High School in 1892. He was
seventeen and one of the youngest in his class. The momentous time was at hand when he must determine his
future vocation. Born in a mining family, tradition dictated
that he go in for mining, but he turned it aside. All through
his High School years the law had beckoned to him. He
saw it as a career that, for one thing, would enable him
to capitalize a gift for fluent speech which had already
manifested itself in school debates. A course in law, however, required a considerable cash outlay, so the youth
determined to earn it himself.

Accordingly, after his graduation from High School he
approached Daly and asked for a job.

"What do you want to do?" asked Daly.

"I want to go into engineering," replied Cornelius.

The upshot was that Cornelius went on the payroll at the
Anaconda mine. It was his first real job. An engineer in a
mine must be a surveyor. The youth showed great aptitude
and eventually rose in rank to be an instrument man, which
meant that he was a surveyor. Often Cornelius was obliged

to get up at four o'clock in the morning to see that the headings did not come together.

On a morning in September 1894, while he was still in the Engineering Department, Kelley met Daly just outside the office. To him he said:

"I am going to quit my job and study law."

Daly's retort was: "Thanks for giving me so much notice." Then, with his habitual sarcasm, he added:

"I will try to get someone to fill your place."

The next day Kelley met Daly again at the same place. Daly's first remark was:

"I am sorry I was so sarcastic with you yesterday. I hope you will give up your ambition to be a lawyer. If you do, I will send you to the Columbia School of Mines and pay all your expenses."

It was a generous offer and would have induced most young men to accept. Kelley, however, was fixed in his purpose and answered:

"Thank you very much but I am determined to be a lawyer."

Came 1895 and an epochal day in young Kelley's life. He entered the Law College of the University of Michigan, receiving his degree in 1898 when he was just twenty-three years old.

During his years at college he worked every summer in the Engineering Department of the Anaconda and other Butte mines. From $60 a month his pay advanced to $125. His chief in engineering was August Christian, who was more than boss, for he became friend and adviser. It was an invaluable experience.

During his service underground in the Engineering Department Kelley had many exciting and sometimes hazardous experiences. One will serve to illustrate his initiative and courage. When he went back to work during his vacation in 1896, he was helper for Sam Barker. They were making a survey in the Diamond mine through a lateral where the cross-cut turned off at the sill. Kelley looked at the ground and realized that it was not safe. He sounded the rock with a small hand axe. This was the usual procedure when a miner thought there was a crack above him. Barker had just been married so Kelley said to him: "You go ahead and take the light and I will follow with the instrument." At this juncture two miners came along. One had a big eight-pound hammer. Kelley asked them to make a sounding with their hammer. One of them, Jerry McCarthy, pounded the rock and then said: "It will stand a thousand years."

Jerry was wrong. As Kelley started to set his instrument, a rock hit him. He had instinct enough to know what was coming and threw himself forward into the cross-cut. He was buried under debris. Barker and the two other miners dug him out. Kelley had sustained a broken leg, a broken shoulder and three broken ribs. Barker and the two other miners, who had all escaped injury, took Kelley to the hospital. After three weeks he was able to hobble around on crutches. He then took up work in the Anaconda office where he was given a desk in the Drafting Department.

The Engineering office was in a two-story brick building not far from the Anaconda mine. The lower floor was mainly a commissary where the top engineers had their meals. On the second floor was the small bedroom that Daly occupied when he visited Butte at that time.

Kelley's principal job was to make a map that would show the connection between the Syndicate on the Hill and the Anaconda group. The map was at a scale of one hundred feet to the inch. Kelley worked day and night under a huge one hundred candle power bulb over white paragon paper. The glare of light on the white paper imposed a terrific strain on his eyes which developed retinitis. This was the forerunner of the serious eye trouble that plagued him in later years. It also made his study at college difficult.

Kelley was able to continue his summer vacation work in

the mines for he was still enrolled in the Engineering Department. He gave his monthly checks to his mother. She did not cash the checks but kept them until he returned to college, thus affording him the money with which to continue his studies.

The year 1898 loomed large in Kelley's life for, in June of that year, he received his law degree. During his summer vacations he had earned enough money to pay for his tuition, but he had achieved more than financial advantage. He had worked in the mines under competent and experienced men and had developed a natural aptitude for engineering. His underground work taught him the routine and technique of mining, an experience that was to be invaluable when he launched his legal career. When, figuratively, he hung out his shingle, he was the best-equipped young lawyer in Butte.

Meanwhile the Kelley family had moved to a large brick house located at 800 North Main Street. With Cornelius home to stay, the Kelleys were united in a happy household.

When Kelley returned to Butte from law school his first impulse was to go in for a political career for which he had a natural aptitude. He was tall, handsome, endowed with Irish charm, quick-witted, with a retentive memory for names and faces—always an invaluable asset in politics. He campaigned for a seat in the State Legislature and, when only three months out of college, was elected.

Kelley could not have entered politics at a more dramatic time. The Montana political pot boiled, for the famous Daly-Clark feud, the war of the Copper Kings, was on. Daly was a Democrat as was Kelley. When the Democratic State Convention met to nominate a State slate Daly bolted it. With Kelley's help he formed the Independent Democratic Party which named Kelley for Congress from the Butte District. He was defeated by the strongly entrenched Republican Party organization, which had put up S. G.

Murray. With a split party opposing them, the Republicans had no difficulty in carrying the state.

Kelley's defeat in the race for Congress was a lucky break for him, for Anaconda, and for the copper industry. With a united party behind him he might have won a Congressional seat in the next election. Beyond that, the United States Senate would have beckoned with all its implications of wider national service. He would have been obliged to forswear a career for which he was so eminently equipped. Thus the ill wind of political defeat blew an immense good.

Previous to the campaign for Congress, William Scallon, then General Counsel for Anaconda, had asked Kelley to be a candidate for County Attorney to succeed C. P. Connelly. Kelley declined the proffer, saying: "Thank you but I prefer to stick to my law practice."

Kelley now settled down to his chosen profession. The leading law firm in Butte was McHatton & Cotter with offices in the Silver Bow Block. The senior partner, John F. McHatton, gave Kelley a desk in the firm's offices.

Kelley's first case involved the apex issue which was to embattle Butte for more than a decade. The client was a man named Poulon. Poulon claimed trespass on his property and on this contention the case was argued. In such a suit it is necessary to produce in court a model of the mine with the alleged trespass, all of it encased in glass. Kelley's experience underground came in good stead. His client lacked the money with which to have a model made by a professional. Kelley constructed a model out of a candle box, painted it blue, and used a red crayon to draw the vein. He conducted the case with such skill that he won a verdict. The damages, or rather the damage, imposed was exactly one dollar. On the day after the trial Poulon left Butte for parts unknown.

Kelley did not receive a penny out of the dollar verdict but he earned much in prestige. The case had attracted attention from press and public. Kelley's reputation as a lawyer was established. As the number of his clients mounted he became a leading member of the Butte bar. Nor was it surprising. His tall, impressive presence, gift of oratory, charm of manner, ready repartee and his resource in impromptu debate, combined to make him a favorite.

In less than a year after Kelley had been given a desk in the McHatton & Cotter offices, Judge McHatton offered him a junior partnership in the firm. He refused it because the firm was chief counsel for Heinze, then waging bitter war on the Anaconda interests. Kelley felt that his first loyalty was to Anaconda where he felt his future lay. Nor was it misplaced as subsequent events amply proved.

For a year after his graduation in law Kelley undertook various cases involving mining disputes and with invariable success. In 1899 he was appointed Chief Deputy County Attorney which took him into the arena of criminal cases. He successfully prosecuted a succession of offenders, some of them the most notorious ever to appear in the Butte courts. He became a master of jury address, eloquently playing on the emotions of jurors in effective fashion. His demeanor, however, always comported with the dignity so essential in a court of law.

Kelley never lacked courage, whether in those early criminal prosecutions or in later years when he was shaping the course of a giant corporation. A case in point was his prosecution of Dan Lucey charged with killing a man named Ryan. The evidence was circumstantial. It evolved about the knife used in the murder. The knife had not been found. Lucey was sentenced to be hanged.

Two days before the date set for his execution Lucey sent for Kelley. When the young lawyer reached the jail the prisoner said to him:

"Come inside the cell. I want to tell you something." The guard immediately warned Kelley, saying:

"Don't go inside. He will try to kill you. The only weapon he has is a stool but it can be used effectively."

To this Kelley replied:

"I am going in. If he attempts anything, shoot, no matter whom you hit."

Kelley went into the cell. Lucey wanted a reprieve, basing his claim for it on the knowledge he possessed about the missing knife that figured in another murder case. He alleged that the whereabouts of the knife had been revealed to him by one of the men involved in the case. Kelley refused Lucey's appeal and he was hanged. Later Kelley obtained the information about the location of the knife.

Kelley's success as criminal lawyer led to an amusing comment. One of the familiar figures in Butte was a phrenologist who went under the name of Professor Smith. He wore a silk hat and frock coat and paraded the streets in this attire, soliciting business. In those days people took phrenology seriously and, as a result, the professor thrived. One of his classic remarks, retailed from mouth to mouth in Butte, was:

"C. F. Kelley is the man whose skill the murderer will seek before he begins to kill."

Kelley's rise as lawyer was matched by his social advancement. The attractive young barrister whose oratorical skill was so effective in court, was in increasing demand as speaker on public occasions, particularly at banquets honoring local or visiting celebrities. His ease of speech, illumined by a ready wit, made his appearances pleasing to eye and ear.

As he stood at the threshold of a notable career, Kelley developed a philosophy about Butte typical of the man. He had watched Anaconda grow from that hole in the Hill into a growing entity with a tremendous future, already assured. When people asked him about the future of the city he invariably replied: "Butte will never be a ghost city." That prediction has been amply verified for today the community on the Silver Bow is richer in mineral and other assets than ever before.

When Daly died in 1900, William Scallon became President of Anaconda, having succeeded him in that office. Because of the opportunity he gave Kelley for his first post with the company and also his distinguished service to the corporation, his career may well be noted. A Canadian by birth, he graduated from McGill University and practiced law in Montreal. After spending a short time in the Lake Superior copper region he went to Butte in 1884 where he started a law practice. Soon he became acquainted with Daly and became his legal adviser. From the beginning of their association Scallon held the trust and confidence of Daly. Beside carrying on his legal work for Daly he assisted him in an advisory capacity in the operation of the Butte and Anaconda properties.

This association led to Scallon's appointment as counsel for The Anaconda Mining Company followed by a similar post, first, with The Anaconda Copper Mining Company and later with The Amalgamated Copper Company upon its organization in 1899. He was almost immediately plunged into the bitter apex litigation with Heinze. When it seemed probable that Heinze's plans to rifle the rich Butte ore bodies would be defeated, Scallon resigned the Presidency of The Anaconda Copper Mining Company and returned to private law practice.

Scallon left Butte in 1910 to open a law office in New York City. After two and a half years he returned to Montana at the request of T. J. Walsh, who had been elected to the United States Senate. He desired that a lawyer of eminent attainments take over his law practice. The law firm of Walsh, Nolan & Scallon was then formed and became one of the outstanding firms in Montana. Walsh never returned to the practice of law, devoting the rest of his life to public service. Nolan died in 1922 and Scallon carried on the firm alone.

At that time D. J.—"Dan"—Hennessy was one of the leading citizens of Butte. At the age of twenty he had arrived in Butte from his native New Brunswick in Canada with exactly fifty cents in his pocket. He saw an apple vendor on the street and bought two apples at twenty-five cents each. Prices were high in Butte for fruit was scarce. Hennessy ate one of the apples, his first food in Butte, and gave the other to a beggar.

Hennessy was alert and personable. He got a job selling men's clothing. Before long he was head man in the Connels Store. In a few years he owned the establishment. He then opened the first Hennessy Department Store which burned down a few days later. Anaconda built the office building on its present site just across the street and named it after Hennessy who opened the department store on the ground floor which still bears his name. With the completion of the Hennessy Building in 1899 the Anaconda organization took offices in it.

Early in his business career Hennessy met Daly. The men became fast friends. It was generally believed in Butte that Daly largely financed Hennessy's business ventures.

The Hennessy and Kelley families were neighbors and friends. Hennessy had watched Cornelius grow up and was proud of his achievements. Early in 1901 he encountered Scallon on the street. After the usual exchange of remarks about the weather and business, Hennessy said:

"You will lose young Con Kelley if you don't hire him."

It did not take Scallon long to make up his mind. A few days afterward he offered Kelley a post in the legal department of his company. Kelley accepted the offer. The man who was to become the dominant factor in the expansion of Anaconda and whose name would be synonymous with it, entered upon his kingdom.

♤ 5

RYAN AND THE AMALGAMATED ERA

WHEN Kelley took over his desk in the Legal Department of Anaconda, his chief was A. J. Shores. Then, as today, the department was housed on the sixth floor of the Hennessy Building. In seniority the other members of the legal staff were W. W. Dixon, J. K. McDonald and DeGay Stivers. On the letterhead of the department, Kelley's name, therefore, was at the bottom of the list. It was characteristic of the man that when he became General Counsel in 1908 he did not change the wording at the top of the letterhead.

With his underground training Kelley was the best-equipped member of the staff to deal with the complex litigation that was crowding thick and fast. The time was ripe for the capitalization of that experience. The Heinze litigation, which was to make Butte an embattled legal camp, had begun. It was to test Kelley's mettle for nearly a decade. He emerged from it the leading mining lawyer of the West. Linked with this was his progressive dominance in the company as far-seeing executive.

The story of the Heinze litigation will be told in detail in the next chapter. Just now the task is to follow the expansion of Anaconda despite the legal turmoil that raged about it.

Up to 1891 the Syndicate had operated the Anaconda and adjacent mines as a partnership. With the financial backing of Haggin, Hearst and Tevis, Daly had laid the solid foundation of his mining enterprise. This had been achieved without corporate form of business. The organization of The Anaconda Mining Company in 1891 achieved corporate status.

Before the expansion of Anaconda is unfolded, however, it is necessary to project the picture of the Butte mining properties and the men who developed them. These properties and their owners, one in particular, were to figure prominently in the drama that was now to begin.

During the decade following Daly's development of the Anaconda claim, other large copper operations came into existence. The success of Daly's venture and the rapid growth of the Electrical Age in America, attracted investment to the Butte district. The major concern among these interests contributed substantially to the opening up of the ore bodies in the area and to the techniques necessary for the treatment of the ores. Among these interests were the W. A. Clark enterprises which were to loom large in the subsequent Butte story. They included the Parrot Silver and Copper Company and various other corporations. Some of these interests operated their own concentrators and smelters in Butte. All contributed to a colorful chapter in mining.

The Parrot Silver and Copper Company was one of the earliest mining corporations in the district, its first claim having been staked out under the old mining law of 1866. It was incorporated in 1880 by Franklin Farrel of Ansonia, Connecticut. S. T. Hauser, later governor of Montana, and A. M. Holter had bought the Parrot claim in 1877. The mine was prepared for production in 1884. Up to 1910, when it was acquired by Anaconda interests, it had produced 240,000,000 pounds of copper. Thereafter its output was combined with other Anaconda production. This company owned Parrot, Little Mina, Bellona, Original Number 6, Adventure, Kanuck, Rialto and twelve other mines.

The Chambers Syndicate, which had started operations in 1882, had gathered for Daly the claims known as the Mountain Consolidated group, already enumerated. These properties constituted a vital part of the later growth of The Anaconda Company. Part of the Syndicate's holdings became the Davis-Daly property. At that time many locaters in Butte, seeing their silver values disappearing, lost enthusiasm for their claims and were seeking buyers. The Chambers Syndicate purchased many of these claims, Daly selecting the ones which most appealed to him for Anaconda.

The Moulton Mining Company owned the Moulton, one of the many which brought an apex suit against Anaconda. Moulton was acquired by Anaconda in 1928.

The Boston and Montana Consolidated Copper and Silver Mining Company marked the advent of the Lewisohn brothers, Leonard and Adolph, into the Butte District. Sons of a merchant in feathers and horsehair in Hamburg, Germany, they came to New York in 1866 to conduct a branch of the family business. Both had energy and big vision. Before many years passed they tired of the prosaic material in which they dealt and turned to metals and mining. They formed the firm of Lewisohn Brothers which became a power in copper. Among other things they organized the United Metals Selling Company, which at one time sold fifty-five per cent of all the copper produced in the United States.

Associated with the Lewisohns in the Boston & Montana were Joseph W. Clark, Albert S. Bigelow and Aaron Spencer, a veteran of the Michigan copper mines. The Lewisohns had purchased rich claims in the Meaderville section of the Butte District from Colonel C. T. Meader and W. A. Clark. Among these claims was the Leonard, named after

Leonard Lewisohn. Other important properties acquired by Boston & Montana were Mountain View, East Colusa, Moose, Badger State, Comanche, Gambetta and Greenleaf. The claims totalled 483 acres adjoining Anaconda properties on the east. At one time Boston & Montana employed 4,000 men, owned important water rights at Great Falls, and a large concentrator and smelter in Meaderville. It was one of the first to install a leaching plant in the area. Boston & Montana was merged with Anaconda in 1910 through The Amalgamated Copper Company. This, however, is a later story.

The Butte & Boston Consolidated Mining Company was organized in 1888 and reorganized in 1896. Lewisohn capital was interested in the development. The company acquired the Sister, La Plata, Free for All, Lone Tree and Gabrella mines. Subsequent mines acquired were the Michael Devitt, Blue Jay, Berkeley, West Gray Rock, East Gray Rock and Silver Bow. Prior to its absorption by Anaconda the company had produced 296,000,000 pounds of copper and paid $1,039,270 in dividends.

The Butte Copper & Zinc Company, incorporated in 1894, owned the Emma mine which later became an important producer of manganese ore of superior quality, the Czarromah, Travona, Fraction, Mountain Central, Bob Ingersoll, Manhattan, Nellie, Ella Ophir, Marie Louise, Railroad, Single Tax and Buck Placer claims. Production by the company was small but Anaconda, as lessee, derived an important output of manganese and zinc from it for war needs during World War I.

Other companies in the Butte district in that early era following Daly's development of the Anaconda mine were the North Butte Mining Company, incorporated by Thomas F. Cole, who was to become a close friend and associate of John D. Ryan, whose properties included the Speculator, Edith May, Gem, Snowball, North Berlin and Tuolumne claims, the East Butte Copper Mining Com-

pany, the Butte & Superior Mining Company with its
Black Rock and Jersey Blue claims, and the Butte & Ballaklava Copper Company which owned the Ballaklava and
Burke claims adjoining the Modoc of The Anaconda Company.

These mines, together with Anaconda, comprised the
major interests that were to be embroiled in what became
the legal mining battle of the century. Blood was to be
spilled, reputations wrecked, millions of dollars deployed,
in a decade of bitter court strife.

The battle of mining interests was matched by the famous Daly-Clark feud which, like the apex conflict, cost
millions and engendered bitterness and hatred that lasted
for years. It would be difficult to find a similar vendetta in
all American history. With the account of the feud, Clark
enters this narrative with compelling interest.

No two men were more different in character, temperament and outlook than the protagonists in their epic struggle. Daly was warm, generous, popular, gregarious; Clark
was tight, starched, ruthless. Daly moved in an ever-widen-
ing circle of friends; Clark was the lone wolf, socially and in
business, an uncompromising individualist. All his properties were operated personally or with his own family.
He did not incorporate his bank and never listed or offered
for sale the stocks and bonds of any of his companies.
Money was Clark's god. It was said of him that "not a dollar got away from him except to come back stuck to another." Daly had no vanity and rejoiced in the success of
his associates while Clark was stiff with pride, jealous, arro-
gant, with a colossal vanity that caused him to bask in flat-
tery. Daly had no political ambition for himself; Clark was
obsessed with the desire to become a power in politics.

Both Daly and Clark had preeminent qualities for leadership but they were manifested in opposite fashion. Each
regarded the exercise of great power as a necessity for the
fulfillment of his ambition and the conduct of his business.

PHOTOGRAPHIC SUPPLEMENT

Marcus Daly

KELLEY SHAFT →

"The Richest Hill on Earth"

James B. Haggin

The Anaconda Mine in 1890

Aerial view of present-day Butte

The Daly Monument in Butte

The Smelter at Anaconda

Early day hoisting in a bucket at Butte

The Kelley Mine

Cornelius F. Kelley—Chairman 1940–1955; Chairman Executive Committee

W. A. Clark

John D. Ryan

International Smelting and Refining Plant at Tooele

Henry H. Rogers

The Great Falls Production Works

PHOTO BY FABIAN BACHRACH

Clyde E. Weed—President

The Cananea Mine and Concentrator

The Yerington Mine

Weed Heights

Roy H. Glover—Chairman of the Board

PHOTO BY BLACKSTONE STUDIOS, NEW YORK

James R. Hobbins
William Scallon

B. B. Thayer
W. H. Hoover

Section of the pit at Chuquicamata

Sulphide Plant at Chuquicamata

The Oxide Plant at Chuquicamata

The Potrerillos Reduction Plant

Location of the El Salvador Mine

Haulage tunnel at El Salvador

Uranium processing plant at Bluewater

The Jackpile Mine

Kenosha Branch American Brass Company

American Brass Company plant at Waterbury

Robert E. Dwyer

PHOTO BY CONWAY STUDIOS CORPORATION, NEW YORK

Reno H. Sales
F. F. Frick

Frederick Laist
William Wraith, Sr.

The Berkeley Pit

Underground electric ore train in the Kelley Mine

Hastings Mill—Anaconda Wire & Cable Company

Anderson Mill—Anaconda Wire & Cable Company

Pot-room at Aluminum Plant

Anaconda Aluminum Plant at Columbia Falls

Clark's directions and commands were often arbitrary. He seldom mingled with his employees, above or under ground. Daly, on the other hand, called himself a miner. He was usually to be found about the mines and in the plants. He was personally acquainted with hundreds of his men, always their friend and frequently their benefactor. In only one detail did they share a kinship. Both fitted into the category of self-made success. Daly, the humble dock worker who became the first of the Copper Kings; Clark who rose from $2.50 a day laborer in a Colorado mine to amass a fortune of $47,000,000.

First a close-up of Clark, the man and his career. William Andrews Clark, to give him his full name, was born in 1839 of Scotch-Irish parents on a farm near Connellsville, Pennsylvania. After attending a local public school and a Wesleyan College in Iowa he studied law for a year. This was too prosaic for a man of his restless temperament so he hired a team, drove to Central City, Colorado, where he got a job as laborer in a mine. A year later he joined the stampede of miners to Bannack. At Bannack he was first bitten by the political bug. He attended a session of the Legislature of the Territory of Montana held in a log cabin. Then and there he decided that some day he would go in for politics. Soon afterward he went to Horse Prairie and located a placer claim. Here he accumulated $1,500, his first stake. With this he bought a mule team and hauled a load of provisions to Salt Lake City which, as he afterward said, he "sold for extraordinarily high prices." Later he opened a store at Blackfoot, a new mining camp. Typical of his business acumen was the fact that he bought tobacco at $1.50 a pound and sold it for $6.00 a pound in Helena.

In those early days Clark developed the golden touch which never forsook him. Then, as later, he converted every activity into gain. With a pack train he bought and sold gold dust, cattle, grain and provisions and carried mail, ending up with a wholesale store in Helena with H. W.

Donnell. This store was then consolidated with a Donnell store at Deer Lodge. The next step in Clark's career was important for the firm branched into banking with G. E. Larabie as partner. The venture proved so profitable that the mercantile end was abandoned. In 1878 a branch bank was opened in Butte with Clark as manager. Donnell sold out and the Butte bank became W. A. Clark & Brother.

Fortune favored Clark. At thirty-three he had become the leading banker, merchant and capitalist in the Territory of Montana and a millionaire. He now embarked on the mining ventures that were to enhance his already great wealth. Years before Daly opened up the Anaconda mine Clark owned Colusa, Original, Mountain Chief and Gambetta and later Moulton. Subsequently the Elm Orlu Mining came into his possession.

The way Clark acquired Farlin's Travona mine was typical of his capitalization of opportunity. Clark had advanced $30,000 to Farlin who had depleted his finances to build a stamp mill at his mine. Unable to meet his obligation at maturity at the Clark bank, he allowed the property to go. Clark's partner, Larabie, was not interested in mines. Clark bought his rights, so the story went in Butte, for a drove of horses. Clark now built the Dexter and Centennial Mills and organized the Butte Reduction Works. By 1886 he owned large Butte real estate holdings and the water and light companies.

Just about this time Clark decided to learn something about geology. He took a course at the Columbia School of Mines in New York. When he returned to Butte he had the twin assets of money and technical equipment for his increasing forays in mining.

Clark loved to bask in the limelight. The first notable occasion for him to shine before the public came when he was Montana State Orator at the Centennial Exposition in Philadelphia. He was not a prepossessing figure on the platform for he was undersized, with bushy whiskers, but he overcame his physical handicap for he was an effective speaker.

When Daly first came to Butte, Clark was already entrenched as leading banker with expanding mining interests. The men became friends. Following Daly's rise after he opened up the Anaconda mine and his growing popularity, Clark came to envision him as a rival for leadership in Butte. Jealousy was a deep-seated characteristic of Clark. This may have been one of the reasons why enmity developed on his part.

Various other reasons have been advanced for the bitter feeling between the men from which sprang the historic feud. The antagonism, however, did not result from controversies affecting mining operations. Many interpreted the feud as a warfare on Butte Hill that found its way into the courts in the form of contests over ore bodies. Nothing was farther from the truth. The fact that some early apex litigation in Butte was instigated by Clark interests, and that one of the last of the apex cases involved a Clark property, the Moulton Mining Company, gave credence to this belief.

The differences between Daly and Clark were grounded in social and, particularly, political rivalries. Daly's resentment was first aroused when Clark wrote a letter to the Walker brothers accusing him of extravagance and unbusinesslike management of the Alice mine. The Walkers sent the letter to Daly. Clark also wrote a similar letter to Haggin after the syndicate began operations on the Hill. It only intensified Haggin's support of Daly. Clark was also charged with the statement that Daly was "uncouth and not a gentleman" and that his Anaconda copper find was "pure luck."

Daly's first opportunity to retaliate was in 1888, when he was largely instrumental in bringing about the defeat of Clark for Territorial delegate to Congress. Clark was humiliatingly beaten by a former book agent, Thomas H.

Carter, later admitted to the Montana bar and subsequently a United States Senator, who won in every district in which Daly had influence, including Clark's own ward. Clark's pride and vanity were sorely bruised. Thereafter the battle lines between the two men were drawn and the feud which embroiled all Montana was on at full tilt.

An interlude in the titanic battle for the United States Senate waged by Clark with Daly opposing his every attempt save the last when he was fatally ill, was the contest for State capital. A constitutional convention had decreed that the people of Montana should name, by vote, their capital city. Helena had wrested the seat of Territorial government from Virginia City in 1875 and held on.

Daly stepped into the picture in 1892 when Montana had been a state for three years. He wanted Anaconda, which he had built, to be the capital. Clark backed Helena and the fight was on.

A primary election to determine the final rivals in a run-off, resulted in a victory for Helena over Anaconda. It was more a duel between Daly and Clark than a contest between two cities. Helena polled 14,010 votes to 10,183 for Anaconda. Butte was third and Bozeman fourth. Great Falls, Deer Lodge and Boulder were also in the running. Popular interest was evident in the fact that out of a total state registration of 51,500, exactly 45,967 votes were cast.

Helena and Anaconda were now the final contestants. In the run-off in 1894 Helena won again. Both Daly and Clark spent huge sums in behalf of their respective cities. It was estimated that the outlay by the two men was more than a million dollars.

The capital fight was a skirmish. The real battle between the Copper Kings was now to begin. It was waged around Clark's ambition to become United States Senator. Again money flowed like water with recriminations mounting higher and higher. It was not only a war of spoken words but written words as well. Daly owned *The Anaconda*

Standard; Clark was proprietor of *The Butte Miner.* In those days anything went, so to speak, in print. Anathema and accusations flew back and forth, for the law of libel then had scant force in Montana.

Clark went to Washington four times with credentials of a United States Senator but he did not qualify for his seat until after the fourth try. In 1889 he was elected by the Democratic division of the Legislature but the Republicans also elected a Senator who was seated. A year later he was again elected but was accused of bribery and resigned. His third fleeting Senatorship resulted from a political ruse. Governor Robert B. Smith, who opposed Clark, left the state to attend a convention. Lieutenant Governor Spriggs, a Clark supporter, took swift advantage of the opportunity. As acting Governor he appointed Clark. There was such a hullabaloo over the appointment that Clark refused to take his seat. In 1900 Clark made his final and ultimately successful attempt. When the campaign for this seat opened Daly was on his death bed in New York. For nearly five years he had circumvented Clark's Senatorial aspirations. Fate now decreed that the lists be closed so far as he was concerned. Clark served his full term in Washington.

So far as Daly was concerned, his political feud with Clark was merely a diverting but expensive episode. Mining was at the very core of his life and to mining he dedicated his ability and energy. The time was at hand when his fondest dreams of expansion would come true.

As the mid-decade of the nineteenth century approached, the fame of Anaconda had become worldwide for Daly had welded the greatest copper-producing concern yet known. The expanding use of electricity created a widening demand for copper and Anaconda was meeting this demand with an ever-increasing production. The financing required by the company was now largely met in New York. The investment capital of the United States had become interested in Anaconda and before long, the financial center of

Europe, which was London, would also have a stake in it.

The old Haggin—Tevis—Hearst—Daly Syndicate was passing out of the picture. Hearst died in 1891. Tevis was to breathe his last in 1899. Haggin had indicated his desire to withdraw from the financial exploits which he had so long carried on. The strain of nearly twenty years of effort to build Anaconda was beginning to tell on Daly. The period of apex litigation, with its myriad law suits and bitter controversies, had just begun.

In 1895, working through the syndicate, and later, through The Anaconda Mining Company, Daly perfected the structure which he envisioned as the greatest non-ferrous metal-producing concern in the world. In the past he had had the benefit of the ample financing of Haggin, the mining sagacity of Hearst and his own broad experience. With these allies, together with Tevis, he had mobilized the mines that tapped the stupendous ore bodies of the Anaconda and other mines. He had reared modern metallurgical works, a transportation system, bought coal and timber lands, organized the Butte Trading Company to provide supplies, the Tuttle Manufacturing Company to replace needed machinery and the Standard Fire Brick Company to make the only brick for furnaces produced in the West. Furthermore, he had reared the town of Anaconda. All this comprised an achievement that would have satisfied any man but Daly was not the type ever to be satisfied. His vision was big, his sense of conception broad, his ideal of production high. He was now to capitalize these assets in the creation of the company that was to be his monument.

In recapitulating his efforts, Daly made a statement of policy early in 1895. In it he said:

"The policy of the Company from the beginning has been not so much to realize immediate returns as it has been to try to lay the foundation for a long life of activity and usefulness. For this purpose, the profits of the Company have been expended in the enlargement and betterment of the plant until today, in its re-modeled, reconstructed, and completed state, it stands without a peer among the copper producers of the world.

"It can be truthfully said that in all the history of copper mining, no enterprise on so large a scale was ever before projected; no equipment for the mining, moving, treating and marketing of copper ores and their products was ever before so thorough, comprehensive and complete; no copper mine ever discovered justified the outlay made upon it and none ever promised such handsome returns on the capital invested. Yielding up its rich treasure at a time when the discoveries of science are revolution-izing the mechanism which moves the commerce of the world, and when the demands of trade are drawing upon this world's visible supply of copper to its utmost capacity, The Anaconda Copper Mining Company enters upon an era of unexampled prosperity which is not alone of merely personal and local in-terest, for while its success primarily benefits those immediately interested in it, its prosperity is also a matter of public concern for the reason that its product enters so largely into the necessi-ties and conveniences of modern business life. No mining enter-prise ever started out under brighter auspices, and none ever promised better returns."

With these words Daly launched The Anaconda Copper Mining Company on June 18, 1895. This concern, which was eventually to take leadership in the production and fabrication of non-ferrous metals, to become a producer of aluminum and uranium, and to rear an empire of operation that stretched from the Great Divide of the Rockies to the slopes of the Andes, would have been born under another name a few days earlier had it not been for a misunderstand-ing between Daly and Haggin, who were in New York, and the Butte offices where the papers were drawn. It was first directed that the new corporation should be known as The Anaconda Copper Company with capital stock of 300,000 shares of $100 par value, the term of existence to be forty years. A few days later Haggin and Daly telegraphed from

New York, directing that the capital structure be changed to 1,200,000 shares, par $25, place of business, Anaconda. W. W. Dixon, Chief Counsel at Butte, replied that such changes could not be made under the law without reincorporating. The result was that a new corporation, The Anaconda Copper Mining Company, was incorporated.

On June 29, 1895 all the property of The Anaconda Mining Company, the stock of which had been held in trust by Haggin, was transferred to The Anaconda Copper Mining Company. These properties consisted of four principal groups, in addition to claims and real estate outside the Butte district. The properties were the Anaconda group, made up of the Anaconda, St. Lawrence and Never Sweat mines; the Mountain Consolidated group which consisted of a series of claims upon a vein system parallel with the Anaconda mine, the principal mines being the Diamond, Modoc, High Ore, Green Mountain and Mat; the Union Consolidated group made up of a number of silver mining claims; and the Anglo-Saxon group which became the Orphan Girl.

As of June 24, 1895, just before the transfer of properties to The Anaconda Copper Mining Company, the stockholders of the old company and their holdings were: Fleming Brenner, trustee, 475,992 shares; J. B. Haggin, 204,-001 shares; J. B. Haggin, trustee, 20,000 shares; Mrs. Phoebe A. Hearst, 299,000 shares; Marcus Daly, W. W. Dixon, Louis T. Haggin, R. P. Lounsbery, H. B. Parsons, Francis E. Sargent and August Christian, each one share.

The Anaconda Mining Company, which now lost its identity, had rolled up an impressive output. Between November 1884 and the incorporation of The Anaconda Copper Mining Company it sold 707,402,130 pounds of copper, 18,567,628 ounces of silver, and 83,349 ounces of gold.

Haggin became President of the new company on July 1, 1895. Moses Kirkpatrick of the Legal Department under Dixon had been named President of the company pending perfection of the organization, Daly was Superintendent, the post he had held from the opening of the Anaconda mine. He had surrounded himself with a group of mining and metallurgical engineers, technicians, accountants and lawyers who were destined to build the enterprise far beyond the hopes and vision of that day.

There now followed a period of rapid development in the technique of mining the Anaconda ore bodies. The complicated vein structures of the Butte Hill posed a problem that demanded the highest skill. This skill was not lacking.

Metallurgical works were rebuilt; electrolytic refining of copper was started. New products and chemicals were recovered from the ores. Costs of treatment were reduced with lower grade ores yielding practical returns. In 1896 sulphuric acid manufacture from the flue gases started. Leaching of tailings from the Old Works was carried on successfully in the Washoe plant. This was a pioneering operation, forerunner of extensive leaching operations by copper companies throughout the Southwest and later in South America.

Within two years after the inauguration of electrolytic refining, one-half of the company's annual output of more than 124,000,000 pounds of copper was produced by this process. The process placed on the market a metal of great purity, a quality that never before had been achieved. It made western copper more competitive in the market with the native copper produced in the Lake Superior region. Refining was gradually concentrated at Great Falls, which was later to be taken over with the acquisition of The Boston & Montana Company.

Cement copper was another development under the aegis of the company. Pumping of underground mine water from the shafts constituted a serious problem and a heavy expense. Copper precipitation by the use of tin cans and scrap iron was first discovered by Frederick Mueller, a miner, and later developed by J. L. Ledford. This operation became an important part of Anaconda operations. The cement copper precipitated from the water pumped out of the mine pays for the pumping costs.

Some idea of the company's operations in its early period is gained from the fact that in the first year after incorporation The Anaconda Copper Mining Company mined 1,355,874 tons of ore, sold 107,036,697 pounds of copper, 4,498,560 ounces of silver and 14,384 ounces of gold for a total of $11,929,903, and had on hand $4,880,020 in metals at the end of the year. The profit for the year was $4,238,-514. For the year 1895–6 the first dividend of $750,000 was paid.

In 1899 Haggin retired as President and was succeeded by Daly. It was the first time he had taken over a high office. Titles meant nothing to this miner, as he was always proud to call himself.

The great production of Anaconda and the fact that the concern had become a vast integrated unit in the copper industry, attracted attention in London, then the world's financial center. A demand for the stock developed there. On November 3, 1895 in a letter to *The Anaconda Standard*, Daly stated:

"After a thorough examination by experts, we have sold one-quarter of the capital stock at a price that makes the properties worth $30,000,000. Since then, a part of this quarter has been sold in New York and London at a price which makes the property worth about $37,000,000. No larger interest than this quarter was ever before offered for sale."

Four-sixteenths of this stock had been sold by the estate of George Hearst. Later three-sixteenths was delivered by Haggin and Daly from holdings originally held by Tevis.

The British stock interest had been acquired by the Exploration Syndicate of London, a concern dominated by the great banking house of Rothschild. Anaconda had become a world citizen, presaging the time when it would become international in scope and operation.

II

As the Nineties neared their close the Butte scene underwent a change. The Daly-Clark feud had left scars but they were not a patch on the larger turmoil that was now to begin. It marked the beginning of the litigation involving title to the greatest and most valuable of the Anaconda ore bodies. Butte became a legal battleground with all the confusion that attends such embroilment.

At this point a new and masterful figure entered upon the Anaconda stage. He was Henry H. Rogers, then active head of the Standard Oil Company. Owner of a large block of Anaconda stock, he also represented major interests in the Boston companies; that is, the Butte & Boston and the Boston & Montana, operating in the Butte district. The first consolidation of mining properties in Butte, leading to the subsequent merger of interests there, was that of the two Boston companies. Standard Oil interests represented by Rogers held large amounts of stock in the Boston & Montana Company and were among the incorporators of Butte & Boston.

A. C. Burrage, who represented Boston and Standard Oil capital, conceived the idea of organizing the Butte mining concerns into a great holding company. He interested Rogers in his plan and also William G. Rockefeller, who was Secretary and Treasurer of Butte & Boston and also an officer and director of Anaconda. Rogers was the President of Anaconda. Other men high in the councils of the Rockefeller-Standard Oil group were among the executives and directors of these Butte companies.

On a trip to Butte to inspect the properties of the Boston companies Rogers studied a map of the hundreds of mining claims which had been filed on Butte Hill. A Field Marshal of Finance, he envisaged opportunities in a big way and realized on them on a big scale. He decided that the Hill, with its rich, concentrated mining ores, was a perfect site for a mammoth consolidation of mining interests. With Burrage he determined to pool all these interests in a company controlling practically all the principal producers of the Butte district.

The time was ripe for such a consolidation. Amalgamation in all lines of industry marked the trend of business, both in corporations that were combined in centralized management, and among employees who organized trade unions to increase their bargaining power. No man fitted more perfectly into the mood, spirit and tendency of the times than Rogers. As a boy in his native Fairhaven, Massachusetts, he worked as a clerk in a grocery store that was one of a chain that operated throughout the state. By means of this combination, the stores were able to buy food cheaper than individual competitors and thereby undersell them. This was the lesson ingrained in Rogers at an early age and it became his guiding star once he entered big business.

When he left Fairhaven to make his way in the world Rogers went to the Pennsylvania oil fields to which speculators were flocking. He had $200 which he had saved out of his pay as grocery clerk. Having decided to go into oil refining, he made an alliance with a schoolmate and started in to learn the business. He put on overalls and boots and worked at the refining stills. Thus began the experience in petroleum that, in the years to come, made him an oil baron and the trusted colleague of John D. Rockefeller, Sr.

Rogers looked the part he played as Wall Street and industrial Titan. Over six feet in height, with white hair, blue eyes, shaggy eyebrows, ruddy cheeks and a forceful walk, he was a commanding and compelling figure. Not until Cornelius Kelley became the dominating force in Anaconda did any personality, directly or indirectly associated with the copper industry, vie with Rogers in dynamic direction.

With Rogers to plan was to act. As a result of his survey of

the Hill properties, The Amalgamated Copper Company
was organized April 27, 1899 under the laws of New Jersey
with a capital of $75,000,000, shares having a par value of
$100. In 1901 the financial structure was increased to
$155,000,000. The proposal to purchase a majority interest
in The Anaconda Copper Mining Company was placed
before Haggin and Daly. Haggin declined to join the enterprise. He received about $15,000,000 for his interest in
Anaconda. Daly was impressed with the plan. He believed
that, for one thing, it was a means of avoiding or settling
the litigation with Heinze which had already begun to
bristle. In this he was mistaken because Amalgamated, as
you will presently see, became involved in a vortex of law
suits. Daly became part of the Amalgamated plan. His interest in Anaconda was estimated to be nearly $17,000,000,
much of which he exchanged for stock in Amalgamated.

The original officers of Amalgamated were Rogers, President; Daly, Vice President; William G. Rockefeller, Secretary and Treasurer. The Board of Directors was comprised
of the officers just mentioned and F. P. Olcott, President of
the Central Trust Company of New York; Robert Bacon of
J. P. Morgan & Company; James Stillman, President of
the National City Bank of New York; Roswell P. Flower,
later Governor of New York; and Burrage. Here was an
aggregation of Wall Street wealth and power which Heinze
was to capitalize in his own devious way to discredit the
company.

Amalgamated took control, by exchange of stock or purchase, of the following companies: Anaconda Copper Mining Company, Boston & Montana, Butte & Boston, Parrot
Silver & Copper Company, Trenton Mining & Development Company, Washoe Copper Company, Big Blackfoot
Lumber Company, Diamond Coal & Coke Company, and
the Mounted Trading Company. Amalgamated also
owned 30,800 shares of The Greene Cananea Copper Company of Mexico, later to become an important asset of Ana-

conda. It also acquired 50,000 shares of The Butte Coalition Mining Company when this corporation was formed to buy out Heinze and end, once and for all, the bitter apex litigation. Amalgamated also held bonds of the Butte & Boston Company and notes of the Washoe Copper Company.

The Amalgamated Copper Company was a holding company, a financial device to acquire control of the important dividend-paying mines. It was in no sense an operating company and took no part in the management and strategy of the subsidiary corporations. Although it did not engage in mine operation it served a useful purpose in bringing together important independent operators and thus expediting their merger when Butte Coalition was formed. The Heinze apex cases, together with the increasing problems in mining, had made it abundantly clear that it was imperative to take steps to centralize management. The following needs had to be met:

1. To make for efficiency and economy under the increasing difficulties of deeper mining, to increase cooperation by reducing costs of functions such as power utilization, pumping, ventilation and safety, and to eliminate duplication of shafts and workings.

2. To allot ore bodies to companies under decisions of sound, unbiased management and thus have the benefit of the best engineering and geological investigation without resort to court action.

The flotation of the Amalgamated stock developed a sensational chapter in American finance. It was entrusted to Thomas W. Lawson of Boston, who was a spectacular and flamboyant operator. His full-page advertisements were marvels of highly colored verbiage which made an effective appeal to the public. Because of the close connection of Standard Oil interests with the company, muckrakers as well as Heinze and his cohorts had a field day. The implication was that Amalgamated was out to trim the public when, in reality, the major purpose was constructive.

Meanwhile, the forces were being aligned for the legal apex battle which shook the state. The battle, however, was not to enlist Daly. He died at the age of fifty-eight. In the late Nineties he was stricken with diabetes, then regarded as incurable but now controllable because of insulin. Vainly he searched Europe for a cure. He returned to this country and passed away at the Hotel Netherland in New York on September 12, 1900. After "life's fitful fever," he was at rest.

Just before Daly died he sent for his old mining partner, Haggin, and told him it would be their last meeting. His mind drifted away from the long years of litigation and jealousies in Butte to the stirring days of early adventure with his colleagues of the syndicate when the future stretched so rosily ahead.

Daly had laid the foundation of a farflung empire. He had helped to launch The Amalgamated Copper Company and had succeeded Haggin as President of The Anaconda Copper Mining Company which became the dominant organization in the various consolidations that eventually led to The Anaconda Company of today. Anaconda had been in the fiber of his being, the very essence of his life.

Services over the remains were held in St. Patrick's Cathedral in New York. Bishop Brondel of Montana officiated. More than a thousand persons in every walk of life attended the obsequies. Interment was in Greenwood Cemetery.

All Montana mourned the loss of the state's outstanding citizen and generous patron, nowhere to a greater extent than in Butte. On the day of the funeral the city was draped in black and hushed in silence. A requiem mass was sung at St. Patrick's Church to an overflowing, grief-stricken congregation. Services were also held in Catholic churches in Anaconda, Helena, Missoula and Centerville. Never before, or since, has Montana paid such a tribute to a departed son.

So great was Daly's impress upon Butte that it was decided to erect a permanent memorial to him. On November 15, 1901 a Marcus Daly Memorial Committee was named. A special committee of three consisting of John D. Ryan, soon to be a director of Anaconda, William Scallon, President of Anaconda, and H. L. Frank, was named to select the type of memorial and its site. Voluntary subscriptions were called for and there was a ready and generous response. A total of $25,000 was raised of which more than $6,000 came from the Butte miners, showing the esteem in which Daly was held by them. It was decided to ask America's foremost sculptor, Augustus Saint Gaudens, to make a bronze statue. Kelley was a member of the committee that went to Washington to conclude the negotiations with him.

The statue was dedicated September 2, 1907 in the presence of a multitude. Kelley, then Secretary of Anaconda, delivered the dedication address. It was an eloquent and touching oration.

Of the passing of Daly, Kelley said:

"To the State of Montana it meant the loss of him who was foremost in the development of her tremendous resources; to some of its communities it meant that he, who had been their creator, their patron and their well-wisher, had been called away forever. To hundreds it meant that the generous friend, the courageous sympathizer, the helping hand, has been forever withdrawn. To the bereaved family it meant an irreplaceable and inconsolable loss of a husband and father of irreproachable integrity and spotless morality.

"Butte, with the majesty of her proud position in the copper world, her shafts innumerable, her ever-busy smokestacks from which the garland of industry constantly emitted a signal of commercial enterprise, Anaconda, with her gigantic industries, Hamilton, with its enormous mills, thousands of contented homes, the most prosperous communities in the world, oh Marcus Daly, are the monuments, more enduring than any of bronze or granite, prouder than any that could be fashioned from marble columns, which you yourself erected, to keep mankind in memory of your grand achievements."

Saint Gaudens excelled himself in fashioning the Daly statue. It shows Daly standing with hat in his right hand, an overcoat thrown over the left arm. A contemplative look is on his rugged face. Originally placed on Main Street near the mouth of the Gulch where Daly first developed the rich copper ores in the Anaconda mine, it was moved to a commanding site near the Montana School of Mines. There Daly stands, enduring in granite and bronze, overlooking the city for which he achieved so much. Under him is this inscription:

"A pioneer miner who first developed the famous properties on the hill overlooking the site of this memorial which is erected by his fellow citizens in tribute to his noble traits of character, in grateful remembrance of his good deeds, and in commemoration of the splendid service he rendered as builder of the City of Butte and the State of Montana."

Daly was gone but his spirit was to live on, incarnated in two men who were to maintain the tradition of the founder and guide Anaconda to its preeminent place in the industrial sun. They were Kelley and John D. Ryan. No two men engaged in a large business enterprise ever developed, and few equalled, a more harmonious, constructive, evenly balanced relationship than this team. Endowed with vision, capacity and resolution, they purged Butte of the apex litigation that threatened disaster, and widened the operations of the company until it became worldwide in scope. With their joint efforts, they recorded an achievement unique in the story of American industrial development.

Like Kelley, Ryan qualified for membership in the lexicon of self-made success. Born at Hancock, Michigan, October 10, 1864, he came from a mining family for his father, John C. Ryan, discovered what is known as the Copper Range mines in the Lake Superior region and was manager of the Hecla mine. In his early life Ryan had no taste for mining or for a college education. At seventeen he went to work as clerk in a general merchandise store at Hancock owned by his uncle Edward, who owned a chain of such stores throughout Michigan. For eight years the young man who was to become a copper magnate, weighed sugar and coffee and cut calico and ribbon lengths behind the counter.

When he was twenty-five Ryan moved to Denver where his brother William lived. For nearly six months he walked the streets hunting for a job. He was finally engaged as lubricating oil salesman for the Crew-Levick Oil Company. His territory was part of the Rocky Mountain area which included Montana.

Ryan had a winning manner and built up a large clientele. On one of his early visits to Butte he met Daly who immediately took to the tall, agreeable, well-mannered young salesman. Ryan encountered only one major obstacle. He could not sell oil to Anaconda. One day he met Daly on the street and said to him:

"It is a curious thing, Mr. Daly, but I can't sell any oil to Anaconda. I simply can't get by Dunlap, that purchasing agent of yours."

Daly pondered a moment and then replied:

"It is too bad, Ryan, but every outfit has a temperamental grouch and Dunlap is a prize grouch."

When Ryan married Nettie Gardner at Houghton in 1896 he was still a $150 a month oil salesman. His courtship led to an amusing story told for years in both Hancock and Houghton. The two towns were connected by a toll bridge over Portage Lake, owned by Miss Gardner's father. The toll was ten cents. Every time, and it meant every night, that Ryan called on his fiancée he was required to pay toll.

Ryan carried on with the oil company for four more

years. Banking had always had a strong appeal for him and he decided to make it a career. In 1900 he gave up his job as oil salesman and moved to Butte where he had a large circle of friends, chief of whom was Daly.

Daly had started the Daly Bank & Trust Company, the outstanding financial institution in Butte. Ryan had been thrifty. With his savings and a generous inheritance from his brother to whom he had been devoted, he purchased an interest in the Daly Bank. The transaction had the approval of Daly, for, upon his death, his heirs chose Ryan to be President of the bank.

As President of Amalgamated, Rogers directed its financial affairs as well as those of the subsidiaries which it controlled. This business was transacted through the Daly Bank. Rogers was impressed with Ryan's ability and personality. In 1904 he brought about his affiliation with The Anaconda Copper Mining Company as member of the Board of Directors. In the following year Ryan was elected President of Anaconda. These were the first major steps which, with Kelley as colleague, were to start him on the way to prestige and power.

As head of Anaconda, Ryan took great pride in his men and particularly their skill as drillers. On one occasion he matched his prize team of drillers against a team from the Calumet & Hecla mines. Ryan went to Michigan with his men and saw them win.

In 1908 Rogers, in failing health, called Ryan to New York to assist him with the business of The Anaconda Company. When Rogers died in the following year Ryan became President of Amalgamated. This necessitated his resignation as President of Anaconda. He continued in the presidency of Amalgamated until its dissolution in 1915. Benjamin B. Thayer, who had been Vice President of Anaconda, succeeded him as head of Anaconda.

Rogers was a temporary figure in the Butte scheme of things. With Amalgamated he had shown a broad and com-

prehending vision and infused a vital energy into the co-
ordination of mining interests. Amalgamated in time became relegated to the past. Ryan, on the other hand, continued to enhance his impress until death removed him
from the picture.

III

The Anaconda Copper Mining Company was six years
old when Kelley joined the legal staff of the corporation.
Henceforth, his career was a steady march to commanding
position. In less than two years Kelley was taking an increasingly active part in the Heinze litigation. His practical
knowledge of mining, as well as his skill in law, combined to
make him an invaluable member of the legal arsenal deployed against Heinze.

The Anaconda legal staff comprised outstanding lawyers
who left their impress upon Montana court history. The
first Chief Counsel was W. W. Dixon, who had been legal
adviser for Daly and the Haggin Syndicate before the partnership assumed corporate form. A. J. Shores, who shep-
herded Kelley when he entered the Anaconda service, became Chief Counsel in 1900.

Kelley's closest legal association, which ripened into a
cherished friendship, was with Lewis Orvis Evans, called
"Orve" by his colleagues and a multitude of others. Here
was a man after Kelley's heart, able, brilliant, resourceful,
intensely human, with a keen sense of humor and a genius
for friendship. He possessed endearing qualities that inspired loyalty among all who knew and worked with him.
Together, Evans and Kelley formed an irresistible team.

In 1870, twelve years after his birth in Utica, New York,
Evans' parents moved to Helena and later to Butte. Evans
studied law in the offices of John F. Forbis with whom,
after his admission to the bar in 1894, he established a partnership. The firm of Forbis & Evans won the esteem of their

fellow practitioners and the respect of courts. It was engaged as counsel for the Butte & Boston and the Boston &
Montana Companies. Subsequently Evans became counsel
for Amalgamated. With Kelley, he was in the forefront in
the battle with Heinze and other major controversies.

Evans was responsible for the establishment of Kelley's
sylvan retreat at Swan Lake located in an unspoiled area of
the Flathead country. Evans, an enthusiastic fisherman, had
discovered the place on one of his piscatorial expeditions.
The heavily forested region, located on the shore of Swan
Lake, was ideal for rest and recreation. Originally Evans
occupied a cabin in an area cleared by the original home-
steader. When the Kelleys visited the place they were enchanted with it. In 1915 Evans and Kelley undertook a
joint occupation of a 137 area clearing, occupying log cabins
that fitted into the atmosphere of the secluded spot. Later
each went on his own. Kelley constructed a group of cabins,
rustic on the outside but with every comfort within. Evans
was his next door neighbor. Kelley expanded his holding
until today he has a domain of 7,000 acres. Here he retires
every summer to rest amid the peace and seclusion of a spot
that invites solace and meditation.

It was not long before Kelley was plunged into the vortex
of the Heinze litigation. The complexities of the law suits
made it necessary for him to work from sixteen to eighteen
hours a day in preparation for a case. During those hectic
years he first manifested his fabulous memory. He was able
to retain in his mind dates, figures and names with uncanny
accuracy. Always in demand as a speaker on civic and other
occasions, he could dictate a fifteen, thirty or forty-five minute speech and then deliver it verbatim without ever refer-
ring to the manuscript.

In the midst of the turmoil of the Heinze litigation Kelley
married Mary Tremblay, daughter of Dr. Joseph A. Tremblay, a prominent physician of Missoula. Behind every man

of achievement stands a woman, his anchor in times of stress and strain, his inspiration when the great things beckon. In Kelley's life that woman was Mary Kelley.

Now began the devoted kinship that was to imbue Kelley with the determination that sped him ever onward and upward. The Kelleys were ideally adapted to each other. Besides being an accomplished violinist, Mrs. Kelley had rare charm of manner and great vivacity. Whether in the Kelley homes in Butte, New York City, Swan Lake or Long Island, she was the perfect hostess. She created a home life that had an enduring influence on her husband's career. Her death in 1955 was widely mourned.

Kelley's twin dedication was to Mrs. Kelley and Anaconda. Sometimes this latter devotion played havoc with household plans. In the early years after their marriage the Kelleys lived for a time in the Largey apartment house on West Main Street. From her apartment Mrs. Kelley could see the Hennessy Building. Often when the children had been put to bed and dinner ready, she looked at the windows of the Anaconda offices. When the lights went out, she said: "Con will be home soon." But Con did not come home soon. Before long she heard the sound of voices down on the street below. Then she would see Kelley, Evans and John Gillie holding a bull session. Frequently they talked for an hour and sometimes longer. Although they had worked all day they were still at it. Dinner over, they would reassemble and resume their talk. Anaconda work, like the old saying about women's work, was "never done."

Although it is running ahead of the consecutive story of Kelley's career, it may be well, at this point, to deal with the famous so-called "Smoke Case," which enlisted Kelley and Evans in litigation that attracted nationwide attention. The issues involved, if decided adversely, would have dealt a staggering blow to all smelters of non-ferrous metal products in the West.

From the time of the company's organization in 1895,

ranchers in the region of the reduction works at Anaconda had made claims for damages to crops and livestock from smelter fumes. These ranchers came to be known as "Smoke Farmers." In the early days of their complaints, settlements involving large sums were negotiated. In 1902, following legal advice, the company engaged a commission of experts who decided that some damage had been inflicted. Claims aggregating $340,000 were paid. In 1903 the company built, at a cost of $725,000, the immense flues and stacks at the new Washoe Works, equipped with devices for removing injurious matter from the fumes and delivering the remaining smoke to high strata of the air where it was widely dispersed. In addition, elaborate experiments were conducted on the actual effect of the surrounding atmosphere on agricultural products. The company itself engaged in ranch production, exhibited its products at fairs and took prizes for crops and livestock.

While company officials believed that practically all damage had been stopped, they were now faced by fresh demands for alleged crop injury. Suits were brought by the Deer Lodge Valley Farmers Association in 1905 claiming enormous damages. The test case was entitled "Fred J. Bliss vs. The Anaconda Copper Mining Company and The Washoe Copper Company." Kelley and Evans, together with specialists, prepared the defense which was a masterpiece of legal and engineering effectiveness.

Trial started in January 1906 before a Master in Chancery, appointed by the Federal Court and continued until 1907. The Master found in favor of the company. Judge Hunt, after denying the injunction sought by the farmers and, upon expert assurance that the preventive measures established at the smelters were effective, dismissed the case on April 26, 1909.

The ultimate victory in the Smoke Case enhanced Kelley's reputation as lawyer. It was a long and tedious grind with experts from many leading colleges testifying. Here, as in so many other cases, Kelley shone as cross-examiner. When the case ended more that 27,000 pages of testimony had been recorded.

The young Kelley was early marked as a leader of men. Despite his exacting labors for the company he took a prominent part in politics. He figured in Democratic State and County conventions and participated in the development of the Silver Bow Club, the Bonita Club, a hunting and fishing club in western Montana, the Butte Curling Club, and the Butte Country Club. His principal hobbies were fishing and horseback riding.

Meanwhile a diverting episode, in which Kelley was the onlooker, stirred Butte. It was the visit of Theodore Roosevelt, then President, in the summer of 1903. When word was received that he planned to stop over in Butte on his way to the Pacific Coast, there arose the red-hot question, "Who will be his host?" It was a ticklish one to answer. The battle lines between Heinze and his henchmen and The Amalgamated Copper Company had been drawn in the apex litigation. Each side strove to outdo the other on such an occasion as the President's visit.

It followed that invitations went to Roosevelt from both sides, thus posing a problem for him. Which invitation should he accept? To complicate the situation, both camps sent envoys to Washington to press their claims. At this juncture a Heinze adherent, posing as a neutral, said to Roosevelt:

"There is a bitter industrial fight going on in Butte. You cannot afford to go there as the guest of either faction. You should go as the guest of the people of Montana or the Mayor of Butte." Roosevelt saw a logical out for him and answered: "I will go as the guest of the Mayor."

The Mayor was Pat Mullins, a blond, corpulent Irishman, elected by Heinze votes. At that time it was no problem for Heinze to win elections in Montana. The Butte miners openly boasted that they worked for Amalgamated but voted for the Heinze tickets.

No time was lost in sending the Mayor's invitation to Roosevelt who promptly accepted. Heinze sent a delegation to Billings to meet the Presidential train. A speech had been prepared for Mullins. When Roosevelt entered the observation car where the delegation waited, the Mayor rose and said:

"Mr. President, I—I—I—oh hell, I never could make a speech," and dropped into a chair. Roosevelt roared with laughter and said: "Bully, Pat, I never could either."

Next morning Roosevelt arrived in Butte. The Mayor had been provided with appropriate clothes including silk hat, tail-coat and cane. He would have been more at ease with a shovel in his hand. After a parade through the principal streets the procession halted at the old Finlen Hotel where Roosevelt was to speak from the hotel balcony. As Mullins rose to introduce the guest of honor he spied his wife standing in the rear. He delayed his speech to introduce her to Roosevelt.

That night the Mayor was host at a dinner for the President. Roosevelt, aware of the situation in Butte, had insisted that an equal number of men from the Amalgamated and Heinze factions be invited. For years a bitter underground fight had been waged between the miners, engineers and superintendents, as well as the officials above ground. Another problem rose up—how to seat the belligerents without starting a free-for-all fight. It was finally decided to seat the Amalgamated men on one side of the long table and the Heinze crowd on the other.

Before the banquet started Jerry Murphy, Butte's Chief of Police, scenting possible trouble, arrived on the scene with two of his men. It was a justifiable precaution. When all the guests had been seated, the master of ceremonies laid a large napkin-covered tray before the President and then lifted the cover revealing a dozen pistols. Every guest had been frisked by the police.

Although Kelley was deeply involved in the law suits that bristled around Amalgamated, he found time for practice outside the company. His reputation as an expert mining lawyer had spread beyond the confines of Montana. He had cases in Tonopah, Goldfields and elsewhere. He had so many outside cases that Scallon said to him: "Are you working for the company or for yourself?" To this Kelley responded: "Make your choice." Scallon said no more, nor did the subject ever arise again.

In 1905 Kelley mounted the first rung of the ladder that took him eventually to the top of the Anaconda hierarchy. He was named Secretary of the company. While this post entailed new duties, it did not distract him from his legal work. Not until he became a top executive did he actively forsake the profession in which he had shone.

In every outstanding personage, whether in politics, industry or, in fact, any other major activity, the thirst for information is paramount. Knowledge is always power. So it was with Kelley. In 1906 he decided to learn all there was to know about mining outside Montana. He started on a tour that took him, first, to Monterrey, Mexico, where he met William C. Potter, who was to become his close friend, head of the Guaranty Trust Company, and a director of The Anaconda Copper Mining Company. He also visited Utah. Here he became acquainted with that giant of mining, Daniel C. Jackling, who opened up Bingham Canyon. Other stops on this trip were at Aguascalientes in Mexico, Dickson where he saw the work of The Tennessee Copper Company, and Tonopah.

Early in his association with Anaconda, as later in the depression years that began in 1929, Kelley manifested a keen interest in one of the vital departments of the company. This was labor relations. In those days labor relations had not reached the stage of high organization and close co-ordination and understanding that prevail today in all the great corporations. There were unions, to be sure, but they were mere aggregations of men without formulated policies. In 1906 Kelley was largely instrumental in negotiating a five-year labor contract satisfactory to both the company and the miners. This working agreement was later developed into a sliding scale of wages based on the price of copper, an arrangement which soon became standard in all the western copper districts. It has been described as the most just and equitable division of wealth ever devised by any industrial concern for its workers.

Steady advancement was now the order in the Kelley career. In 1908 he was named General Counsel. His work was predominantly of a legal nature until 1911, when he was elected Vice President. It was eminently fitting that his successor as General Counsel should have been Evans, his close friend and colleague in so many legal battles. Evans held the post until his untimely death in 1931. Although Kelley's duties became administrative he never lost the lawyer's critical outlook and ever since has constantly safeguarded the legal interests of the company.

Soon after his accession to the Vice Presidency, Kelley and John Gillie went over to Anaconda and made a careful inspection of the smelter there. On the way back to Butte, Gillie, able but a confirmed pessimist, whom Kelley had known since he was a boy, said:

"Now, Con, I want to tell you one thing. For God's sake, don't ever build any more plants. The plant at Anaconda is more than the Butte mines will ever need."

Kelley disagreed. Under his stimulation the smelter was entirely rebuilt. The process was completely changed under Frederick Laist and, as Kelley put it, "Anaconda was on the way."

The reference to Laist marks the entry of a man upon the Anaconda scene who was destined to perform prodigies of constructive work for the company. It is pertinent, therefore, to get his background and his training at this point because henceforth he will loom large as a vital contributor to the corporation's development at home and abroad, whether in copper, zinc, uranium or aluminum.

Laist graduated from the College of Chemistry of the University of California in 1901, was instructor of chemistry at the University of Utah in 1903 and entered the employ of Anaconda in 1904 when he took over a position in the laboratory and Testing Department. From that post he rose successively to become Chief Chemist, Blast Furnace Superintendent, General Superintendent, Metallurgical Manager of the Montana plants, General Manager at Anaconda and Great Falls, General Metallurgical Manager of all the company properties and, finally, Vice President in charge of Metallurgical Operations to become the foremost metallurgist in the non-ferrous metal field.

As Vice President, Kelley had a large part in the further rebuilding of Anaconda. In 1911 the Boston & Montana Company, which had been merged into Anaconda, had a separate smelting plant at Great Falls, already a great Anaconda metallurgical center. Anaconda had been shipping 5,000 tons of ore a day to Great Falls 175 miles away, to wash sixty per cent of the tonnage into the Missouri River. Kelley and Laist decided that it was unbusinesslike to ship the ore to Great Falls when it could easily be hauled twenty-six miles to Anaconda and treated in the larger plant there. Kelley's idea prevailed and the big expansion of Anaconda began.

Figuratively, copper was now infused into Kelley's blood. With this energizing element stimulating his every endeavor, he rose to be the last of the Copper Kings. Following the death of Ryan, the story of Kelley became the story of Anaconda—a serial of high and outstanding service.

♤ 6

THE BATTLE OF THE APEX

NO CHAPTER in the long story of Anaconda was so beset with turbulence as the period of the Heinze litigation which may well be termed the Battle of Butte. For more than eight years a bitter and spectacular contest was waged in which violence flared, lives were sacrificed, hatreds engendered. The fight was above and below ground. Biased judges made a mockery of justice. Cases before them were generally lost before they were tried, only to be won on appeal. Heinze was revealed as a prize poacher and plunderer, an industrial buccaneer with a Napoleonic complex. In his attempt to be a Colossus astride the richest hill on earth, he plunged Butte into a legal turmoil unparalleled in mining history. It cost Anaconda and the associated companies $1,000,000 a year to defend its rights and circumvent the predatory tactics of Heinze. The Daly-Clark feud was a minor engagement compared with the titanic struggle that he initiated.

Clearly to understand the legal controversies that embroiled Butte it is necessary to explain what lay at the root. All the law suits sprang from different interpretations of the apex law. To go back for a moment, in the early days of the gold rush to California, the miners made their own laws.

The pistol and knife, and sometimes the lynchers' noose, were employed to ward off claim jumpers. This rough and tumble procedure preceded the employment of the injunction to safeguard properties. Those early California miners, once they resorted to peaceful methods of protecting their rights, were influenced by the Spanish laws prevailing in the gold fields as well as the ideas of Cornish miners. These laws decreed that miners should possess a vein in its dip into the earth; that is, between the vertical boundaries of the claim. The first federal mining law enacted in 1866 grew out of this western conception.

As the years passed friction arose over overlapping veins. In consequence, the Congressional Act of 1872 was passed. Generally known as the "apex law," it became a strong incentive to prospectors but it also embodied evils and became the basis of ruinous litigation, particularly in Butte.

In apex law physical existence of a vein must be established within the surface confines of claim ownership. The intersection of a vein at the surface is known as the apex. The law guaranteed the owner the right to follow that vein downward even when it led under the surface holdings of claims located beside it. The extra-lateral rights thus bestowed, therefore, allowed the miner to mine far beyond his side-lines. There would never have been any litigation, perhaps, if the veins were continuous from surface down but frequently they were not. They are crooked, or faulted, or broken up and sliver off in many fine veins like a horse's tail and sometimes are cut off at various places by worthless rock.

If a vein leading down from the surface is lost near the vertical side-wall of a claim, and a similar vein of identical ore is found below it, or to one side in an adjoining claim, the question arises—who is to decide whether the second discovery is a geological continuation of the first? Here, in a maze of geological complexities, was the crux of the litigation that shook Butte. It remained for Heinze to capitalize it profitably to the fullest and most reprehensible extent.

The pattern of apex litigation had been set in the so-called King-Amy Silversmith cases fully a decade before Heinze launched his forays. Involved in this action were the Amy and Non-Consolidated lode claims. The vein in dispute was being mined for gold and silver. The ore was in the Amy discovery vein which dipped northerly from the Amy into, and within, surface boundaries of the Non-Consolidated. Plaintiff brought suit July 5, 1887 to determine rights to portions of the vein being mined by the Non-Consolidated owner.

This suit was the first apex controversy of record in the Butte district, and also the first of the few from the area to be considered by the Supreme Court of the United States. It was the opinion in this case that finally established the rule of law that where the apex of the discovery vein crosses both parallel side-lines of a location, the side-lines become end-lines and the claim can have no extra-lateral rights in the direction of the lines originally designated as end-lines. The rule, thus formulated, had important application, not only in Butte but in other mining districts.

F. Augustus Heinze's debut in Butte was far from auspicious. He arrived in 1889 when he had just turned twenty. Reared in Brooklyn, his forbears had been Jewish, Yankee and Irish, a racial blend that contributed to a magnetic personality. He was of robust physique, handsome, debonair, with an ingratiating manner that charmed friend and foe alike. No one who met this personable young man in that first year in Butte dreamed that in his sturdy breast burned the ambition to become what in present day terminology is called a big shot. Nor could they foresee that he would ignite a powder train that exploded into a bang that shook all Butte to its depths.

Heinze got a job as surveyor with the Boston & Montana. His pay was $100 a month. As surveyor for Boston & Montana, he acquired his first knowledge of the riches that reposed beneath the granite of the Hill. That knowledge, and the additional data he acquired, were to be capitalized to the fullest extent.

Heinze was quick to grasp an opportunity. He studied the field and came to the conclusion that smelting costs were excessive so he decided to build a smelter. This required capital, so he went to New York to raise it. It was tribute to his winning way and effectiveness as a salesman, that he interested the great banking house of Baring Brothers, second only to the Rothschilds in the realm of international finance. Before the deal could be consummated the Barings failed.

Heinze then worked on the editorial staff of *The Engineering & Mining Journal* in New York, compiling copper statistics. He did more than compile figures, for he learned the name, history and potentialities of every copper concern in the United States. He also became acquainted with the Lewisohns who operated United Metals and acquired a knowledge of copper selling.

Luck was with Heinze. At this point he inherited $50,000 on the death of his grandmother. He went to Europe, studied at several universities and also took a course in the School of Mines at Columbia University. He was now a linguist and a man of the world.

Returning to Butte, which was now to be his stronghold, he revived his scheme to build a smelter and organized the Montana Ore Purchasing Company. Next he took a lease on the Estrella mine, owned by James A. Murray. He negotiated a sliding scale of royalties based on the grade of ore produced. Heinze offered Murray fifty per cent on all ore running over fifteen per cent copper and nothing on second-class ore. Since the mine was in first-class ore Murray signed up. Henceforth and until the lease expired, every ton of ore raised from the mine ran under fifteen per cent.

Scruples never bothered Heinze. He had manipulated the grade of the ore so that Murray got the low-grade output while he managed to keep the high-grade ore, turned it over to the Montana Ore Purchasing Company and pocketed all the proceeds. It was a typical Heinze operation to be duplicated in many versions in the years to come.

Murray discovered the deception, sued Heinze and won a judgment in court. Later a private settlement was effected. This was the first law suit in which Heinze was involved. It was small potatoes, so to speak, compared with the dozens he instigated to clutter up the Montana courts.

During the period of the Heinze litigation there were times when as many as forty court actions were pending between Heinze and Amalgamated. Only three apex controversies came up for trial. These were the Rarus-Michael Devitt, the Rarus-Pennsylvania and the Nipper-Anaconda. The extremely important Minnie Healy-Leonard dispute arose over veins and ore bodies of greater value than those of all other Heinze apex actions combined, but it did not get beyond preliminary court proceedings. The Copper Trust case embraced points of law as to the right of a junior location spread over the vein already covered by senior locations.

Many of the suits started by Heinze, such as the Fairmount, L. E. H., Liggett and Foster Addition were fishing excursions. Others, too numerous to mention, might be designated as nuisance or patrol raids, conceived solely for the purpose of securing information or to cause annoyance. In many of the actions of this class there was scant mention of veins or ore bodies and few got beyond the original complaint and answer stage. At one time Heinze had thirty-two lawyers, including a brother, A. P. Heinze, imported from New York, working for him. The brother's job was to find hypothetical holes into which F. Augustus could poke a law suit. It is not surprising that the litigation instigated by Heinze was called "court house mining."

Heinze's methods were characteristic of the man. His technique was largely based on pillage and piracy. When, for example, he acquired the Rarus claim, located near the center of the richest area in the Hill, he provided himself with a lease of operations from which he was able to make underground incursions upon surrounding property. Another was his Nipper claim. In court he set up the allegation that the ore bodies in adjacent ground which he was mining, had their apices in his claim. He developed the theory of an "umbrella apex" by which he claimed title to ore bodies in all directions. This theory was upheld only by the judges whom the Heinze faction elected and was repudiated in the Supreme Court of Montana.

Heinze followed another method of promoting controversy by making himself or some of his associates, partners in other concerns, mainly the Amalgamated. They would then make false claims against the company whose stock they held and ask for a receivership.

One of Heinze's most potent assets lay in his influence with the miners. He made them extravagant promises and put them over through sheer eloquence. He was an effective soap-box orator, a rabble-rouser to the nth degree. His constant promise was for "a full dinner pail," the slogan he adopted from the McKinley-Bryan campaign. He claimed credit for the eight-hour day when, in reality, Amalgamated had adopted it before the enactment of the law by the Montana Legislature.

Through his political alliance with W. A. Clark, who was always eager to join any faction that opposed the Daly interests, Heinze wielded immense power at election time. Although the miners worked for Amalgamated, they voted for the Heinze-sponsored tickets; hence the pliable lower court judiciary that bowed to the Heinze will and obeyed his behests.

Heinze was an adept propagandist and he employed this medium overtime. Amalgamated's association with Rogers, William Rockefeller and other leading Standard Oil executives gave him a target that he employed for his purposes.

On the platform, or rather soap box, and in his newspaper, *The Reveille*, he pilloried Standard Oil. He stamped the oil company as an "octopus," with "tainted" money that perverted every national issue through its immense resources. He painted the corporation as a menace to the economic peace and political security of Montana. A characteristic, ridiculous Heinze accusation was: "Standard Oil controls all the lamplight of the nation and now it is intent on controlling the electric light through manipulation of copper."

At that time the main offices of Standard Oil were at 26 Broadway in New York. Heinze pictured the building as a Satan's sanctuary, repository of every abuse in the capitalistic code. Standard Oil, in his fulminations, meant "vested interests," then, as today, the favorite objective of the demagogue.

All this misrepresentation was grist to the miners' mill and also to a considerable body of people not involved in mining. It made for a degree of class hatred which Heinze was quick to adapt to his own purposes.

Still another phase of the Heinze technique was revealed in what came to be known as the "fake bond" episode. In many cases Heinze was required to post bonds. In his Federal Court cases he was also required to give large bonds as a guarantee for accounting upon the final disposition of the various cases. In one instance his bond was fixed at $950,-000. He organized the Delaware Surety Company in New York to provide the bonds. In a hearing before the State Supreme Court he was required to furnish an additional bond of $350,000. Again he named the Delaware Surety Company as bondsman. The court became suspicious and appointed a commission to investigate the bonding company. The surety company was found to be without assets or even desk room. Its directors were relatives of Heinze and his brother. They also included a dress goods agent, an employee of a lace store and a dry goods salesman. The

Supreme Court then required that the surety should be made a cash bond.

These, then, were some of the devices and subterfuges employed by Heinze in his ambition to tear apart the organization that Daly and his associates had reared and to rifle the richest ore bodies on Butte Hill. It was an artful and mendacious program without precedent.

Before the curtain rises on the Heinze litigation it is important to disclose the character, or rather the lack of it, of one of the principal actors who, in the phraseology of the theater, had an important supporting part. He was William Clancy. Born in Missouri, he had turned up in Butte some years before the apex suits began to bristle. He had little knowledge of, and less consideration for, the law. Clancy became what is known as a curbstone lawyer and was more at home in a saloon than in a court of law. Described as "a moose of a man," because of his heavy build, his white beard failed to give him a semblance of dignity.

In 1897 the Heinze political forces elected Clancy to the District bench. He had been a candidate for Justice of the Peace, a position requiring no qualification in the law under Montana statute. His Heinze supporters, who had captured the Democratic convention, elevated Clancy's candidacy to the Silver Bow bench. There were two District judges on the Silver Bow bench. The other was John Lindsay, against whose honor and integrity no suspicion ever arose. No such immunity was bestowed on Clancy who became a Heinze henchman.

Under the rules of the court, cases filed were alternated between the two judges, the odd numbered ones going before Judge Clancy and the even numbered ones before Judge Lindsay. By some legerdemain, all the Heinze cases were set before Clancy, even when Amalgamated lawyers took care to file cases in such order that under the rule they should go before Judge Lindsay.

Clancy became a fountain head of injunctions always

favorable to Heinze. It followed that the Heinze attorneys never lost a case before him. He closed down by injunction several of the largest mines in Butte and enjoined the mining of many valuable ore bodies. On the slightest pretext he granted to Heinze inspection orders to enter Amalgamated mines while he refused the same right to the company. He levied heavy fines on Heinze's opponents for refusing to obey his orders. Supervisory writs and other mandates from the Supreme Court he took "under advisement." Some of them were never heard of again. It was one method of giving Heinze ample opportunity to mine valuable ore bodies from disputed ground.

During the course of the long litigation John F. Forbis, an attorney for the Boston & Montana, made this statement: "It would not be an exaggeration to say that I have engaged in hundreds of hearings before Judge Clancy in this litigation. In six and a half years we obtained in his court only two fruitless injunctions."

In court Clancy was a burlesque of judicial dignity. While on the bench he would sit with his feet cocked up on the desk before him, gazing vacantly out of the window and filling a capacious brass cuspidor with expertly aimed tobacco juice. This performance was carried on while some of the foremost mining lawyers of the country were expounding their cases and eminent geologists were giving expert testimony. Usually he came to life only when an exception was made by a Heinze lawyer and was promptly sustained. He was never known to render a decision unfavorable to Heinze. If it had not been for the higher courts, which invariably reversed Clancy, Amalgamated would have faced disaster.

The only time Clancy reversed a decision favorable to Heinze resulted from one of the most dramatic episodes in the long litigation. Heinze owned a fractional claim between the Mountain View and St. Lawerence mines, which he had given the high sounding name of Copper Trust. This fraction was seventy-five feet long, ten feet wide at one end and tapered to a point at the other. Heinze claimed that the Anaconda vein apexed in this fragment of a claim. Application was made in 1898 in Clancy's court for an injunction to halt operations on the Anaconda, Never Sweat and St. Lawrence mines on the ground that all these operations were being conducted on ore bodies which were owned in part under the Copper Trust location.

Clancy, ever ready to serve Heinze, issued the injunction without delay and the three great mines were closed. It meant the layoff of three thousand miners. The date was December 20; the weather bitter cold. Christmas was at hand. The miners were determined to get back to work. A mob of miners assembled and then started with a rope for the court house where the judge had his sleeping quarters. "Hang Clancy," was the cry from the thousands of throats.

Amalgamated officials quickly warned Clancy of his danger. He sent word to Amalgamated headquarters that he would revoke the injunction as quickly as the lawyers could draw up the papers. He said that he had been "wheedled" into signing the injunction without understanding the contents. The miners were appeased and by midnight had returned to work. The injunction had lasted fourteen hours.

Clancy was slovenly in appearance and careless in his habits. Stories about him abounded in Butte. This one is typical. One morning as he wended his way to court he met an acquaintance who stopped him and said:

"Judge, I'll bet you a dollar that I can tell you what you had for breakfast this morning."

"You're on," replied the judge.

"Ham and eggs," said the acquaintance as he lifted Clancy's beard, exposing egg and ham fat stains on the vest.

"You lose," retorted Clancy. "That was yesterday's breakfast."

Meanwhile Heinze was enlarging his domain. He bought the Glengarry claim, long regarded as worthless and opened up a rich body of ore. He built his smelter which added to his growing riches. By this time Heinze was a social lion. His handsome presence, beguiling manner and lavish hospitality made him a favorite, particularly with the women. "Fritzie," as they called him, had become something of an institution in Butte.

Heinze's horizon now widened. He had established a reputation and it was not restricted to Butte. He learned that there was need for a smelter at Trail in the Kootenay region of British Columbia where mining operations had been started. He journeyed to Trail, built the smelter and constructed a narrow gauge railroad from Trail to Rossland. Heinze now settled down to expand in his own peculiar way. He needed publicity so he bought *The Miner*, the only journal in the district. Now began the type of campaign that was later to win temporarily for him in Butte. He wanted a target that could be shaken down and he found it in the Canadian Pacific railroad. There had been criticism of the road's inadequate service. Heinze bore down on this opportunity in his paper, excoriating the railroad. The railroad then woke up to the fact that there was a serpent in the community. Heinze now proceeded to get a land grant from the Dominion Government and announced flamboyantly that he would build a narrow gauge railroad to the Pacific Coast. The chances were that he had no intention of building the line, but bluff was part of the Heinze technique. He could always cash in on it. The Canadian Pacific fell into the trap and bought Heinze out for more than a million dollars.

Heinze returned to Butte in fine fettle. He was now in the money, a full fledged capitalist with new dreams of conquest. The field was wide open; rich pickings awaited him on the Hill. In Clancy he had a willing ally. The protracted turbulent apex litigation was now to begin.

On a lower slope of Butte Hill was the Rarus claim, soon to be a storm center. Heinze's manager had told him that

the mine was difficult to work and practically worthless,
that what valuable mineral there was in it belonged to the
adjacent Boston & Montana because the ore bodies under
the Rarus apexed on Boston & Montana ground. Heinze
saw the opportunity for a quick turnover. Apex was now to
be a sort of magic wand to convert unfounded representa-
tions into easy money.

Heinze then bought Rarus and offered it to A. S. Bigelow, President of Boston & Montana, for $250,000. He
made the offer in Bigelow's Boston office. Bigelow was a
Bostonian of the old school. He regarded Heinze as a young
upstart and indignantly turned down his proposal whereupon Heinze said:

"If you want fight, I will give it to you. Before you and I
have finished, I will give you a fight that will be heard from
one end of this continent to the other."

That prophecy was to be fulfilled. Before the smoke
cleared Bigelow's entire fortune had been wiped out in the
contest.

Meanwhile Heinze had begun to mine on the Rarus and,
through his Rarus shaft, was encroaching on Boston &
Montana ore bodies. Heinze believed he had a trump card
for, in his work as surveyor for Boston & Montana in his
first year at Butte, he acquired a knowledge of the workings
of the property.

Bigelow now brought suit to enjoin Heinze from mining
any more ore in the Boston & Montana. This injunction, in
the words of an historian of Butte, "had such a prolific
brood of pestiferous offspring that for a time it looked as
though the mighty Amalgamated Copper Company might
be overwhelmed by the sheer number of them. They were
like seven-year locusts, only these locusts kept multiplying
throughout the years the fight lasted."

Before the suit came to trial Amalgamated had been
formed with Boston & Montana part of the big consolidation. Heinze now was confronted by the fact that instead of

a single company he had, as opponent, a powerful group of companies united in a common interest and equipped to fight back on a large scale. And fight back they did. The battle was about to begin.

Heinze had just celebrated his thirtieth birthday. He was already, as a Montana commentator on his operations put it, "the most adept pirate in the history of industrial privateering." He was rich, popular and the world of Butte, as he saw it, was his oyster.

Heinze had set up an organization of mining companies gathered under a holding concern called The United Copper Company, capitalized at $80,000,000. It controlled five operating corporations with a total capital of $12,500,000. The units involved were the Montana Ore Purchasing Company, the Nipper Consolidated Copper Company, the Minnie Healy Copper Company, the Corra-Rock Island Copper Company, and the Belmont Copper Company. To serve his purposes he also formed, later on, other corporations which were highly useful because he could transfer properties in litigation to them to avoid service under injunctions. Three of these more or less phantom companies were the Johnstown Mining Company, the Chile Gold Mining Company and the Hypocka Mining Company.

Heinze's tactics in the Rarus case, around which was to develop a maze of law suits, were peculiarly indicative of his methods throughout the apex litigation. Although enjoined, Heinze continued to extract ores not only from Boston & Montana but also from the Michael Devitt mine which adjoined Rarus, the Pennsylvania and the Leonard. He then got the Johnstown Mining Company, formed for this purpose, to assume responsibility for the ore taken out of those mines. Since they were not parties to the injunction, he felt that he was free to go ahead with his predatory move.

Heinze did not always get away completely with his illicit operations. In the Michael Devitt case he looted the mine of $1,000,000 worth of ore and was fined $20,000.

Amalgamated failed to receive damages in a civil action against the Johnstown Mining Company because, being a phantom, it had no assets.

The long-drawn apex litigation involved many legal complexities too baffling for lay explanation. It was nearly always the same story of biased injunctions and technical controversies, whether in the Rarus-Michael Devitt; Copper Trust-Anaconda, Snohomish; the Tramway-Butte & Boston; the Snow Bird-Anaconda; the Minnie Healy-Miles Finlen-Boston & Montana; the Rarus-Pennsylvania; the Nipper-Anaconda, or any of the many other cases that burdened the court calendar. They necessitated the employment by Amalgamated of special counsel and geological experts, thus imposing huge outlays. In the end, victory was for Heinze in the District Court and reversal in the higher tribunals.

In 1901 Amalgamated's difficulties were enhanced by the Heinze-supported election of Edward W. Harney to the District Court bench. Of the same ilk as Clancy, he was never swayed by the letter of the law but by prejudices. He was a Heinze creature, molded to mete out illegal confiscation without the slightest basis of justice. Between Clancy and Harney, Amalgamated was beset by twin evils.

The bitter legal battles were matched by physical warfare underground. While the batteries of lawyers fought bloodlessly in court with oral arguments and expert testimony, miners employed by the companies involved, waged what was sometimes hand-to-hand conflict. Heinze miners, ignoring court orders to admit Amalgamated workers to appraise the value of ores stolen in Heinze raids, forcibly resisted entry. Many of the miners were armed. To resist entry into the properties which the court ordered open, they used unslaked lime, boiling water and dynamite. Immense damage was wreaked on shafts, timber and machinery. The warfare also took toll of human life.

To comprehend what happened, it is necessary to review

the Michael Devitt case briefly. It will serve as a case history of the time, effort, cost and subterfuge employed in only one phase of the litigation instituted by Heinze.

The Michael Devitt mine had been put up for sale in 1897. A five-sixth interest was purchased by the Butte & Boston Company. The remaining one-sixth was owned by Heinze. The Butte & Boston Company sued Heinze for $161,000, the value of ore which it claimed he had taken from the Michael Devitt through his Rarus workings. There were thirty-six expert witnesses, including Heinze. The Heinze witnesses alleged that the vein containing the ore in dispute lay at its apex in the Rarus claim. This was disputed by the Butte & Boston witnesses.

Federal Judge Knowles found that five-sixths of the ore taken out of the Michael Devitt workings by Heinze belonged to the Butte & Boston Company and left the determination of its worth to the jury. The court had enjoined Heinze from further mining in the Michael Devitt. Heinze and his agents were held in contempt for violating this injunction. In July 1898 the United States Circuit Court of Appeals reversed the decision of the trial court, the injunction was cancelled and the case remanded for retrial.

Now followed the familiar Heinze tactic. Heinze's Montana Ore Purchasing Company immediately put a hundred miners to work in the Michael Devitt. A new restraining order was served. Thereupon Heinze leased the Rarus mine from which the Michael Devitt was being worked, to the Chile Gold Mining Company, which went on mining the ore. When the Chile Company was restrained, Heinze personally continued mining the ore because he had not been included in the restraining order. Again, the familiar Heinze maneuver. In 1899 Heinze obtained an injunction from Clancy restraining the Butte & Boston from producing ore in Michael Devitt.

The second trial of the case opened in 1900 in Helena before Federal Judge Knowles. The Boston Company had now come into the fold of Amalgamated. Heinze at once began one of his vicious newspaper campaigns against the company. After forty-five days of testimony the jury returned a verdict in Heinze's favor. Amalgamated then proved in court that one of Heinze's writers had prepared the newspaper articles. The judge now ordered a third trial. Both sides were under injunction against removing any ore from the disputed ground.

No action was taken in the case for nearly four years. In 1902 Heinze conveyed his interest to the Johnstown Mining Company. Working through the Rarus shaft he disregarded the injunction which still held, on the ground that the Johnstown Company was not subject to it. He ran crosscuts to the Michael Devitt ore and started mining rapidly. He bulkheaded all openings to other mine workings with concrete.

Amalgamated was determined to find out at first hand just what was going on. Reno H. Sales, then geologist and later chief geologist of Anaconda, with two miners entered the mine at night by a roundabout underground route at serious personal risk and found mining of ore in progress. Amalgamated applied for an order of inspection and Judge Knowles granted it. Heinze climbed out of a window in his office and went into hiding to avoid service. On Heinze's allegation that Judge Knowles was biased, Judge James W. Beatty of Idaho was sent to succeed him.

Heinze was now brought before Judge Beatty and given the choice of admitting Amalgamated engineers into the Michael Devitt workings or paying a fine of $2,000. Heinze then ordered the stopes to be blasted so that his looted tonnage of ore could not be measured and appraised. Amalgamated got court permission to drive a cross-cut into the Michael Devitt. Two Amalgamated miners were killed when Heinze workers exploded dynamite passed down the upraise after it had been connected with the Heinze workings.

A year after Sales and his two miners went into the Michael Devitt, Heinze was called before Judge Beatty, charged with unlawfully taking more than a million dollars worth of ore from the mine. He was fined $20,000 and his engineers $1,000 each. He still had a profit of $980,000. The irony was that Heinze had not been tried for theft but for contempt of court. That was one way Heinze got away with litigation.

The climax in the welter of law suits was reached in the spring of 1903. Heinze had planted agents in two Amalgamated subsidiary companies as stockholders. They were instructed to bring suit in Butte demanding a receivership for Amalgamated on the ground that it was an "illegal trust." Clancy also had under advisement legal questions involving the very existence of Amalgamated. He announced that he was preparing to render a decision in these vital matters, including the right of Amalgamated to do business in Montana.

Clancy's decision, as was expected, was in favor of Heinze in all the issues involved, including the hard-fought Minnie Healy case. The most drastic aspect of the decision from the bench was that Amalgamated was doing business in Montana in violation of the state law.

This time Amalgamated knew how to strike back effectively against injustice and corrupt court procedure. Within a few hours after the decision had been rendered, all properties controlled by Amalgamated in Montana and adjoining states were closed down. The Butte mines, the Anaconda smelter, the copper refineries at Great Falls, the lumber mills near Missoula, the coal mines and the company stores were all deserted. Most Montana business was affected by the shutdown. More than 20,000 miners and kindred workers were out of jobs, and thousands of clerks, service workers and railroad employees were laid off. Industry was paralyzed because mining was the life blood of the Montana economy.

Heinze, in his unbridled ambition for money, prestige and power, had overreached himself. Because of his obsession the innocent bystanders, so to speak, were now the victims of his folly.

In the hour of economic distress, feeling against Heinze mounted. Thousands of miners gathered to confront him. He sent word that he would address them on the Court House steps. Once more his glib tongue served its purpose. He made one of his demagogic speeches, vilifying the Standard Oil interests associated with Amalgamated, shouting: "Rockefeller and Rogers are seeking to control the executive, the judiciary and the Legislature of Montana." If he had inserted his own name instead of Rockefeller and Rogers, it would have been the truth. The mob cheered the tirade, not really knowing what they were yelling about. Heinze had a respite but not for long.

Frantic efforts were made to bring about the reopening of the mines. Governor Joseph K. Toole and others sought to intervene in what had become an impasse, imperilling the normal life of the entire state.

The situation was resolved by Scallon, President of Anaconda. He hit upon a plan under which Amalgamated was willing to resume operations. This was the so-called Fair Trial Law. It called for the assembly of a special session of the Legislature to enact a law permitting a change of venue in cases where there was suspicion that the trial judge was prejudiced; when there was reason to believe that a fair and impartial trial could not be held in his court; when the convenience of witnesses and the ends of justice would be promoted by a change; or when, for any cause, the judge was disqualified.

Governor Toole called the special session for November 11, 1903. The Fair Trial Law was enacted and the mines were reopened.

The Fair Trial Law was a body blow to Heinze. No longer could Clancy and Harney dish out injunctions to harass Amalgamated and impede its orderly progress. Although frustrated, Heinze still had a nuisance value which he kept alive.

The Parrot Company was the first to take advantage of the Fair Trial Law, having its case transferred from Clancy's court. At this time Heinze had instituted a large number of suits against other companies controlled by Amalgamated. The court declared these suits to be "harassing and malicious." When Clancy, in 1903, gave Heinze the right to survey many of the Amalgamated properties, the Parrot Company appealed to the Supreme Court and secured a change of venue. Heinze then started new cases in the Federal Court after having changed the place of incorporation of several of his companies to New York State.

Kelley was in the forefront of the Heinze litigation. His thorough knowledge of mining, combined with his legal skill, made him an invaluable associate of Forbis, Scallon and Evans.

On one occasion Kelley became so incensed over a biased ruling by Clancy that he strode up to the bench and said to the judge:

"You blankety blank. I would like to pull every whisker out of your face."

Clancy, roused from his usual somnolence, yelled: "Jail that man. I cite him for contempt of court."

A deputy, friendly to Kelley, took him out of the courtroom and that was the end of the matter.

Kelley had an active part in the effort to impeach Harney. William Wallace, later Solicitor General of the United States, had been retained by Amalgamated as counsel to present the articles of impeachment. He became ill and the prosecution of the case for impeachment fell on Kelley who presented it to the State Senate Committee named to hear the evidence.

Kelley had obtained the services of two detectives who were loaded with damaging evidence against Harney.

Brought to Helena, they were to testify before the Senate Committee. Heinze adherents knew the detectives were in town and were determined that they should not testify. They had posted guards at the courtroom door to prevent their entry. The detectives, however, made their way into the Committee room after a scuffle at the door. One of the detectives, a woman, then took the stand and gave the testimony hostile to Harney. The moment she sat down she and her associate were arrested, charged with perjury and put in jail. The Heinze-dominated local court fixed a cash bond of $50,000 for their release.

It was now half past ten at night. Kelley needed the witnesses but how and where was he to get $50,000 cash at that hour? He met the emergency by calling up Ryan at Butte. Between them, Ryan and Dan Hennessy raised the $50,000, put it on a locomotive with an armed guard, and sped it on to Helena. A writ of habeas corpus was obtained and the detectives were released.

Kelley was also conspicuous in the Minnie Healy–Leonard case which involved one of the richest ore bodies in Butte. Boston & Montana owned Leonard and Heinze, the Minnie Healy. The case concerned the usual Heinze unlawful procedure. When Harney, following the dictate of his master, decided the case in favor of Heinze, Kelley filed a motion for a new trial. He also filed fifty-five affidavits containing concrete evidence of Harney's dissolute life and his unfitness to sit on the bench. Harney refused to hear the case, whereupon Kelley obtained a Writ of Mandamus from the Supreme Court to compel him to do so. Harney then sent word that he would jail anyone who presented the motion for a new trial based on the affidavits.

Harney's threat did not deter Kelley. At that time Butte swarmed with Heinze spies, gunmen and detectives. Nearly every man connected with mining carried a pistol. In self-defense and to combat the Heinze gangster tactics, Amalgamated had its force of detectives charged with the security of its top executives.

When Kelley went to court to make the motion for the new trial he was accompanied by a guard named Danny O'Neill who had been a deputy sheriff. As Kelley reached the courtroom he found it crowded. All Butte knew of the antagonism that flamed in Harney for Kelley. Harney had made open threats to kill Kelley and on one occasion was only deterred from it by Kelley's coolness and contempt. The spectators were therefore primed for a real show.

A Heinze gunman was planted in the court near the bench. Kelley took O'Neill up to where he was sitting and said to him: "Sit here. Watch this fellow. If he makes a move at me, kill him."

Harney was glaring malevolently at Kelley when he rose to present the motion for the new trial.

"Upon what grounds?" asked Harney.

"The motion is based on the corrupt, dissolute and absolutely false conduct of the presiding judge in this case, as disclosed by the affidavits on file," replied Kelley.

Harney now retorted:

"I don't want to hear those affidavits. The motion is overruled."

"Thank you, Your Honor," said Kelley as he strode from the room.

Kelley argued the case before the Supreme Court which, on technicalities, refused to overrule the lower court. The case emphasized the degradation of the District Court under both Clancy and Harney and the difficulties under which the Amalgamated lawyers worked to get fair hearings. It would be difficult to find parallel instances in all American legal history.

Meanwhile the Heinze cases dragged on while a plan was being formulated, based on an honest difference of opinion, as to the identity and ownership of ore bodies. The Fair

Trial Law had demonstrated that fictitious claims to titles could be beaten, but it did not eliminate Heinze or put an end to his pernicious practices. The remedy was now at hand.

The inevitable conclusion had been reached that if the mines of Butte Hill were to operate economically, all possibility of conflicting claims should be removed. This could only be brought about by a single ownership of all the mines in the area. Such a consolidation meant lower operating costs and improved working conditions in the mines, extended development of research in both mining and metallurgy, and the early use of hydroelectric power without which the mines could not long survive.

The first essential step toward such a consolidation was to bring the properties owned by Heinze into Amalgamated ownership. Heinze, with his devious schemes, was always pressed for money to keep his perilous operations in Butte afloat. It had been clear all along that much of the litigation that he initiated had been for the purpose of building up a valuation to be sold to Amalgamated.

Ryan had become President of Anaconda in 1905 during the most turbulent period of the Heinze litigation. Although essentially a man of peace yet with a strong personality, he abhorred conflict and dissension. He now set to work to put an end to the ruinous litigation and to bring about a reasonable settlement. This meant the elimination of Heinze as a troublemaker.

In February 1906, Ryan, Kelley and Thomas F. Cole incorporated The Butte Coalition Mining Company, under the laws of New Jersey, with a capital of $15,000,000, par $15 a share. It owned the Red Metal Mining Company which was its operating concern. Butte Coalition was organized mainly for the purpose of buying out the Heinze properties. After some negotiations Heinze agreed to sell all his holdings in Butte for $10,500,000. Fifteen years previous he was making $100 a month as surveyor in the Boston & Montana. His golden dream had been realized.

Heinze transferred the following properties to Red Metal:

By the Montana Ore Purchasing Company: The major interests in the Rarus and Johnstown claims, one-third of the Tramway, one-half of the Snohomish, two-thirds of the Mountain Chief, one-half of the Highland Chief, two-fifths of the Vulture, 108 lots in Butte and a number of other mining claims;

By the Johnstown Mining Company: Fractional interests in the Rarus, Johnstown, and Pennsylvania and one-eighth of the Minnie Healy;

By the Minnie Healy Mining Company: Part interests in the Minnie Healy and Lake claims;

By the Corra-Rock Island Mining Company: Corra and Rock Island mines and interests in the Snoozer, Blackfoot, Robert Emmet and other claims;

By the Nipper Consolidated Copper Company: Interests in the Nipper and other claims;

By the Hypocka Mining Company and the Guardian Copper Company: Small interests in the Minnie Healy claim;

By the Belmont Mining Company: 67½ acres of fractional claims in the southeast part of the city of Butte. Besides these properties, the Butte Coalition Company also bought control of the Alice Gold & Silver Mining Company which owned 340 acres of mining claims.

It is an illuminating commentary on Heinze's activities that when he was bought out, one hundred and ten suits, pending in the Butte District Court and involving claims totalling more than $70,000,000, were dismissed. For the first time in nearly a decade, the Butte courts were free to proceed with normal business, untrammeled by bias and bicker.

Despite the cost in time, money and exasperation, the

apex litigation served a constructive purpose. It was primarily responsible for the exhaustive underground study which revealed invaluable knowledge of the geology of the district. The Butte Hill was thoroughly mapped for the first time. An even greater benefit was the consolidation of properties which made for improved mine operation and metal production economies and, as the years passed, vast expansion. As one mining expert put it:

"Had the mining companies, as they existed in 1888, attempted to continue as individual entities, Butte would have been a ghost town in less than thirty years. Property consolidation thus saved for Montana a prosperous and ever-growing community, and for the nation a tremendous supply of copper, zinc, lead, manganese, silver and gold."

Heinze now had his millions. He went to New York dreaming of new worlds to conquer only to find physical and financial disintegration in the end. A fleeting hour of glory, however, preceded the twilight of his career. He founded his own bank, the Mercantile National, and launched the brokerage house of Otto C. Heinze & Company. With this equipment he started in to be a power in Wall Street. In this new essay for prestige he lacked the tools with which he had extorted wealth in Butte. There were no biased judges to enforce his predatory tactics, no gunmen to back his forays. He was up against the master manipulators of high finance in a game beset with pitfalls for the amateur, the boaster and the overconfident. Heinze, the embryo Wall Street Napoleon, filled this bill.

Heinze made two errors of judgment which cost him dear. The first was that he revived his United Copper Company, which was still in existence, and organized a pool in it. The second was his alliance with Charles W. Morse, then head of an ice trust and a notorious stock market manipulator. Heinze's pool collapsed under the drive of experienced Wall Street operators. His loans were called; his bank and brokerage firm failed. He was practically cleaned out. The worst was to come. Heinze and Morse were indicted for fraudulent banking practices. In this instance his luck did not forsake him. Morse was convicted and served a term in a Federal prison while Heinze was acquitted.

Saddened and disillusioned, Heinze returned to Butte. He still owned a mine in the Coeur d'Alenes and a tunnel in Utah. This time he could find no apices to connect with Amalgamated properties. Distance lent safety to them. The trump card, which he had played so successfully, was gone and with it the thrill that had animated him during the years of the long litigation.

When he had just turned forty Heinze married Berenice Wheeler, an actress who gave him a son. The marriage ended in divorce two years later. In 1914 he died of cirrhosis of the liver at Saratoga, New York. He was just forty-five. Into those four and a half decades he had packed several lifetimes of colorful industrial adventure.

Heinze sought to be the dictator of Butte and Wall Street. Like all dictators he suffered the fate that invariably overtakes them. The political dictators have fallen because the will of the people ultimately prevailed. Heinze's eclipse was born of vanity and cupidity. His meteoric career can best be summed up in these words: "He came like wind and like water he went."

YEARS OF EXPANSION

THE END of the Heinze litigation and the departure of the chief trouble-maker from the scene enabled Anaconda to embark on its orderly productive course. With the passing of Heinze the aura of synthetic romance that had enveloped him and given color to Butte, vanished. Efficiency was now the order of the day. The time had arrived when The Anaconda Copper Mining Company would advance toward its full stature in the industry.

The year 1905 was historic in the annals of the company because of two events that stemmed from it. Ryan had become President of Anaconda and Kelley was advanced to the Secretaryship. Now developed the teamwork between them, born of close friendship and mutual trust, that was to initiate and develop practically every major phase of the progress of the company.

Kelley had first met Ryan at a dinner given for Ryan by Jack Liggett, member of a Montana pioneer family. Ryan was then head of the Daly bank. The men clicked immediately. Ryan was the businessman and banker; Kelley, the master of mining law and of corporate organization. By temperament Ryan was calm and judicial with an unerring judgment. Kelley was more animated with a comprehending vision. Both were doers with undaunted courage; both were endowed with qualities of bold leadership. They worked in such close and intimate cooperation that it was well-nigh impossible to differentiate between their individual accomplishments. Ryan was forty and Kelley ten years younger when they merged their talents. The disparity in age, however, did not affect their teamwork. Once they joined their gifts they formed a combination rare in the conduct of an industrial organization. There has been an irrevocable logic in the life of Kelley and it was matched by a no less invincible logic in Ryan.

It was obvious to Ryan and Kelley that wise procedure dictated the purchase of properties rather than going to court to determine the vexing apex problems arising out of mine operations. This had been accomplished with the Heinze settlement. Moreover, rich as the Butte areas were, they could not afford costly litigation. The answer, therefore, lay in consolidation even where no conflict threatened. Geologists had warned, and experience seemed to indicate, that sooner or later, questions of title and identification of ore bodies at great depth must arise, no matter how friendly or cooperative might be the spirit of the owners. As mines went deeper the technical staffs of independent enterprises differed as to the entire mineral structure of the Hill. Hence the need of consolidation.

There were other difficulties. One was in the control and disposal of water which coursed through the vein structure to the deepest workings, bringing a heavy cost burden. The multiplicity of operating shafts constituted another cost that threatened the future of the district as an economical producer. Problems of ventilation and the high temperatures of many workings presented a serious study for engineers. It was deemed inevitable that electricity must come into the mines to replace steam power. Steam-operated pumps exhausted their hot vapor into the already vitiated atmosphere of the mines, complicating the heat and ventilation problem. Open pit mining had been developed in the por-phyry deposits of Utah and elsewhere, proving that copper could be produced more cheaply than in Butte. Expert opinion supported the conclusion of Ryan and Kelley that if Butte was to continue as a major production center, sub-stantial economies in overhead cost must be brought about.

Meanwhile there was a change in executive direction. On June 10, 1909, Benjamin B. Thayer succeeded Ryan as President when the latter became President of Amalgam-ated on the death of Rogers. Thayer contributed an inter-esting chapter to the Anaconda story. Born in San Francisco he graduated in mining engineering from Lawrence Scien-tific School of Harvard University. He was a classmate of William Randolph Hearst whose father, you will recall, was a member of the syndicate that opened up the Anaconda mine. Thayer went to Butte immediately after graduation. It was generally believed that the George Hearst association with Anaconda influenced him to seek a career in Butte.

In Butte, Thayer started as a miner and soon became shift boss. Although an engineer, he knew every phase of mining from personal experience. He filled every position in The Anaconda Company from miner to President, the post he held for six years. When Amalgamated was dissolved and Ryan took over the Presidency of Anaconda, Thayer con-tinued as Vice President to the end of his life.

Came 1910 and a year of decision. Events were now shap-ing for the much-desired consolidation. Plans had been laid for the dissolution of Amalgamated and the disposal of its assets.

On February 15, 1910, Thayer, in a circular letter, called a special meeting of the stockholders of Anaconda to con-sider a proposal to increase the capital stock from 1,200,000 shares, par value $25, to 6,000,000 shares of the same par value and to amend the articles of incorporation so that the company might acquire and hold the securities of other corporations. It was necessary that two-thirds of the stock be voted and more than this amount was represented at the meeting in person or by proxy. After the increase in capital stock was voted a resolution was unanimously adopted to increase the authorized capital from $30,000,000 to $150,-000,000 and to purchase all the property and assets owned by other corporations which had been under Amalgamated control, by issuing to them amounts of capital stock of The Anaconda Company as follows:

Boston & Montana, 1,200,000 shares; Butte & Boston, 300,000 shares; The Washoe Copper Company, 380,000 shares; Trenton Mining & Development Company, 120,-000 shares; Big Blackfoot Lumber Company, 300,000 shares; Red Metal Mining Company, 500,000 shares; Parrot Silver & Copper Company, 90,000 shares; Alice Gold & Silver Mining Company, 30,000 shares.

At a meeting of the Board of Directors of Anaconda held in New York on March 24, 1910, a report made by Professor James F. Kemp, professor of geology in the School of Mines of Columbia University, and Herman A. Keller, another eminent mining expert, was read. It stated that it was their conviction that the proposed consolidation was highly desirable. It approved as equitable and fair the advantages to be gained by all the participating companies in facility of mining, economy of development, hoisting and pumping. Highly important was the assertion that the complicated question of apex rights, which increased as the mines grew deeper, would be eliminated.

Two months later an agreement to purchase was concluded with all but one of the companies involved. This company was the Alice Gold & Silver Mining Company, which had issued 400,000 shares of stock. Of this, Amalgamated, through Butte Coalition, owned 359,721 shares. In April, 1910, Anaconda purchased all the property and assets of Alice for 30,000 shares of its stock. A group of minority stockholders objected and instituted a suit to annul the sale. Now followed a long legal controversy which ended

when the life of Alice expired in 1930. With the wind-up of
the company Anaconda purchased the properties for $1,-
500,000. Thus Anaconda, which had originally purchased
the Alice property in 1910 for 30,000 shares of its stock, now
bought back that stock, plus accumulated dividends.

Kelley's corporate craftsmanship was never demonstrated
in more convincing fashion than in the unification of the
properties which now came under Anaconda control. This
is what he did: First, he made a schedule. There were corporations in Utah, Montana and Massachusetts, organized
under the laws of those states. It was necessary to bring all
under a common ownership, which was accomplished.
Then Kelley appointed a committee consisting of the operating management of each corporation. He then named a
Super Committee which included Kemp, Keller and
George M. Church, a noted accountant, who had been a
director of Amalgamated and Anaconda. Each of these
committees, representing individual management, made a
study of their property and a valuation of the unit in terms
of common stock participation. Their reports were submitted to the Super Committee and a final adjudication was
made, as already indicated.

With the unification of properties, The Anaconda Copper
Mining Company began its march toward eminence in the
industry. In a little more than a decade it would be a power
in two continents and also extend its operations in half a
dozen states. Henceforth, the keynote was expansion.

After the absorption of the principal properties controlled
by Amalgamated, Anaconda purchased several of the properties owned by W. A. Clark. These included the Original
and Stewart mines and the Butte Reduction Works. The
transaction was effected through Amalgamated which paid
$5,500,000 for the properties and then transferred them to
Anaconda in exchange for 112,500 shares of Anaconda
stock. This acquisition was brought about by Ryan and
Kelley.

The terms of the transaction were $1,000,000 cash and nine promissory notes of The Anaconda Company for $500,000 each. Following the Clark-Daly feud, Kelley and Clark became close friends. Clark, who was getting deaf, frequently sought Kelley's advice at meetings and relied on his judgment.

Anaconda had become flush with money so it was decided to advance payment on the unpaid Clark notes which amounted to $1,500,000. Kelley went to see Clark at his office in 20 Exchange Place in New York to close the deal. It was a hot Saturday afternoon in May. Clark, in his shirt sleeves, was working at his desk, scratching away on papers. Kelley said:

"Senator, what are you doing down here on a hot Saturday afternoon?"

"Well, I will tell you, Con," answered Clark. "I have two bids for blowers for the smelter I am building at Clarkdale, Arizona. The bids are so nearly the same that I am figuring out the difference in weight in order to ascertain the difference in freight." It was characteristic of Clark that this multimillionaire should quibble about a comparatively few dollars in freight cost.

Kelley then broached the object of his visit, saying:

"I came down to see you about these promissory notes of Anaconda."

Clark's face fell for he thought Kelley's mission was to ask for an extension. One of the notes was due in June.

"Yes," replied Clark, "what about them?"

Kelley then said:

"Mr Ryan and I have discussed the matter and we think we would like to anticipate the payment of the remaining notes."

Clark leaned forward, cupped his ear and said:

"You want to pay off the note about due now?" to which Kelley answered:

"No, we would like to pay off all three."

Clark pondered a moment and then said:

"I just got so much cash I don't know what to do with it. If you insist on paying the notes, all right, but I prefer that they run to maturity."

"No," said Kelley, "we have the cash and we want to pay now." If Kelley had asked for an extension he would have been turned down.

Anaconda paid off the remaining notes. The company took the entire purchase price of $5,500,000 for the Clark properties in less than two years out of the Original and Stewart mines.

Clark owned the United Verde in Arizona, one of the wonder copper mines out of which he amassed a fortune. Kelley greatly desired to acquire this property for Anaconda with the backing of J. P. Morgan & Co. Kelley talked to Clark repeatedly about selling the property. The invariable answer was: "United Verde is not for sale." Once he did say to Kelley: "If ever I decide to sell it, you will be the first to know."

Kelley had three friends, Thomas W. Lamont, Dwight Morrow and Thomas Cochran, in the Morgan firm and he enlisted their aid in trying to put over the purchase of United Verde. Cochran said: "Anything is for sale at a price." Kelley had asserted that he was willing to pay $50,-000,000 for United Verde. The bankers arranged a meeting with Clark in the board room of the First National Bank where Clark had his New York bank account. This episode is worth relating if only to reveal how Clark started that bank account. He had acquired a number of gold bars in his bank at Butte, so he shipped them to New York to open his account in the First National. The bars were worth more than two hundred thousand dollars. It was probably the first time that an account was started in a New York bank with gold bars.

The bankers got nowhere with Clark when they met in

the board room of the First National. They dangled the $50,000,000 offer before his eyes to no avail. With Clark's declaration, "United Verde is not for sale at any price," the meeting ended.

Anaconda had meanwhile widened its sphere of operations with two important acquisitions. In 1909 the International Smelting & Refining Company had acquired from the United Metals Selling Company all the capital stock of the Raritan Copper Works at Perth Amboy, New Jersey, the Raritan Terminal & Transportation Company, and the New Jersey Storage & Warehouse Company. International then began to operate the copper works at Raritan and a smelter at Tooele, Utah. A smelter at Miami, Arizona, was under construction. It had financed the building of the Tooele Valley Railroad and the International Lead Refinery at East Chicago, Indiana.

In April 1914, Anaconda acquired all the assets of the International Smelting & Refining Company through an exchange of 330,000 shares of Anaconda stock for the 100,000 shares of International stock outstanding. With the dissolution of International, Anaconda organized the International Smelting Company with a capital of $15,000,000 consisting of 150,000 shares, par value $100. Anaconda transferred to the new company the Tooele smelter and the Miami plant in exchange for 95,000 shares of International Smelting and advanced the money for the completion of the Miami smelter. Subsequently the name of the International Smelting Company was changed back to International Smelting and Refining Company, a wholly owned subsidiary. It acquired the assets of the Raritan Copper Works and the International Lead Refining Company, also wholly owned subsidiaries. As a result of these transactions the entire issue of 200,000 shares of International Smelting & Refining Company stock came into the possession of Anaconda. International Smelting brought Anaconda into four states and pointed the way to the combination of mining with fabrication which was to give the company a twin prestige.

Through the acquisition of all these plants and facilities and their consolidation into the International Company, Anaconda was enabled to have all its metallurgical operations in the United States, outside Montana, under a single concern. It was an important step toward economical operation and compact organization.

On June 9, 1915, the Amalgamated was dissolved. Ryan returned to the Presidency of Anaconda while Thayer became Vice President in charge of mining operations. By this time Kelley was Vice President with increasing responsibilities.

One of the major problems that confronted Ryan and Kelley after the consolidation was to bring about lower costs in the production of metals which had to be marketed in competition with those of the low-cost producers in the United States and elsewhere. The question of cheap, practical electric power for the mines, smelters and refineries had assumed increasing importance. With the development of new metallurgical processes the demand for electric power became more insistent. Ryan, with Kelley as associate, met the need with the formation of the Montana Power Company in November 1912. It not only solved Anaconda's power problem but performed a vast service for all Montana.

The employment of electric power in the mines and reduction plants began in 1907 when electric locomotives were introduced in the underground workings at Butte. Prior to that time horses and mules were used for underground haulage. Earlier, this work was done by hand with wheelbarrows. The major amount of power used in the mines in Butte prior to the organization of Montana Power was generated by steam plants at the mines. This type of power was becoming exceedingly expensive as the mines went deeper and greater amounts of power were necessary for both mining and hoisting. At that time the power cost was in the neighborhood of $120 per horse power year.

The remedy for this excessive cost lay in hydroelectric power which had been developed only to a limited extent in Montana. Long before they were harnessed by the power-conscious disciples of a mechanized civilization, the streams of Montana had proved their worth to man and beast. On turgid rivers and turbulent creeks wild game had slaked their thirst and, with primitive equipment, the Indians had caught their fish. Up the long reaches of the Missouri, Lewis and Clark poled their rude pirogues on their historic journey of exploration.

It was on the Missouri, appropriately enough, that Montana's first hydroelectric development was launched in 1871 at Black Eagle Falls a few miles above the Great Falls, with a primitive 8,000 horse power plant. Two years later another plant was erected on the opposite bank. These plants were operated by the Great Falls Water Power Company and the Town Site Company to serve the Boston & Montana which had built a smelter at the site. Other power companies subsequently organized were the Butte Electric & Power Company and the Missouri River Electric & Power Company and their subsidiaries.

Ryan envisioned the possibilities of increased hydroelectric development and the economy it involved for Anaconda properties above and below ground, particularly in the excessive cost of electricity from steam. He realized that the answer lay in a combine of the various existing electric generating capacities and transmitting the power to the local centers at Butte and Anaconda. Since he and his associates had substantial interests in these companies he was able to emphasize the advantages that would result from such a customer as Anaconda. His wishes prevailed. At his instigation and under his direction, the Montana Power Company was organized on November 12, 1912. He

assumed the presidency and filled the office until his death
in 1933.

Anaconda played an important part in the growth of
Montana Power. It is doubtful if a utility with a small number of residential customers thinly spread out over a wide
area could successfully serve them with low-cost electricity
and later natural gas, unless it had very large consumers to
help pay for an extensive transmission system. Anaconda became the largest user of Montana Power electricity and
natural gas.

To form Montana Power, Ryan merged all the power
companies already mentioned and later on, the Great Falls
Power Company and the Thompson Falls Power Company.
The newborn corporation found itself in possession of eight
hydroelectric and four steam plants at widely separated
locations. Ryan, despite the load of executive responsibility
he was carrying as head of Anaconda, set to work to expand
the use of hydroelectric power not only for Anaconda and
its properties but for the entire State of Montana. Today his
name is blessed in thousands of homes, schools and farms, to
say nothing of mines and plants, as the giver of cheap, constant electric power. The onetime Volta plant now bears
the name of Ryan. If Ryan had performed no other service,
his instigation of Montana Power would alone have given
him a high and enduring place in the industrial history of
Montana.

Anaconda was quick to take advantage of the expanded
hydroelectric facilities. The Butte, Anaconda & Pacific
Railroad, including all its spurs to the mines on Butte Hill,
was completely electrified in 1913. This electrification was
the first use of high voltage for operating trains under heavy
load conditions. Engineers representing railroads in the
United States and Europe came to Butte to study the pioneer operation. For one thing, it served as a test in transportation by electric power on mountain grades. For another, it was found that in drawing heavy trains over steep

grades the electric locomotives could use their motors as generators in braking the trains down the grade and return to the power line almost as much electric energy as had been required to move the trains up the grade.

Ryan's vision saw beyond the employment of hydro-electric power in mines, smelters and refineries. The success achieved in the electrification of the Butte, Anaconda & Pacific led to a historic innovation. Thanks to his suggestion and promotion, the electrification of great railroads was inaugurated. The first was the Chicago, Milwaukee & St. Paul which electrified its mountain divisions and brought to Montana the distinction of having the then longest stretch of electrified railway in the United States.

One of the most important innovations under Ryan's presidency of Montana Power was the introduction of natural gas in 1931. It was brought from the fields in south central and western Montana to cities which the company was already serving with electricity. This project, initiated during the lowest point of the depression, was inspired by Ryan's courage which never failed him. Without his enterprise, natural gas fuel for the people of Montana would have been deferred for many years.

Immediately after its introduction, the Anaconda properties at Butte were piped for natural gas. Its introduction was a boon for the company. Operations in the Southwest had proved that natural gas practically served all purposes in smelting processes as efficiently and far more economically than coal. Negotiations were initiated for providing the plants at Great Falls with natural gas fuel. Subsequently service for the use of natural gas was inaugurated at Anaconda. All coal-burning apparatus was replaced with gas burners.

Electricity, however, more than held its own as a replacement for coal. An additional demand for electric power developed when Laist originated the electrolytic process for the reduction of zinc. Units for this treatment were installed

at Anaconda and Great Falls. A fundamental requirement
of this process was low-cost electric power which Montana
Power was able to provide.

The fact that two of the major load centers, Butte and
Anaconda, were 150 miles from the principal sources of
generation at Great Falls, meant that Montana Power necessarily became one of the pioneers in long-distance transmission of electric energy. Steel tower lines were constructed
and the high voltages necessary for long-distance transmission, initiated. This was a radical innovation at the time.

In 1928 the American Power & Light Company acquired
virtually all the outstanding common stock of Montana
Power and acted as a holding company until holding was
terminated by order of the Securities and Exchange Commission. Direct ownership of the securities was returned to
individual stockholders on February 15, 1950.

An amusing incident occurred after Ryan had moved to
New York. He had interested some prominent New York
financiers in Montana Power and invited them to visit
Montana and inspect the properties. He got in touch with
Kelley, then Vice President of Anaconda, to provide hospitality for the guests. Accordingly Kelley arranged a dinner
at the Silver Bow Club.

The New York party expected to meet a miscellaneous
gathering of hard rock miners with a sprinkling of cowboys
in ten gallon hats. A surprise awaited them when they arrived at the club. An elaborate banquet table, laden with
flowers, awaited them. Scarcely had they recovered from
the sight of the table and the beautifully decorated dining
room, when they received another shock. Kelley, the host,
and his fellow members of the reception committee appeared in immaculate dinner coats and were entirely at
home in them. The New Yorkers believing they were in the
traditional Wild West, had not bothered to don evening attire.

The hit of the evening came when the orchestra, com-

posed entirely of miners and recruited from the Boston &
Montana mine band, played a program. The band leader,
Sam Treloar, also a miner, had composed a parody on a
song, popular at that time, entitled "Has Anybody Here
Seen Kelly?"

When the time came for Kelley to make a few remarks
the orchestra suddenly burst forth in song:

> "Has anybody here seen Kelley,
> "Kelley with the thin light hair?"

Needless to say, the song and the gracious and generous
hospitality made the evening memorable for the visitors.
They returned to New York with a new conception of the
West.

One of the dramatic figures in the development of Butte
and Montana passed from the scene when W. A. Clark
died in 1925. His principal properties had been purchased
by Anaconda in 1910. Three years after Clark's death his
remaining holdings were bought by Anaconda. They included the Clark-Montana Realty Company; the Montana Hardware Company; eighty-seven per cent of the
Moulton Mining Company; the Elm Orlu Mining Company; Timber Butte Milling Company; the Mayflower and
West Mayflower mines; the Butte Street Railway Company; *The Butte Miner*, a newspaper; and some scattered
mining claims. Among the other Clark properties of importance that also passed to Anaconda in this transaction
was the pioneer bank of W. A. Clark & Brother and the
Western Lumber Company.

Kelley participated in the succession of mergers and acquisitions, carrying at the same time responsibility for the
complex legal problems involved. His was an increasingly
variegated task, taking toll of time and energy.

The acquisition of the major mining properties in the
Butte district was now complete. All were mobilized into a
single system of operation under Anaconda management

with a single staff of executives, engineers, technicians and legal counsel. The way was open for a common level system throughout the district and also for a unified program of drainage, haulage and ventilation. The company was now able to concentrate its energies toward more efficient and economical operation.

With the introduction of electric power and natural gas, Anaconda's fuel problems were solved. Another problem now confronted the company. It was ventilation, a major requirement in mining, particularly at deep levels. Ventilation, the life blood so to speak, of the miner, was now to enjoy the benefits of unification.

Although the Anaconda properties had ventilation facilities from the beginning, it was not until February, 1918, that the company organized its Ventilation and Hygiene Department, the first concern in the metal mining industry to institute such a department. Eighteen large, surface, reversible modern mine fans provide the primary ventilation circuits throughout the mines of Butte district, displacing over 3,000,000 cubic feet of fresh air per minute. As an example of the astounding environmental changes within the Butte mines, six and one-half tons of fresh air are being drawn into, and displaced from, the mines for every ton of ore which is hoisted to surface. During one month in 1955, approximately 600,000 tons of ore were hoisted. It meant that nearly four million tons of air were circulated through the Butte mines in August 1955.

Over one thousand small fans provide the secondary or auxiliary ventilation system. These auxiliary fans operate primarily, blowing on more than forty miles of air transmission duct. The major part of the air transmission duct used underground is of the flexible type. Approximately thirty miles of new flexible air transmission duct are placed in the Butte mines each year.

The material from which The Anaconda Company prepares its flexible air transmission duct has an especially woven nylon fabric as a supporting base which is coated with a high quality neoprene. This particular fabric was developed by The Anaconda Company. The fabric is inert to acid water, mold and fungi and has an exceptionally high tear resistance. Over 10,000 horse power is direct-connected to ventilation equipment. This is sufficient electrical energy to serve as a utility for the city of Helena and its vicinity.

Two large air conditioning systems service underground workings in the northwest area of the Butte district. One plant delivers 1,200 tons of refrigeration per day and the second plant can produce 1,500 tons per day. In the first instance this is the equivalent cooling produced by a block of ice one foot square and eight miles long. In the second instance the cooling produced is equivalent to that of a block of ice one foot square and ten miles long. This ingenious method of air conditioning is entirely an Anaconda development.

Complete conversion to wet drilling was accomplished in the mines owned by the company in 1925. In 1936 research work conducted by the Ventilation and Industrial Hygiene Department disclosed that dust emanations during drilling operations were a direct function of the quantity of water delivered through the drill steel to the cutting face of the bit. As a result of this work all modern air percussion drills are provided with a water needle of desirable diameter. Considerable research work has been done by the Ventilation and Industrial Hygiene Department with the cooperation of the United States Bureau of Mines relative to the various types of equipment and methods for providing desirable environment.

Anaconda pioneered in another essential mining operation since it was the first organization in this country to use electrostatic precipitation underground. In its quest to produce desirable environment in the mines the company developed a compact and highly efficient dust collector which is now available to all industry, and also designs for contaminant control for surface plants.

When Mother Nature bestowed her gifts on the richest hill on earth, she accompanied her presentation with an excessive burden in the form of extremely high temperature rock gradient. The rock temperature at the 4,200 foot level is 127 degrees Fahrenheit. If no ventilation were provided, the temperature of workings at this horizon would be higher.

As a result of all this development the Butte mines today are much cooler than they were twenty-five years ago despite the fact that they have advanced considerably in depth. The miners are healthier and therefore happier.

Like every other important Anaconda development, the timber holdings came in for unification. Daly, with his great foresight, had begun the acquisition of forest lands to provide the timber so necessary in the mines. Following his death the timber acreage was increased until it reached 386,137 acres, which means two and a half billion board feet of standing timber. Formerly the company sawmills were located at Bonner, St. Regis and Hamilton in Montana and in Hope, Idaho. Following the consolidation idea, all milling is concentrated at Bonner.

Bonner is a one hundred per cent Anaconda community for the mill is the town and the town, the mill. Nearly 500 men work in the mill and as many more in the woods. The company has its own fire department, hospital and ambulance, and donated the ground for a school and two churches. All timber operations are under The Anaconda Company Lumber Department.

Conservation of one of our most valuable natural resources animates company policy. When trees are cut down, a sufficient number of adjacent trees are left to provide natural feed source for renewal. Thus it is not a question of "woodman spare that tree" but woodman renew that tree.

Forty per cent of the 100,000,000 board feet cut during a

year is used in the mines where packaged timber handling saves time, money and manpower. The remainder is disposed of in nine retail yards of the Interstate Lumber Company, a wholly owned Anaconda subsidiary, and to independent retail dealers in Montana and as far east as New York State.

The foundation of Anaconda was reared on copper and copper has continued to loom increasingly large in company progress and prestige and always will. In 1919, however, the company embarked on what was to become a progressive program of diversification of product. It purchased 3,600 acres of phosphate land together with a number of mining claims near Soda Springs, Idaho, at a cost of $650,000. The property is located in one of the richest known phosphate rock areas. Some phosphate properties near Garrison, Montana, were also bought. The company constructed a plant at the metallurgical works in Anaconda for production of a high quality fertilizer.

A town known as Conda was built at the mines, seven miles from the main line of the Union Pacific Railroad, which constructed a branch to the property. Within a short time Anaconda became one of the world's largest producers of phosphate fertilizer. The rock is crushed in a plant at the mine and shipped to Anaconda where it is processed with sulphuric acid derived from the smelting operation in the reduction works. The fertilizer contains one of the most essential plant foods.

Remote location of the Anaconda fertilizer plant from the intensively cultivated agricultural Middle West made it impossible to ship the ordinary superphosphate to these areas because of the heavy freight rates. Laboratory tests under Laist, at Anaconda, created a process of combining sulphuric acid and phosphate rock for the manufacture of phosphoric acid. This phosphoric acid was then used to treat the phosphate rock. In this way a product was produced of approximately three times the quality of phos-

phoric acid as was available in the superphosphate fertilizer then in commercial use. The new fertilizer was called
treble-superphosphate. It is in wide demand throughout the
sugar beet growing regions of the West and in all areas
where the maintenance of the fertility of the soil is necessary.

II

The impact of World War I imposed tremendous responsibilities, as well as difficulties, for Anaconda. As in the
second global conflict, the company rose to the emergency
through trial but without error. Throughout those years of
economic derangement which affected all large industrial
concerns, Ryan's qualities of leadership rose to new heights
with Kelley standing shoulder to shoulder in every critical
emergency. Their vision, courage and resource were never
more manifest than in those devastating years that "tried
men's souls."

When hostilities broke out in August 1914, the price of
copper was low. Immediately the cost of labor and materials rose. Ryan led the movement to set and maintain copper
prices at a level adequate to offset the abnormal cost of production. Even at the prices finally established, Anaconda
and other producers emerged from the war with financial
loss. Ryan made his fight with negligible support from other
producers. Happily his dealings with the government were
principally with a man who knew the copper business and
who, through his long business experience, could evaluate
facts, needs and figures. That man was Bernard M. Baruch,
chairman of the War Industries Board.

There had been complete demoralization of the copper
market at the outset of the European war. For three months
after that fateful August of 1914 the price of copper was not
even quoted on the market. In November 1914, copper sold
at 11.1 cents a pound. Then the price soared but little was
bought at the high figures save the small lots held by
brokers.

When it became certain that America would enter the war and that the compass of industry would be set for military needs, the Navy and War Departments notified Baruch of their immediate copper requirements. The Army desired 25,510,000 pounds of copper and the Navy, 26,000,-000 pounds. Ryan wrote Baruch on behalf of all the principal producers, offering to provide this amount of copper at 16.6739 cents a pound, the average selling price of the metal over the period from 1907 to 1916. This was little more than half the current market price. When the producers offered to supply the government with the 51,510,000 pounds required by the Army and Navy, wages at the mines and smelters were based on a price in excess of 31 cents a pound. Costs had risen beyond all previous levels in the industry.

With our entry into the war the price of copper was fixed at 23.5 cents a pound. Since the agreement on the price made with the War Industries Board established a precedent, it may be well to reproduce it:

"On September 21, 1917 the price of 23.5 cents was definitely fixed in the form of agreement between the government and the producers. It was approved by the President, subject to revision after four months, the short period being established for the purpose of allowing any producer, consumer, or other interested party to appear and present reasons, if any, for increasing or decreasing the price. It is interesting in this connection to note that . . . no consumer, public or private, nor official of our own or any other government, appeared to object to the price as too high. The fact is that the fixed price of copper represented a smaller advance over prewar normal than that of perhaps any other commodity. This was the first negotiated price-fixing arrangement ever established by the United States Government. Despite many hardships and obstacles the American copper producers played their part and contributed to the successful prosecution of the war in a way second to no other industry. There are ample grounds for the belief that the prices fixed by the government worked hardship on many operators."

This opinion was corroborated by Professor F. W. Taussig, a member of the government's Price Fixing Board, who said in his publication, *Price Fixing by a Price Fixer:*

"If iron and steel, coal and coke, heavy chemicals, cotton, wool, wheat, corn, sugar and meat, be classed along with copper as the absolute war essentials, it is found that the advance in copper over prewar normal allowed to copper, was less than half the average granted to all these other products."

The price of 23.5 cents for copper remained in effect until July 2, 1918, when it was advanced to 26 cents a pound to compensate partially for increased cost of wages, supplies and advances in freight rates made by the government when it took over control of railway operation.

Anaconda met the mounting war demands with increased production. Electrolytic refining of zinc had been perfected at Great Falls in 1916 and 1917 and this meant a large-scale production of zinc of the highest quality. It was also planned to enter rod and wire drawing in a new plant at Great Falls, a project later carried out.

As the war progressed with urgent government demands for metal, Anaconda registered record marks of production. In 1916 the company's plants produced 671,421,689 pounds of copper, a new high. Of this total, 283,505,657 pounds came from company mines. During the same year Anaconda produced 20,906,439 pounds of zinc. In 1917 the output of zinc was 50,624,524 pounds due to new and expanded plant facilities.

Anaconda met another need. Manganese for war purposes came into big demand. Before 1914 we obtained the major part of our supply from abroad. Submarines had reduced the foreign supply to a minimum. There was no alternative but to turn to domestic sources. Anaconda made a large outlay to produce manganese from the Butte ores and again measured up to its responsibility.

So, too, with ferro-manganese. In 1918, at the solicitation of the government, Anaconda started production of the metal. Five electric ferro-manganese furnaces were installed at Great Falls. Three had started operations with a program for production of 1,000 tons a day when the Armistice was signed. With the advent of peace the demand for ferro-manganese ceased and the furnaces were shut down and dismantled.

Ryan's outstanding services as industrialist were suitably recognized in May 1918, when, having served as Red Cross Commissioner for the Wounded, he was appointed Assistant Secretary of War and placed in charge of aircraft production. The war ended soon thereafter but Ryan had laid his plans, and had so perfected airplane output that 23,000 planes a year could have been delivered.

When Ryan went to Washington as Assistant Secretary of War, Kelley advanced to the presidency. With Ryan in Washington the terrific burden of Anaconda leadership, together with the added responsibilities attendant upon the war effort, fell on Kelley's shoulders. He met the challenge with his customary skill and capacity for work.

With peace proclaimed in 1918, new problems and responsibilities faced Ryan and Kelley. Before them loomed the difficulties arising from the economic dislocation due to the war. That, however, was only one phase of the problem. During the war, all plant facilities had been greatly expanded and output stepped up to the limit. The increase in production finally became in excess of our requirements or the ability of the United States and its Allies to fabricate the metal. Ryan and Kelley, with other leaders in the industry, warned the government of threatened disaster to copper mining. Suggestions were made for the release of manpower for other essential war work. The government at Washington was adamant in its refusal to curtail production and ordered continuous output.

The inevitable result was that with hostilities over and war profits ended, inventories showed enormous quantities of copper at the refineries, in the hands of producers, the government, and the Allied powers. Foreign and domestic demand had receded to such an extent that the United States had a copper surplus.

Ryan realized the necessity for a letdown in production which meant curtailment of personnel. At this juncture Baruch called the industry to Washington and said to them:

"Our soldiers will be coming back and we must have work for them. We know here at Washington that you are producing more copper than you can sell, but we want you to keep your mines open and have jobs for our boys when they return."

There was nothing to do but to keep the mines open with copper stocks piling up. The difficulties in the industry were increased by a great flow of reclaimed secondary copper into the market. Millions of pounds of metal, retrieved from the battlefields of Europe, were returned to the market after a single process of purifying and melting. Copper fell from 25 cents a pound to 12 cents.

The copper market became stagnant with no sales recorded. *The Engineering and Mining Journal* refused to make a quotation on price from November 11, 1918, when the Armistice was signed, until February 1919, when it quoted a price in the 15 cent bracket.

The situation confronting the copper producers was one of the most serious in the history of the industry. It remained for Kelley to show the way out. To comprehend what he accomplished it is necessary to explain just how the copper companies were involved not only with their topheavy surplus but with their involvement with the banks. A bank would accept a ninety-day draft of a copper company, collateralized with an adequate supply of copper. It would then sell the draft to the Discount Corporation which would endorse it. Having two names on it, the draft would be eligible for rediscount at the Federal Reserve Bank in New York at the prevailing Reserve Bank rate. To the Federal

Reserve rate, ½ per cent was added, the originating bank charging ¼ per cent, and the Discount Corporation ¼ per cent for their respective endorsements.

Early in 1920, the New York Federal Reserve Bank announced that it would not renew discounted drafts collateralized with tangibles like copper at the end of their maturity, except for one-half the amount. This, of course, forced the sale of collateral.

To avoid having the copper collateral sold at Sheriff's sale, Kelley and some of his associates evolved the plan of organizing a Webb-Pomerene corporation named the Copper Export Association. Any copper sold to it could be resold only outside the United States.

The copper companies now sold 200,000 tons of copper at 10 cents a pound, plus its agreement to pay each contributor proportionally as much more as it received on the resale. The Export Association then sold investment bankers its five-year seven per cent notes for $40,000,000. These notes, having the 200,000 tons of copper as collateral, plus the obligation of each contributing company for its proportion of the total sum, were then resold to the public. The underwriters' commission was 2½ per cent, in addition to the seven per cent rate of the notes. This financing saved the copper companies from what otherwise would have been a very serious situation. Ultimately, the Copper Export Association sold the 200,000 tons of copper for more than 10 cents a pound. The average price of copper did not rise to about 14½ cents until 1928.

Only by such a bold and summary plan as was embodied in the Copper Export Association, could the copper industry have been placed on a sound economic basis. It served its purpose, set up a landmark in the industry, and made every copper producing concern debtor to Kelley and his associates.

Ryan realized the disadvantages under which the copper companies were placed in the New York financial district.

The metropolitan banks knew little about copper collateral and less about the operation and potentialities of the mines. Ryan, with his keen banking sense and his long experience in the Daly bank at Butte, organized the Copper Bank in New York, which provided the facilities so necessary for copper financing. Subsequently the Copper Bank was merged with the Mechanics Bank which later became the Mechanics and Metals Bank.

During the war the various European nations had changed their metal procedure, both in sales and distribution. At the outset of hostilities England had found herself practically without any supply of copper and we were forced to provide it. For years three leading German syndicates had marketed all the copper in Europe. With peace Britain, in particular, set about reorganizing her copper business. For one thing, the British Metal Company was organized to take over all metal distribution.

It was therefore necessary to find out just what was happening in the European metal market. Largely at Kelley's instigation a committee was formed to go abroad and make a survey. Kelley was named chairman. His associates were Walter Douglas of Phelps Dodge, Adolph Agassiz of Calumet & Hecla, and Joseph Clendenning, sales head for American Smelting & Refining Company. Stephen Birch of Kennecott and Solomon Guggenheim went along but were not members of the committee.

The committee was organized in proper fashion. Douglas was named commissioner for hotels and reservations; Birch, for food and delicacies, while Kelley took over responsibility for liquid refreshments. The party set off in great style on the Red Star liner, *Lapland*.

The trip was marked by one amusing incident. Douglas had cabled for reservations at the Savoy Hotel in London and had received what he thought was a reservation. When the party reached the Savoy, Douglas was told by the room clerk that there were no reservations. Dumfounded he made inquiries and found that for some reason he had cabled the hotel the price of copper on the day the cable was sent instead of specifying the number of rooms. Rooms were found to be available despite the fact that the hotel was crowded with Allied officers returning from the various fronts.

The committee then started its investigation. The decision was reached that the best way to handle American copper in England was through a British corporation. Kelley then organized the British-American Copper Company.

The committee went to France where the Versailles Peace Treaty was being framed. Baruch was there as President Wilson's chief economic adviser. He insisted that Kelley join the conference and give his views on the international metal situation from the American standpoint, which he did.

One Sunday morning Baruch called on Kelley at his hotel and asked him to go for a walk. When Baruch wants to discuss an important matter he invariably asks his man to take a stroll or join him on a park bench. President Wilson had returned to Washington. Baruch said to Kelley:

"Con, I have received a cable from the President asking me to ask you to remain in Paris until the end of the peace conference."

To this Kelley replied:

"If the President really wants to see me, cable him to cable me personally."

Kelley had no desire to remain in Paris so he cabled Ryan to ask him to come home. On receipt of the cable he was able to tell Baruch that he was urgently needed in New York.

Back in New York with his mission accomplished, Kelley resumed his place at Ryan's side. Although physically removed from the Butte scene, he kept in close touch with every activity there. Beginning with his early association with the company he had taken the lead of labor relations, one of the most important company departments. In 1906 he had persuaded the miners to enter into the five-year contract satisfactory to the company and to them, and in 1912 had brought about the just and equitable sliding scale of wages, based on the price of copper, an arrangement which became standard in Western copper districts.

Although company relations with the miners remained friendly, there were sporadic outbreaks of warfare between the unions. For years there had been smoldering enmity between the Butte Miners Union and the American Federation of Labor. The most violent clash was on Labor Day 1914. Labor Day was always celebrated in Butte with a parade. When the procession got under way, the president of the Butte Miners Union was dragged from his horse by a mob of I.W.W. organizers who had refused to join in the parade and a free-for-all fight ensued.

Meanwhile a gang of hoodlums had joined in the melee. One of them shouted "Burn the Union Hall!" The mob forced the engineer of a nearby mine to lower a dozen of them down the shaft to the powder magazine where they seized half a dozen cases of dynamite. They then proceeded to blast the Union Hall until it was a shambles.

Dissatisfied with this destruction the hoodlums then cried: "Let's blow up the Hennessy Building." This meant that the Anaconda offices were endangered. When Kelley was apprised of the threat he sat calmly at his desk and said:

"All right. We will stick here and go down with the building."

The threat to bomb the building was not carried out but terror reigned in Butte for days. The Socialist city administration refused to take action. Finally the Governor of Montana was persuaded to send in militia, a military court was set up, and the prinicpal hoodlums who had incited the miners to riot, were convicted and jailed. Life in Butte in those days was far from dull.

To resume the sequence of the Anaconda story, while the Copper Export Association saved the industry from financial disintegration, the copper surplus remained. In consequence, the mines were shut down in 1921. Depression stalked business. Under the rapidly fluctuating conditions of the times it was necessary to maintain closer ties between the operating departments of the company in Butte and the offices in New York at 42 Broadway where policies and production programs were formulated. Operations of the large production forces in the West had to be more closely supervised. All the while, despite adverse conditions in the industry, improvement in methods was being made and investment in plant and equipment increased. There was urgent need for closer coordination between the operating departments in Montana and elsewhere in the West. Ryan and Kelley were confined more and more to their New York offices because of plans being formulated for further safeguarding the company under the prevailing conditions.

In March 1922, James R. Hobbins was appointed assistant to the President of Anaconda with offices in Butte. He was placed in charge of all the company's Western operations, particularly the mines. He was well equipped for the post. A native of Madison, Wisconsin, he had worked as surveyor and construction engineer. His first important post was with the Great Falls Power Company. Later he became manager of the Northern Montana Division of the Montana Power Company holding this post until he joined Anaconda. Hobbins was so successful in coordinating western operations that he was made Vice President in 1923, and Executive Vice President in 1936, the position he held until April 1940, when upon Kelley's elevation to the Chairmanship of the company, he became President. Such was the rise of a gifted executive whose sudden and untimely death in 1949 was deeply and widely mourned.

In this country nothing is easier to start than a smear

campaign. It is a phase of human weakness that people are apt to believe the worst instead of the best in a man. Misinformation is more readily accepted than the truth.

Ryan and Bernard M. Baruch, Chairman of the War Industries Board, became the victims of just such a campaign. In 1921 it was alleged in Congress that both men had engaged in copper price-fixing and profit-making during the war and later when the industry was in the midst of one of its worst depressions. No accusation could have been more unfounded. Baruch, even then a Presidential adviser, had given his services devotedly and unselfishly to the nation; Ryan, a devout churchman, was the soul of integrity.

In a letter to Finis Garrett, a member of Congress, dated March 1, 1921, President Wilson shamed the accusers of Baruch and Ryan. In this letter he said:

"My attention has recently been called to certain attacks made in the House of Representatives charging that certain men who rendered distinguished service in the war had profited out of the Government as a result of the fixing of the price of copper. These charges and intimations have been satisfactorily answered, but a statement of the facts in the matter of the fixing of the price of copper during the war on my part, may further clarify the situation.

"As a matter of fact, Mr. Bernard M. Baruch and Mr. John D. Ryan, whose names have been linked with irresponsible gossip in connection with the fixing of the price of copper, had nothing whatever to do with the price-fixing negotiations which finally resulted in the statement I made fixing the price either at the time the price was fixed, or subsequently thereto. Judge Lovett acted as Chairman of the Committee which considered the first price-fixing of copper and after due consideration, recommended to the President in September 1917, that he had fixed the price at $23\frac{1}{2}$ cents per pound on condition that the wages of the employees of the copper companies should not be reduced below the then prevailing price which was based on 27 cent copper.

"A year later a readjustment of the price was made necessary by the increase in railroad rates and costs of supplies, and after negotiations which extended over many months, a further increase was recommended by Mr. Robert Brooking, Chairman of the Price-Fixing Committee of the War Industries Board. Neither Mr. Baruch nor Mr. Ryan had any part in these two negotiations which resulted in the fixing of the price announced by me. The prices were fixed only after independent investigation by the Federal Trade Commission as to costs of production."

After stating how the copper industry had placed all its resources at the disposal of the Government, the President continued:

"To state that either Mr. Baruch and Mr. Ryan had influenced the action of the Federal Trade Commission . . . or attempted to dictate the recommendations either of the War Industries Board or the Price-Fixing Committee, is utterly foolish and without foundation of any kind."

In closing the President said:

"I cannot allow this occasion to pass, without again expressing my great confidence in Mr. Bernard M. Baruch and Mr. John D. Ryan whose names have been unfortunately connected with this matter. There was not a suggestion of scandal connected with either of these gentlemen in any of the war activities in which they played so notable a part, and I wish before the closing days of this Administration again to say how admirably they served the needs of the Nation, and how unselfishly they devoted their fine talents to the Government in every crisis which faced us during the critical days of the war. In every transaction which they handled for the Government in the varied activities in which they played so distinguished a part, they were actuated by the highest patriotism."

In that critical period of the early twenties, Ryan and Kelley demonstrated their faith in the future of America by committing themselves to a program of mine development and the acquisition of new properties to meet increased demands for copper and other metal products which they felt would develop in the near future. Their faith was justified. Before two years passed Anaconda had met this need with the purchase of a mammoth concern that wrote another chapter in industrial history.

$\triangle$ 8

"FROM MINE TO CONSUMER"

AS THE third decade of the twentieth century began to unfold, the copper situation became increasingly perilous. With the Anaconda mines shut down, huge metal stocks piled up at smelters, prices at low ebb, and the economic dislocation following World War I still creating stagnation, there was need of bold and courageous action to set the wheels of production into motion again. Ryan and Kelley met that need in a transaction that dramatized their faith in America and its potentialities for recovery and progress.

Ryan and Kelley realized that it was imperative to seek outlets for the output of Anaconda then inert. These outlets would permit a constant flow of metals from the plants at all times even when there might be a temporary surplus of metal in the market. Their studies led them to the inevitable conclusion that Anaconda must enter the field of fabrication. The field of fabrication was well served by long established concerns, many of them valued customers of Anaconda. These concerns were also suffering from the adverse economic conditions of the times. Fluctuations in metal prices prevented them from ordering large consignments of copper and zinc and also made it difficult, if not

impossible, for producers to adopt firm, long-range productive schedules.

Ryan and Kelley were convinced that a merger between
producer and fabricator of non-ferrous metals would 'be
highly advantageous to both for it would bring benefit to
the public through the elimination of intermediate costs,
as well as the creation of other economies under the slogan,
"From Mine to Consumer." Such was the situation, and
such were the possibilities, in the middle of 1921.

There was no need for Ryan and Kelley to look far afield
for the fabricator to which they could wed Anaconda. That
fabricator was The American Brass Company, a giant in
brass, and the largest fabricator of non-ferrous metals in
the world. Like Anaconda it stood supreme in its field.

American Brass represented an evolution in metal fabrication that added a glowing chapter of achievement to the
story of American industry. It made the Naugatuck Valley
of Connecticut the cradle of brass in this country and projected Waterbury as the Brass Capital. The Connecticut
brass industry has a heritage that reaches to the roots of
the nation and embodies a story rich in romance and picturesque detail.

Without the technological advances that accompanied
the growth of the brass industry, many of our present day
conveniences would not have been possible. The development of electric power, the modern methods of communication, the rapid strides in all forms of transportation, the
building of better homes and the countless items for use
within those homes, the field of medical research, the irrigation of lands for farming, the processing of foods these, and
countless other phenomena that are today accepted as a
natural part of the American way of life, owe their existence,
at least in part, to the small beginnings of the Connecticut
Yankee pioneers in the brass industry.

During the colonial period England had a monopoly on
brass production since the British were the pioneers in the

direct fusion of copper and zinc to make brass. Oddly enough, the brass industry in Connecticut owes its origin to the manufacture of tin ware. In 1740 William and Edward Pattison started the manufacture of culinary vessels and household articles from sheet tin. These products were sold by pedlers who developed a farflung trade system that extended throughout the Colonies into Canada.

The brass era was now to dawn. It began with the manufacture of buttons, first for military uniforms and later for civilian attire. Up to 1837 only wooden clocks were in use. In that year Chauncey Jerome perfected a one-day brass clock, the use of which gave brass additional impetus. Then came the production of pewter and britannia ware and the first nickel silver produced on this side of the Atlantic.

These, and kindred ventures, formed the background of the brass industry in Connecticut. The industry was localized in the valley for two reasons. One was that the soil was not suitable for agriculture, the other lay in the fact that the pioneers in the industry stayed there. From the efforts of those stay-at-homes sprang the brass industry.

In those early days copper was difficult to obtain. The pioneer brass workers got their copper by purchasing old stills, kettles and discarded ship sheathing. Paul Revere's copper mill at Canton, Massachusetts, the first in the United States, was a boon.

The infant brass industry labored under a serious handicap because it lacked skilled workers who were practically all in England. Brass-making in Britain was an ancient and secret craft. The workers were organized in a guild which enjoyed Parliamentary protection. Export of brass workers was prohibited by law. The reason, of course, was that the British saw a threat to their prestige in the youthful industry springing up in the Naugatuck Valley.

It remained for Connecticut Yankee ingenuity to circumvent the British ban. Israel Holmes, a former employee of the Scovills, pioneer brass manufacturers, and subsequently

founders of four important brass concerns, got to England
on some innocent pretext. While there he engaged half a
dozen skilled brass workers. He put them into casks and
rolled the casks aboard a ship bound for America. The men
were released as soon as the vessel was out of sight of land.
Before reaching the American shore they reentered the
casks which were floated ashore at night at the mouth of the
Naugatuck River. After three of these expeditions Holmes
had recruited thirty-eight skilled workmen who formed the
nucleus of the new brass industry. Descendants of some of
those smuggled workmen still live in Waterbury and work
in the brass mills there.

One family operation will illustrate the fiber of the men
who created the brass industry. In 1770, Henry Grilley, who
had learned the brass process from an Englishman in Boston, came to Waterbury and, with his brothers Silas and
Samuel, started to make pewter buttons. At that time it was
a household industry. A few years later Abel Porter and
his brother Levis, settled in Waterbury, associated themselves with the Grilleys under the name of Abel Porter &
Company, and undertook the manufacture of buttons from
sheet brass. They were the first in America to employ the
modern method of making brass by direct fusion of copper
and zinc. This involved the first rolling of brass in the
United States.

Another pioneer whose name is written large in the
annals of Naugatuck Valley was Israel Coe. He built one
of the first brass mills at Walcottville. Here he started the
manufacture of brass kettles, the first of their kind to be
fabricated in this country. The name Coe is intimately associated with American Brass. In 1940, John Coe, no relation to Israel, became President of the company and later
Chairman of the Board. In 1952, his son, John A. Coe, Jr.,
was named President and is today the efficient head of the
company.

With men of this caliber the production of brass expanded. Progress in related fields had been reflected in the industry. The perfection of the brass clock, the making of nickel silver, the use of wire for the making of pins, hooks and eyes, the invention of the spinning process for making hollow ware, the development of the burner for kerosene oil and of rim fire cartridges, and the invention of the extrusion process, all marked the successive steps in the advance of the industry. Of all of these, the application of electricity to industry and the demand for the use of the metal in large quantity in this connection, were easily the most important.

One interesting fact in connection with the early stages of the brass industry was the organization of the American Brass Association, formed in 1853, which formulated the earliest trade agreement in the United States. It was signed by every brass mill in the valley. It was originally concerned with prices. Later it sought to regulate production by a pool which saved more than one manufacturer from serious loss. By 1884, the Naugatuck Valley was producing 85 per cent of the rolled brass and brass ware in the United States. This was made possible by the development of half a dozen concerns which were ultimately to become part of American Brass.

The advisability of consolidating some of the existing brass companies seems to have taken root about 1870 but nothing definite was done about it until 1893 when the State of Connecticut issued a special charter authorizing the formation of a new company to include various brass concerns. The plan failed to materialize and the charter was extended first to 1895 and then to 1897.

Consolidation, which marked the approach to the Anaconda–American Brass deal, now got under way. On December 14, 1899, the Coe Brass Company of Torrington, the Waterbury Brass Company and the Ansonia Brass & Copper Company joined under the name of The American Brass Company. A year later the Benedict & Burnham

Manufacturing Company and, in 1902, Holmes, Booth &
Haydens came into the American Brass fold. In 1901 the
present Kenosha, Wisconsin plant entered as a subsidiary
of the Coe Brass Company. Coe Brass had also acquired the
Chicago Brass Company. All these firms represented the
backbone of the brass industry and, through years of meritorious service, had advanced to high place in the industry.
American Brass was originally a holding company but became an operating company in 1912.

It was peculiarly fitting that Charles F. Brooker should
have been named as president of the combine. As president
of Coe Brass he was the first to envision the need of a combination of brass interests and had worked hard for its
consummation. Nor was any brass executive so well qualified for the post he now assumed.

Brooker's career was in the best tradition of American
self-made success. Born on a farm near what is now Torrington, he did his stint on the place, rising before dawn, milk-
ing cows and running barefoot in summer. Irked by this
drudgery he got a job when he was twelve in a Torrington
general store and later worked as clerk in a Waterbury store.

When Lyman W. Coe started the Coe Brass Manufacturing Company he hired young Brooker, then seventeen, for a minor job. Before long Coe realized that in
Brooker he had the makings of an able executive. When he
was twenty Brooker was head of the sales department where
his maxim was "Service and Quality," which he nailed to
the masthead of American Brass once he assumed leadership. At twenty-three Brooker was an officer of the company. From that time on, until his death in 1927, he was a
commanding figure in the industry, the Dean of Brass.
Brooker made many trips to Europe in the interest of his
firm. The governments of Russia, France, Italy and Spain
knew him well. When he formed American Brass the units
comprising it were making approximately two-thirds of all
the brass used in the United States.

A human interest story that bears on American Brass must precede the account of the Anaconda–American Brass merger. One of the bulwarks of American industry is the so-called "small business," so often reared from humble start. Frequently the "small business" is of such strategic value that it becomes an eventual part of a large concern. Such an instance is afforded by the French Manufacturing Company, now a unit of American Brass. Its story is one of those typical instances of how ambition, skill and perseverance have their high reward.

Decades ago Fred W. French was a skilled employee of the old Benedict & Burnham Company. In time he advanced to be superintendent of the Seamless Tube Plant. During all the years when he worked in overalls at a bench he dreamed of building his own plant for the production of small-diameter seamless tubing. Being of inventive mind, he made many contributions to the development of the product. In 1905 French realized his lifelong ambition. He established the French Manufacturing Company in an abandoned feed house with two employees. One was his son, Leon R. French. From that modest beginning the French Manufacturing Company developed into an important productive unit specializing in very small-diameter seamless tubing and copper tubing. It established a national reputation for the production of precision tubing in diameters ranging from the size of a human hair to three-fourths of an inch. Fred French sold his business to American Brass in 1929 but continued as active head of his old company. In 1934 the company became the French Small Tube Branch of American Brass. French remained in the business until his death in 1943 when his son took over. He retired in 1955.

The approach to the merger of Anaconda and American Brass was casual. One day in 1921 Ryan and Kelley sat at lunch at the Recess Club in New York. At a nearby table sat Brooker. The Anaconda chieftains had been considering a union with American Brass for some time and, as it developed later, so had Brooker. They had a community of problems, born of great expansion during the war and lack of outlet for products with peace.

As soon as Ryan and Kelley spied Brooker, Ryan said: "I am going over to sound out Brooker on a merger deal." He had previously met Brooker on several occasions. With this he walked over to where the squat, goateed head of American Brass was sitting and said:

"There is something I would like to discuss with you."

Brooker asked him to sit at his table, whereupon Ryan said:

"This is too important a matter to talk over here. Could you come down to my house on Long Island this evening and we can have a full discussion with Mr. Kelley?"

The three men met that night at Ryan's house near Manhasset. In a session that lasted until midnight the preliminaries for a merger were talked out. This was the first step toward what became a historic transaction.

In the ensuing months Ryan and Kelley visited all the plants in the American Brass set-up. While their aides scrutinized reports, inventories and all other related documents, American Brass made the same survey of Anaconda. By this time 1922 had dawned. Both sides were receptive but no purchase price had been agreed upon.

In January 1922 Ryan and Kelley visited the Coe plant at Torrington. At the conclusion of their stay they started by car for New Haven to board a train for New York. Half way to their destination Kelley said:

"Let's fix the price we think should be paid for American Brass. You write your estimate on a sheet of paper and I will do the same."

With this Kelley tore two sheets out of a notebook and handed one to Ryan. When they compared estimates it was found that Ryan had written $43,000,000 and Kelley, $47,000,000. The purchase price, finally agreed upon, was

$45,000,000, or midway between the two estimates Ryan and Kelley had jotted down on those pieces of paper. The consolidation was signed February 12, 1922.

Since half of the purchase price was in cash, it was up to Ryan and Kelley to raise $22,500,000. They set out one morning to find it and succeeded in accomplishing their purpose before nightfall. The first subscribers were William G. Rockefeller and his son, Percy. The second was Thomas Fortune Ryan.

The merging of Anaconda and American Brass represented one of the largest deals in American industrial history up to that time. American Brass had outstanding 150,000 shares of stock. All but 53 of these were acquired by Anaconda through an exchange of Anaconda stock and the payment on the basis of three shares of Anaconda and $150 in cash for each share of American Brass. Later the 53 outstanding shares of the Brass Company were acquired. Anaconda now owned 100 per cent of American Brass. The brass empire had been joined with the copper empire. Together they represented a mammoth enterprise, biggest in its field.

When the merger had been agreed upon Ryan issued a statement at Waterbury in which he said:

"The time has come when we cannot compete in the industry if we control only one stage of the business. Anaconda is not now able to operate its mines at a steady and economical rate. We have had high prices during periods of scarcity and low prices during periods of depression. The American Brass Company has not been able to pledge steady production and employment to its workers because it has not been able to book orders far in advance, not knowing what the cost of raw material would be. This is a faulty condition, and we believe that great benefits will arise by reason of the proposed merger.

"The raw material supply will be assured at steady prices, and the manufacturer can then book his orders with the certainty of obtaining material at reasonable costs. In this way, from the mine to the consumer, there can be one just and fair profit, and the industry will be stabilized."

With a century and a half of experience, research and efficient management behind it, American Brass today represents a highly organized and closely coordinated enterprise far beyond the hopes and dreams of the pioneer brass makers with their almost primitive household operations. Those small timbered homes with their slow hand labor, became mills and, in time, the early mills developed into huge plants humming with every mechanical device and every phase of research known to the making of brass.

American Brass has divisions in Waterbury, Ansonia, Torrington, Buffalo, Detroit and Kenosha, Wisconsin, for the production of copper and copper alloys in the forms of sheet, strip, tube, rod, wire and extruded shapes. The fabricating units are the American Metal Hose Division at Waterbury and Mattoon, Illinois, where products are flexible metal hose and tubings; the Waterbury Brass Goods Division which turns out eyelets, grommets, stampings in all metals, and the French Small Tube Division at Waterbury with a single product, small-diameter seamless tubing.

At this writing two important plants are under construction for American Brass. One is the Los Angeles Division which is a brass mill for producing all brass mill products. The other is the Aluminum Division at Terre Haute, Indiana. This fabricating facility is a logical extension of Anaconda's entry into the aluminum field which began with the operation of the plant of The Anaconda Aluminum Company at Columbia Falls, Montana. The Terre Haute plant will be a completely integrated aluminum mill for making aluminum coiled sheet, tube, rod and extrusions. Raw material will be fed from the Columbia Falls plant.

American Brass entered the international field with its wholly owned subsidiary, Anaconda American Brass, Ltd. of Canada. This acquisition had a pioneering background.

The first brass ever turned out in Canada was produced by the Canada Brass Rolling Mills at New Toronto in 1905. Five years later J. F. Brown took over the concern under the name of Brown's Copper and Brass Rolling Mills. This name was retained until 1922 when Anaconda bought the business machinery, and good will, and later the land and buildings. It then became Anaconda American Brass, Ltd. At the time of the purchase only copper and copper alloy sheet, rods and shapes were produced.

Anaconda rebuilt and enlarged the plant which, in 1922, covered seven acres and employed 300 persons. Today it comprises thirty acres with 1,500 employees. In 1932 a tube mill was completed, turning out the first copper tube to be pierced in the Dominion.

Two important innovations have been developed at the new Toronto plant. One is a method of producing extruded rod which drastically reduced the butt and core scrap. The other is the floating plug method by which very long lengths of tube can be drawn on a block with a considerable saving of scrap.

The company contributed its full share of output in World War II. It took over the operation of two government owned plants, Canada Strip Mill, Ltd. at New Toronto and another mill of the same name at Montreal. Subsequently the company purchased the Canada Strip Mill at New Toronto which was converted into a new rod mill. Anaconda American Brass, Ltd. has not only greatly enhanced the prestige of Canadian industry but has also forged an enduring economic bond between the two nations.

When American Brass was formed in 1899 the industry had survived without benefit of technical staffs. Scientific copper metallurgy was practically nonexistent in Waterbury. A bold precedent was now to be established. A. P. Hine, superintendent of the Coe Brass Manufacturing Company, hired a chemist and set up a laboratory of sorts.

When the post of chemist fell vacant in 1902 Hine cast about to find a successor. Happily for American Brass and the entire industry, his choice was W. H. Bassett. He faced a difficult task because the word "metallurgy" had not yet been applied to brass mill processes.

Bassett built a laboratory and organized a technical staff for the study of mill processes, the physical characteristics of alloys, and their application to end uses. Copper and brass were scrutinized under the microscope for the first time. The entire field of metallography and grain structure came under study. At long last, the potential impact of science on the brass industry was recognized.

Behind the beginning of this significant movement stood Bassett, pioneer and pathfinder. He evolved exact brass and bronze formulas and emerged as the father of copper-alloy technology in the United States. From his efforts stemmed an enormous progeny of copper alloys.

The corrosion of condenser tubes early engaged Bassett's interest and he became an authority on the subject. His ten-year tests led directly to the establishment of his corrosion research laboratory.

By the end of World War I it had become apparent that the technical needs of the several divisions of The American Brass Company could not adequately be served from a central department. Accordingly, a plant metallurgist was established at each division. As the complexities of the work have increased, these plant metallurgists have, in turn, established laboratories, both chemical and physical, and have staffed them with qualified people, so that the metallurgical needs of buying, processing and selling are covered, not by remote control but by intimate, personal association, while the central department at Waterbury coordinates and furnishes help where the local facilities are inadequate.

Bassett died in 1934 at the height of his career for he was only sixty-six. He was the unquestioned dean of brass metallurgists. No man before, or since, has spoken with such authority or exerted such an influence on brass technology.

Bassett's successor, H. C. Jennison, carried on in the tradition of his predecessor. Upon his death in 1938 John R. Freeman took over, soon to be engulfed in wartime conditions. The Technical Department of American Brass attained new heights of dedicated accomplishment in those war-torn years.

Research today is conducted on a broader scope than ever. Technical supervision of mill processes is increasingly comprehensive and the basic knowledge for regulation of such processes is constantly broadened. The study of metallurgical problems in the mills is in competent hands. The staff of metallurgists who serve sales and the customer are engineers of sound education and experience. They include men familiar with electrical engineering, who are deeply versed in the mysteries and vagaries of corrosion, who understand the complexities of welding and its applications, who know the problems of the power plant, and who are familiar with marine affairs from fisherman's boat to battleship. The technical contributions of American Brass are still first in the industry.

With such a research organization it is not surprising that American Brass is distinguished for numerous "firsts" that have not only created a variety of new products but have also simplified many phases of the copper and brass fabrication. The list is so long that it is possible only to enumerate a few of the outstanding achievements.

Before metallurgical chemistry was established to the point of making qualitative or quantitative analyses, the company developed the first notable American copper-base alloy by exhaustive experimentation with alloying elements. The result was Tobin Bronze, the first alloy produced for salt water service, still the overwhelming choice for power boat propeller shafting. Tobin Bronze plates covered most of the hulls of the American Cup defenders when these racing yachts were constructed of wood.

American Brass made a significant contribution to copper metallurgy with the development of the copper-silicon group, marketed under the trade name Everdur. This marked the first time silicon had been successfully alloyed with copper, creating a group of engineering metals with strength and fabricating qualities comparable to steel, and corrosion resistance superior to copper. Everdur is widely used in pressure vessels, water distribution equipment, hardware, electrical conduits and many other applications.

In the Nineties the company made the first cupro nickel alloy tube, named the Benedict Nickel. It is a durable condenser tube for marine condensers. The first customer was the British Lighthouse Service. Admiral Dewey's flagship, *Olympia*, in the memorable Battle of Manila Bay, was tubed with Benedict Nickel. The company also invented a so-called semi-anneal to relieve stresses in tubes and prolong their service life.

A notable innovation was the importation by American Brass of the first extrusion presses used in the United States for making a product similar to drawn shapes. Another important importation, also a first, was the Manesmann process for forming tube blanks from heated cylindrical billets.

Still another important innovation came in 1924 following a ten-year study of the corrosion resistance of copper and copper alloys to all types of potable waters. The findings indicated that an alloy of 85 per cent copper and 15 per cent zinc—85 Red Brass—was the most durable pipe material for potable waters. This led to economy in rust-proof plumbing which, up to that time, was considered a luxury only to be used by very wealthy home owners.

In 1933, American Brass metallurgists announced the successful development of a process for producing wide sheets of thin sheet copper in unlimited lengths by electro-deposition. The product was named Electro-Sheet. Bonded to building paper, it is used as a flashing for windows, doors and building weatherproofing to shield electric and electronic equipment, and for electrical circuits in radios and television sets.

During World War II when nickel had such high priority that the use of cupro nickel alloys was limited exclusively to the United States Navy, American Brass developed and patented a new ten per cent cupro nickel alloy which, after carefully adjusted percentages of iron and manganese, approached in durability the 30 per cent nickel alloy which the Navy was using exclusively for condenser tubes and tube sheets. This new alloy has proved its high resistance to turbulently flowing sea waters and is performing an important function in conserving the supply of nickel.

One of the company's original products is Formbrite which puts a new gleam in brass. It has a superfine grain structure that makes products more lustrous and more scratch-resistant.

American Brass metallurgists did much pioneer experimentation in the development of copper-aluminum alloys and developed two which are notable for special applications. Avialite, an aluminum bronze, was perfected for parts in airplane piston engines, such as valve stems and seats. It has the durability and resistance to heat to withstand the high temperatures and pounding to which these parts are subjected during flight. Tempaloy, another special aluminum bronze, is employed for heavy duty and high-speed service in power boat propeller shafting.

When radiant panel heating was somewhat shrouded in mystery, the company published a simplified formula for calculating heat output and laying out an adequate system of panels. This was of great help to heating contractors who did not have graduate heating engineers on their staffs. To further simplify the installation and calculation of radiant panel heating, American Brass engineers designed a machine-formed prefabricated panel for ceilings and floors named P.G. The name is devised from the words, panel grids. The P.G. panels provide many economies. The system can be installed at a lower cost than a conventional radiant heating system.

One more innovation will serve to round out this partial list of American Brass "firsts." Developers of color TV were stalemated for want of a metal from which to fabricate the essential shadow screen. This screen, consisting of thousands of minute holes etched in a thin sheet of metal, had to have absolute accuracy in spacing and aperture size. No existing metal had the precise qualities necessary for making this screen on a commercial basis. The problem was presented to The American Brass Company metallurgists who developed a new cupro nickel alloy with a nominal composition of 94 per cent copper and 6 per cent nickel, which has the precise qualities for the screen. This development has gone a long way to make color TV possible.

American Brass has the largest rolling mill in the industry for rolling heavy copper and copper alloy plates for condenser tube sheets, and for the heads and shells of tanks and vessels for storage of hot water and for processing uses. During World War II, the Detroit Division rolled 70–30 cupro nickel plates for the tube sheets of the main condensers of 72 U. S. Navy battleships, 1,367 destroyers, 1,440 escort vessels, 44 landing craft, 616 carriers and cruisers, and 16 miscellaneous ships, a total of 3,555 vessels.

The resource and resiliency of American Brass were tested and not found wanting in the great flood of August 1955, the worst disaster in the history of the northeastern United States. Several of the plants at Waterbury, Torrington and Ansonia were in the path of the rampaging waters. Millions of pounds of copper and copper alloys, billets, cakes and wire bars were tossed about like toothpicks. In the Waterbury Division the water reached a height of seventeen feet. Roadbeds were washed out; whole sides of buildings torn away. The total damage to American Brass aggregated $15,900,000.

As soon as the water subsided, John A. Coe, Jr., President of American Brass, made the reassuring statement to the community: "We will rebuild where we are." Other American Brass plants took over the unfilled orders of the plants out of commission and customers cooperated with sympathy and tolerance. Rebuilding was begun at once. By the end of January 1956, normal production in rebuilt plants was under way. It represented a stupendous task of rehabilitation.

II

Anaconda's second venture into fabrication resulted from the acquisition of a group of highly organized plants which were combined in The Anaconda Wire & Cable Company. Like the parent organization, it is a giant in its field, the largest manufacturer of wire and cable in the United States, as well as a pioneer in the development of many phases of copper and brass output.

To the layman, wires and cables are products connected with lighting and carrying power to run gadgets and machines. This, of course, is true, but the layman would be amazed if he knew the multiple, variegated and complex uses in which wire and cable are employed. Insulated wire has been called the life line of the nation because it touches every one of our 168,000,000 people in some way in their waking and sleeping hours. What wire and cable do in the air, on and under water and ground, in homes, mines, transportation, communication, planes, elevators, radios, television sets, factories, kitchen gadgets, automobiles; in fact, wherever power is transmitted and employed, comprises a story rich in research and achievement and not without its element of romance.

One of the miracles of present day life in America is the fabulous increase in the use of electricity. The consumption of electric energy has doubled every ten years for the past three decades, with a corresponding increase in the demand for electrical conductors. As electricity has been extended to new uses, new lines and types of electrical wires and cables have been required. Anaconda Wire & Cable progress has closely paralleled the growth of the electrical industry. To-day in its seven plants, the company produces a wide variety of electrical wires and cables for public utilities, mines and railroads. It also turns out bare cables for the overhead transmission and distribution of electrical power at all voltages and also magnet wire for electrical apparatus, as well as electrical conductors for industrial, commercial and residential use. In the company's research and development laboratories at Hastings-on-Hudson, Muskegon, Michigan, and Marion, Indiana, there is continuous effort to improve existing products and to create new lines of manufacture for wider and more efficient service.

What might be called the predecessor history of Anaconda Wire & Cable can be traced in a direct genealogical line to the beginnings of the copper and brass industry in this country. This is born of the fact that its roots are closely related to plants of The American Brass Company, some of whose concerns were pioneers in the industry in the Naugatuck Valley and thus helped to inaugurate the era of brass in the United States.

Another root of the story goes back to 1888 when the Norwich Insulated Wire Company of Harrison, New Jersey, completed the first impregnated paper cable which had hellically wrapped paper tapes impregnated with oil and covered with an extruded lead sheath. In 1891 the Norwich concern was succeeded by the National Conduit & Cable Company which, in turn, was absorbed by American Brass. This plant later became the present day Hastings-on-Hudson works of Anaconda Wire & Cable. The completion of the sequence of Anaconda Wire & Cable development came when it became a fabricating division of what was then The Anaconda Copper Mining Company, now The Anaconda Company, plus three independent plants and two more divisions in California.

One of the roots of Anaconda Wire & Cable was the rod and wire mill built by Anaconda at Great Falls in 1918. The expansion in the use of hydroelectric power in Montana and other sections of the West following the establishment of the Montana Power Company, created a heavy demand for wire and cable. It was to meet this demand that Anaconda built the Great Falls plant. One of the earliest operations of the mill was to supply the copper cable used in the electrification of the Chicago, Milwaukee & St. Paul Railroad. The contract called for 440 miles of cable at a cost of just over $5,000,000. The Great Falls plant also supplied the cable for the electrification of the Butte, Anaconda & St. Paul Railroad which connects the Butte mines with the reduction works at Anaconda. The experience gained in these two contracts for the manufacture of copper and copper alloy cables was of inestimable value to the mill and to the future of Anaconda Wire & Cable. It led subsequently to the selection of the merged company for other important electrification operations which included the Pennsylvania Railroad and the Cleveland Union Terminal.

In the decade following World War I there was a tremendous expansion in the electrical industry in the United States. New utilities were organized and vast hydroelectric projects undertaken. The entire country became crisscrossed with a network of power lines. Many manufacturers who supplied the materials for these utility concerns were valued customers of Anaconda and The American Brass Company. The products of the Great Falls rod and wire mill were in increasing demand. The plant was doing a capacity business principally in copper bars which other concerns drew into wire.

It became evident that substantial economies in manufacture could be effected if several large concerns operating in the field of wire and cable could be brought together under unified management. In consequence Anaconda Wire & Cable was organized in February of the memorable year of 1929. Little did the organizers dream that before this fateful year ended, the country would be in the throes of the most devastating panic it had ever known, or that in 1941 we would be engulfed in a global war. Anaconda Wire & Cable weathered these two major dislocations and advanced onward to new and progressive peaks of prestige and production.

H. Donn Keresey was instrumental in organizing Anaconda Wire & Cable. He had been head of the sales organization of The Anaconda Company when it was operating the Great Falls rod and wire mill and was well acquainted with all the manufacturers who were its customers. Some of the most important of these manufacturers merged their businesses with Anaconda Wire & Cable. Keresey has been President of the company since its inception.

In 1929 the Great Falls mill with an established reputation, became part of the nucleus of Anaconda Wire & Cable. One of the first companies taken into the merger was the Tubular Woven Fabrics Company whose President, W. E. Sprackling, is now Executive Vice President of Anaconda Wire & Cable. The Pawtucket plant, which was sold in 1946, produced building wires, portable cords and tubular hose.

The other independent plants included in the merger were: Inland Wire & Cable Company, located at Sycamore, Illinois, the Marion Insulated Wire & Rubber Company at Marion, Indiana, the Maring Wire Company with plants at Muskegon, Michigan, and Anderson, Indiana, the Hastings Wire & Cable Corporation at Hastings-on-Hudson, New York and the Kenosha plant of American Brass. In addition to these plants, Anaconda Wire & Cable took over a concern on the Pacific Coast, which had originally been organized as a selling unit for the Great Falls mill. It became The Anaconda Wire & Cable Company of California. For several years the company operated two wiredrawing mills in California, one at Oakland and the other at Orange. Subsequently the Oakland plant was sold and coast operations were concentrated at Orange. This plant is one of the largest in the West.

Various changes have been effected since the inception of Anaconda Wire & Cable. In 1932 the company consolidated its Kenosha facilities with those of its plant at Sycamore, which had been known as Inland Wire & Cable, largest producers of bare and insulated wire and cable in the Middle West. Kenosha operations were then suspended. The Hastings plant, acquired from American Brass, was first engaged in the production of electrical building materials. Later it turned to bare and insulated wire and cables and conduits.

The plant at Hastings-on-Hudson is the largest individual unit in the group of seven making up Anaconda Wire & Cable and is the headquarters division of the company. Here are located the executive division of the manufacturing branch, and also the principal research and development laboratories. The Anaconda Company owns 70.63 per cent of the outstanding stock of the company.

Anaconda Wire & Cable was requested by a group of businessmen in Mexico to cooperate in establishing a wire and cable plant in their country to meet the increasing demand for these products. As a result, the company owns a minority interest in the venture which is called Conductores Electricos S.A. de C.V. A wire and cable plant as well as a copper rod mill were completed in 1955. Under Anaconda guidance, a competent Mexican management was installed.

The promotion program of Anaconda Wire & Cable, operative since 1937, is unique. The company was the first and, up to the present time, the only one to conduct national non-commercial programs which benefit every segment of the electrical industry. The initial campaign bore the title of "Industrial Modernization." Another, "Preventive Maintenance," was carried on during World War II. It was followed by "Wire Ahead" and "Power Up," designed to increase the electrical efficiency in industrial plants. "Full Power Ahead" was designed to enable the home owner to achieve electrical adequacy for maximum electrical living.

Like its sister units in the Anaconda organization, The Anaconda Wire & Cable Company has recorded an impressive list of innovations both for war and peace. First, the more dramatic contributions to the national defense. Since 1934 the company has designed and furnished most of the intermediate and high-power long wave radio antennas for the United States Navy located in many parts of the world. The largest are suspended on 600 foot steel towers and cover an area approximately one mile long by one-fourth of a mile wide. These assure shore-to-ship communication at all times. The design and fabrication of complete antennas is a project not normally included in the scope of a wire and cable company's engineering activities but Anaconda took on the job with commendable success.

These super installations are located at Annapolis, Panama and Honolulu. They enable the Navy Department to keep in touch with ships on any waters anywhere in the world. Nothing like them has ever been achieved before.

Early in the defense program when the supply of tin was foreseen to be critical, a substitute coating consisting of lead with antimony and cadmium as alloying elements for easy processability, was developed in the company laboratories and named Anacondalay. This product greatly reduced the amount of tin so vitally needed. Free licenses and technical know-how were made available to other wire manufacturers. A patent was obtained in 1950.

When shipboard cable, both power and communication types, passes through bulkheads, external packing glands prevent the passage of water around the cable. Water, however, does pass through interstices inside the cable, impairing efficiency. In 1942 the Navy Department requested cable manufacturers to develop suitable methods for sealing cables against water penetration. Anaconda was the first manufacturer to create a satisfactory product that met all requirements.

With the outbreak of World War II, Germany introduced the magnetic mine in large quantities. More than a million tons of British shipping were destroyed by this device before its secret was learned and defensive methods developed. In July 1940, the United States Navy Department approached several American cable manufacturers with the information that one means employed by Great Britain involved the use of floating cable.

With little more information than this, the manufacturers were required to design and fabricate buoyant cable. Cable of this type had never before been manufactured in America. The requirements were severe and unusual for the industry. Experience, design and manufacturing data were not available and it was necessary to initiate an intensive research and development program, while at the same time instituting an expanding rate of production. Of the manufacturers approached, Anaconda Wire & Cable Company was the first to produce a buoyant cable and has continued to lead in its development and production. Later developments disclosed that the purpose of the buoyant cable was to produce a magnetic field in coastal waters of sufficient intensity to detonate a planted magnetic mine at a safe distance from the minesweeper.

Soon after our entry into the war the Naval Ordnance Laboratory asked Anaconda Wire & Cable to design and manufacture a variety of special coils. One of the most important was the magnetic mine search coil which would sense the approach of a ship and initiate the triggering sequence which would explode the mine at the proper moment. These coils were precisely wound on a high-permeability metal core less than three-fourths inch in diameter and nearly four feet long. The core pieces are very sensitive and easily damaged. Hence, great care was necessary in handling them throughout all the manufacturing processes. When finished, the coils were molded into a watertight rubber jacket, an operation which previously had never been accomplished successfully. All of the attendant problems were solved on, or ahead of, schedule, and many thousands of coils successfully manufactured. A chain of these coils can ring a port and make it immune from sudden attack.

Early in the fall of 1941, work was started for the United States Navy to design an acceptable type of compass compensating coil and develop methods of producing it. This is the device which fits around a ship's compass and nullifies the magnetic effects of degaussing cables in order to insure correct readings of the compass. It is an assembly of several special electromagnet coils in a sealed container. The design characteristics and construction were entirely new, and a tremendous amount of research was required to solve the many problems encountered. This work was done expeditiously and successfully. Anaconda was the principal and largest producer.

Many types of special cables are required in connection with the guided missile program, cables for internal wiring within the missile itself, cables for interconnecting the various equipments on the ground, and break-away cables for supplying power and control connections to the missile up to the instant of takeoff. All of these are designed to meet uncommon and severe requirements, and usually incorporate large numbers and varieties of conductors. Anaconda has designed and manufactured a number of different types of cables for these applications.

Anaconda's contributions to the activities of peace are no less important than those dedicated to war effort. In the Hastings-on-Hudson plant is housed one of the most unique operations in cable research. It was inspired by the fact that few electric circuits transmit full load continuously. The change from a maximum in the daytime to a minimum in the evening, is called "a daily load cycle." To measure this load cycle Anaconda Wire & Cable has devised a so-called cyclic aging test which measures the expected life of the cable during service. It is accelerated aging, achieved by an elaborate set-up in a laboratory which is equipped to subject the cable to daily on-and-off current loading which will raise the conductor temperature above its rating in service and, at the same time, subject it to voltage two to three times its rated operating voltage. The loss in the insulation of the cable is measured automatically each minute during the duration of the test which continues from one to one and a half years. The increase in this insulation loss is a measure of the expected life of the cable during service. Through rigorous twenty-four hour testing cycles simulating actual but more severe conditions, high voltage insulated cable is tested for long life and stability. In these tests, Anaconda not only beats the clock but the calendar as well.

Mark Twain once said that "everybody talks about the weather but nobody ever does anything about it." He was wrong in this oft-quoted remark because Anaconda *does* something about it. Weather is another unique operation at Hastings-on-Hudson. It is achieved with the Weatherometer.

Electric cables are installed in all sorts of surroundings and hence may be subject to the ravages of the weather, sun, ice, de-icing salts, oil and gasoline, brackish waters, acids and alkalies in the soil, and to attack by animals, birds, insects and fungi. The effect of sun, rain and cold are measured in a testing chamber which automatically subjects the samples to ultraviolet light exposure, water spray and freezing in a predetermined cyclic schedule. Many years of natural weathering can be approximated in a few weeks of such testing. The best proof of a cable's suitability is experience in actual service, but it is not usually possible to wait so long. The Weatherometer obviates this wait.

Still another unique aspect of Anaconda research goes on in the bacteriological section of one of the laboratories at

Hastings-on-Hudson. It is the study of the resistance of various cable constructions to termites and certain bacteria. It is just one more indication of the thoroughness of Anaconda research to insure the adequacy of its products.

Through its intensive research Anaconda Wire & Cable has created a long line of new products, all to the end of durability and service. Among them are Oxhoff, a chemical cleaning process important in relation to magnet wire production; Duraline, which safeguards workmen and trees from accidental contact with inadequately insulated conductors; a new rubber compound named "Type ANW," an insulation with high heat resistance; Densheath, for low voltage application; ATV-225, a shielded television lead-in line which minimizes pick-up of interference; Carbonblack, which prolongs the life of a cable; Carbobraid, a wire braid that supplants the aluminum braid formerly used to cover ship cables; Vitrotex, a magnet wire insulated with alkali-free glass-fiber yarn, heat resistant and comparable to steel; and a nylon magnet wire, also heat resistant, and synthetic resins.

Anaconda has also developed a new brand of copper, "Hy-Therm," which has improved annealing qualities and increases current loadings; the F-3 Lead-Alloy Sheath, which prevents cable expansion and contraction due to temperature changes; and the Type CB Cable, an important Anaconda "first," to prevent deterioration of insulating oil.

Plans have been completed for a new high-voltage research laboratory and expansion of the present laboratory facilities at Hastings-on-Hudson. These laboratories will be among the finest and best equipped in the wire and cable industry. They will include a 3,000,000 volt lightning generator, the highest voltage testing facilities in the industry.

These additional laboratory facilities are necessary to conduct the research and development required to extend manufacture of high-voltage insulated cable beyond its present limit of 69,000 volts. A greater demand for extra-high-voltage cable is expected with the continued rapid growth of electric power systems which, at present, is at the rate of one hundred per cent in ten years. The new laboratory will be ready in 1957.

With all these affiliations and acquisitions, The Anaconda Company became a vast mining, reduction and fabrication organization, gigantic in stature, with a know-how in every phase of the non-ferrous metal industry. It has reared an organization of geologists, mining engineers, metallurgists and fabricators preeminent in their field, whose talents were sought in every branch of the business.

The multitude of metal products that flow from Anaconda mines and plants obviously require a highly organized selling organization. This is provided in The Anaconda Sales Company which was organized June 9, 1922. In 1934 the United Metals Selling Company transferred its assets to Anaconda Sales and was dissolved.

Kelley became President of Anaconda Sales in 1934 and was succeeded by Robert E. Dwyer. On Dwyer's retirement as President of The Anaconda Company in 1956, Thomas A. Campbell, a Vice President of Anaconda and Executive Vice President of Chile Copper and Chile Exploration, became head of the company.

Forty per cent of the Anaconda Sales operations are with Anaconda Company subsidiaries. The remaining products are sold throughout the United States and all foreign countries except Russia. The principal products are copper and its by-products, zinc, lead and aluminum. Active head of Anaconda Sales is William E. Kennedy, Executive Vice President, who began as office boy at the age of fifteen. In 1957 he had rounded out fifty-five years of service.

🔱 9

ANACONDA IN CHILE

ON A slope of the Andes in northern Chile not far from the border of Bolivia stands an impressive monument to Anaconda enterprise. Here, nearly ten thousand feet above sea level, has been reared a productive community in an area once the habitat of Indians. For this is Chuquicamata, site of the world's largest known copper deposit, mightiest bastion in all the domain of the red metal. Its transition into a vast open pit operation with a town of 25,000 people enjoying every modern facility, is one of the wonder stories of mining without precedent in the long and adventurous narrative of industrial endeavor.

Immense as is the operation at Chuquicamata, it is only part of the Anaconda copper development in Chile. To the south lies Potrerillos, the mine that marked the company's entry into the republic. To replace its waning output is the El Salvador property fifteen miles away. Still a fourth operation is the Africana not far from Santiago. Here, then, is a chain of properties, each with a distinctive background, that guarantee an abundant future supply of the indispensable metal.

Copper has a twofold significance for both the United States and Chile. Since 1940 we have been obliged to import forty-one per cent of our copper requirements. Chile supplies twenty-four per cent of this amount. Copper is the economic life blood of Chile, mainstay of the republic's fiscal system. A change in the price of copper is likely to upset national budget calculations.

Because of its magnitude and its domination of the Chilean copper scene, it may be well to deal first with Chuquicamata. In no other country has the production of copper projected such a picturesque background. It is linked with the romance of the Spanish Conquest of the New World and spans a unique era in metallurgy. Long before Columbus reached the shore of America, the Atacama Indians, predecessors of the Incas, fashioned copper with stone hammers. They blew through long canes to enliven the fires of their crude adobe melting furnaces. Copper was fashioned into weapons and also for more utilitarian uses. It became a bell around the necks of the llamas, a knitting needle or a necklace for women.

In 1535, when the Indians were taking advantage of the night winds to force the draft in their furnaces, came the rumble of the Conquistador advance. Diego de Almagro, companion and rival of Pizarro, conqueror of Peru, swept down in search of gold, the lodestar that had led Cortes to Mexico and now the fickle beacon that lured Almagro on into what became Chile. He found no gold, only a gleaming red metal that the natives were converting into practical uses. Almagro and his mailed soldiers rode scornfully over the treasure that is now Chuquicamata. They returned in disgust to Peru, their only booty copper shoes for their horses.

There is evidence that long before the Spanish conquest the Atacama Indians had produced copper. Primitive tools and mummified early miners have been found in the old workings. As in the Sahara Desert along the Nile, the extremely dry atmosphere preserves human beings and tools from oxidation and decay.

Down the years the Atacama Indians plugged away at their shallow diggings, producing ore that assayed up to fifty per cent copper. Use of the metal widened. With the arrival of the priests, copper bells called the pious to worship, copper utensils appeared in the rude homes. When revolt against Spanish rule flared, copper was fashioned into cannon and became one of the instruments for liberation. By 1876 copper had begun to come into its own. Camps sprang up on the barren Andean flank, the modest beginning of the development that was to roll up billions of dollars.

Modern exploitation did not commence, however, until after the War of the Pacific which spanned the years between 1879 and 1881. Chile emerged from the war as the dominant power on the west coast at the expense of Peru and Bolivia.

In the Eighties and Nineties, Chilean and British engineers established small, shallow workings and smelters on the mountain side. For years the copper was packed on llamas and mules and sent down ten thousand feet to the coast or the nearest railway. Life and labor were difficult on the arid terrain. There was not a bush or a blade of grass to relieve what has been well termed "the repelling beauty of the desert."

All the while, reports of the huge copper deposits on the mountain side trickled out. Several English concerns began to operate in a modest way on the scene. A large area of the outcrop became honeycombed with shallow mine workings, some of them at a depth of forty or fifty feet. Other operators, attracted by the reports of the quality and extent of the ore deposit, were awed by the grim environment and departed for more congenial climes.

It remained for Albert C. Burrage, a Boston capitalist, who had been one of the organizers of Amalgamated, to find the key that unlocked the copper Golconda of the Andes. Like so many others he had learned of the great deposit but, unlike so many who merely nibbled at the prospect of big development, he did something about it.

In 1910, Burrage visited the area, studied the property and became convinced that it could be profitably operated on a large scale. He obtained options on the entire mining territory at Chuquicamata from the Chilean government and from the English companies who were carrying on sporadic operations. This was the first step in what became the historic development of the world's greatest copper deposit.

Burrage offered his options to M. Guggenheim Sons in New York nor was his choice misplaced. The story of the Guggenheims is one of the most diverting in all the history of American metals. Nowhere is there a more effective illustration of the capitalization of opportunity that democracy holds out. In 1848, Meyer Guggenheim, a Swiss immigrant, arrived in New York in the steerage and shouldered a pedler's pack to earn his first money in the country of his adoption. From that humble beginning sprang the famous Guggenheim dynasty, for Meyer became the father of seven sons, a septet that made metal history in mining, smelting and refining. The leader of the family was Daniel whose vision and courage made the first large scale development of Chuquicamata possible.

Although the Guggenheims operated as a family, following their father's solemn injunction, it was to Daniel that Burrage first submitted his proposition. Daniel and his brothers were impressed with Burrage's description of the Chuquicamata area and its possibilities. They sent engineers to study the property and received a favorable report.

In 1912, the Guggenheims organized the Chile Exploration Company in New Jersey to take over the Burrage options. This corporation became the operating end. During the same year the Guggenheims incorporated the Chile Copper Company in Maine. Within a few months another Chile Copper Company was incorporated in Delaware. In 1913, the directors of the Chile Copper Company formed in

Maine, transferred all its properties to the Delaware corporation. When these transactions were completed, all stock of the Chile Exploration Company, as well as all other rights and property held by it, were turned over to Chile Copper Company of Delaware and the Maine corporation went out of existence. The Chile Copper Company was organized for the purpose of holding the capital stock of Chile Exploration, issuing bonds and employing the proceeds for the development of Chuquicamata and all its installations.

No mining area anywhere offered such a challenge to man's resource, courage and ingenuity as was presented by Chuquicamata when the Guggenheims took over. The country was barren and forbidding; sand and rock dominated the area. The natives said: "It looks like rain every seven years," but the rains never came. Drinking water had to be brought in ox carts. Winds howled over the granite wastes. Suitable food was difficult to obtain. There were no roads. The nearest civilized community was the port of Antofagasta, 165 miles distant.

There was another challenge. The low grade ore, and there was a mountain of it, could not be smelted in the ordinary way because of the chlorine in it. It meant that an entirely new process had to be devised. This was accomplished by E. A. Cappelen Smith, consulting metallurgist for the Guggenheims, and a new chapter in the history of copper extraction was recorded. Instead of treating the ore by concentration and smelting, as is the usual procedure, it was subjected to leaching out the copper in huge vats and precipitating it by electricity. The Chuquicamata ore was the first of the porphyry coppers to be leached.

The Cappelen Smith process was so successful that the Guggenheims purchased the Chuquicamata property in 1912. Since the various corporate organizations have already been enumerated, we can now go into the development of the property.

Early drill holes proved that the whole mountain was ore

which grew gradually into astounding size. In 1913 the engineers estimated a 100,000,000 ton reserve; then 200,000,-000 and finally 600,000,000. These original estimates fell far short of the mark because today the ore reserve of Chuquicamata is estimated at one billion tons, the world's greatest copper body.

With the purchase by the Guggenheims, development of Chuquicamata on a large scale got under way. Actual operations began in May 1915. A power plant to run the plants was built at Tocopilla. This was the first big installation.

In connection with the construction of the Tocopilla plant is an interesting story which shows how Yankee ingenuity triumphed over wartime obstacles. When the Germans declared war in 1914 all the machinery for the plant, built in Germany, was on piers in Hamburg and Bremen or on ships headed for Tocopilla. The problem was to get the essential equipment to Chile. John K. McGowan, the first non-Guggenheim to be made a partner in M. Guggenheim Sons, went to Europe to iron out the situation. The United States was then a neutral and he was free to act. After long negotiations with the Allied governments he made a deal by which the machinery in transit and the remainder on the piers in Germany, would be transferred to Allied bottoms, in exchange for copper sorely needed for the conduct of hostilities.

Once the power plant went into operation, things began to hum at Chuquicamata. Steam shovels, once used on the Panama Canal excavations, bit into the grim mountain sides, starting the vast rim with its succession of benches which today constitute one of the wonder sights of mining. A seventy-mile pipeline from a stream up in the Andes brought in the much-needed water; roads were built, through a long transmission line flowed ample electric power. All this was on a scale never attempted before in a mining venture. Chuquicamata, because of its reserve and massive development, soon became a byword throughout the domain of copper. A community of 15,000 people, including workers, officials and their families, sprang up.

There now impended the greatest transaction in all mining history. In 1922, as you have seen, Anaconda bought American Brass with its tremendous capacity for output. This output required a vast amount of copper. It was in excess of what the Anaconda Montana mines could produce although they were then turning out a million pounds of copper a day.

Ryan and Kelley realized that it was imperative to secure additional sources of copper supply. First they undertook negotiations with the Utah Copper Company. These failed because of the large interest owned by Kennecott Copper which made a deal on a satisfactory basis impossible. Every other possible alternative in the United States was explored to no avail.

Ryan and Kelley now focussed their interest on the great Katanga open pit operation in the Belgian Congo. No purchase was possible here because of the close connection between Katanga and the Belgian government. One byproduct of the negotiations did develop. Kelley went to Brussels to discuss with Fernand Pisart, head of Katanga, the possibility of a joint sales operation but the results were negligible.

The failure of these negotiations was the proverbial ill wind that blew good. One day Kelley's friend, Thomas Cochran, partner in J. P. Morgan & Company, asked Kelley to come in to see him. To Kelley, Cochran said:

"Why doesn't Anaconda buy Chuquicamata? As you know, it is the biggest copper deposit in the world."

Kelley needed no urging. Together with Ryan, he went to see Daniel Guggenheim and negotiations began in 1921. The Guggenheims were loath to sell, which was not surprising. Ryan and Kelley persisted and finally on March 15, 1923, Anaconda took over Chile Copper for $77,000,-

ooo, the largest cash transaction known in Wall Street up to that time. It meant that fifty-one per cent of Chile Copper was sold at $35 a share. Capitalization of Chile Copper was 5,400,000 shares, par value $25 a share. Southward the star of the Anaconda empire had set its way.

Although it is running ahead of the story chronologically, the final Anaconda-Guggenheim deal may be narrated here. In the spring of 1928 there was an enormous demand for copper, here and abroad, with the price advancing to high levels. Copper shares soared. Ryan and Kelley still persisted in their desire for complete control of Chile Copper. Ryan proposed to Daniel Guggenheim an exchange of Anaconda shares for the remaining Chile Copper shares.

By the fall of 1928 the copper market was still booming. Negotiations between Ryan and Daniel Guggenheim went on continuously. It appeared to be a favorable time to acquire the remaining Chile shares when Anaconda stock was quoted at a high figure. Finally, on January 21, 1929, and after more weeks of discussion, a basis for conversion was announced to take over the remaining 2,200,000 shares of the Chile Copper Company at 73/100 of a share of Anaconda for one of Chile. This conversion had been agreed upon with Daniel Guggenheim. Some of the other members of the family were holding out for 80/100 of a share of Anaconda. Anaconda shares were selling at about $150. Stockholders were then offered subscription rights at $55 for the new Anaconda issue. The other Guggenheims then agreed to the conversion. The offer was made officially by The Anaconda Company, January 23, 1929, and 2,073,003 shares of Chile were turned in for conversion, giving Anaconda 98.41 per cent ownership. On June 30, 1940, this had increased to 98.50 per cent. Today it is 99.50 per cent. Thus was concluded a mammoth transaction.

With Anaconda in command, Chuquicamata took on new and expanded life. Output was increased by technical improvements. In 1929 the mine produced 300,000,000 pounds of copper. Despite increasing production the geology of the great deposit had not been completely explored. In 1930, Reno H. Sales was sent down to make a complete survey. By careful study and much detailed mapping, he solved the structural problem of the ore body. Based on his solution, three new churn holes were drilled. They went much deeper than the general run of holes up to that time. The results obtained from this drilling and the correct understanding of the geological structure, made it possible to add at least 200,000,000 tons of ore at an average grade of 2.75 per cent copper to the reserve. It meant that Chuquicamata now had a reserve of a billion tons. The three drill holes not only proved the existence of the additional high grade ore but also demonstrated that a good grade of ore continued to much greater depths than had been proved from earlier drilling. The fact that the deep drill holes are still in high grade porphyry ore at their deepest points is of the greatest importance to the future of the property.

The original plant at Chuquicamata was designed to treat 10,000 tons of oxide ore daily. Additions to the plant and improvements in processing brought the capacity up to 480,000,000 pounds yearly. In 1942, after our entry into World War II and at the request of the United States Government, additions to plant and more mine equipment yielded a further production of 50,000,000 pounds annually, making a total capacity of 530,000,000 pounds when operating 335 days a year.

It now became evident that a production of this magnitude could not be maintained from oxide ore for any extended length of time due to decreasing grade, and the depletion of the oxide ores which had been the only type of ore mined up to this time. Nature, in her mysterious alchemy, had wrought a change in ore. By 1948 a large tonnage of sulphide ore was being exposed in the pit and was bypassed in the mining operations as far as possible. Continued removal of oxide ore, however, turned up greater tonnage of the sulphide which, up to this time, could not be treated because no plant was available at Chuquicamata for the processing of this type of ore. It was therefore necessary to build a sulphide plant completed in 1952 to treat 30,000 tons of ore a day. The sulphide plant marked the beginning of a new cycle of development. Pending the completion of the plant, 8,000,000 tons of sulphide ore were stockpiled. The vast body of sulphide ore underlying the depth of the open pit insured a supply of copper for many years to come. The oxide ore yields twenty pounds of copper to the ton; the sulphide, thirty pounds to the ton.

Despite the predominance of sulphide ore, the oxide is still being mined and treated. There is also a combination oxide-sulphide ore which gets a dual treatment, first by leaching and then by sulphide plant process. Thus, to the greatest concentration of metallic wealth in the world, Chuquicamata adds a variety of ore seldom found elsewhere.

Many were the difficulties that had to be surmounted at Chuquicamata. The problem of an adequate supply of industrial and potable water will serve to illustrate what had to be met and overcome. The mine is located in one of the most arid of all regions. The yearly rainfall averages less than one-tenth of an inch and then only when the capricious rain clouds are kindly disposed.

A ton of water is needed for every ton of ore concentrated. Industrial water was only one aspect of the problem. Potable water is required in large quantities. In the early days water was brought in from the nearest railroad in casks loaded on ox carts. Water at Tocopilla was first provided by the evaporation of sea water. When the company built a spur of the rail line to the mine the water came in tank cars. As the mine expanded and the community grew, this process proved wholly inadequate. Today four pipelines supply the mine and its people with water.

Potable water amounting to 4,500 metric tons per day is conveyed in the Toconce pipeline from springs fifty-nine miles due east of Chuquicamata. This water is used not only for drinking but also for boilers and other needs requiring high quality. For industrial water at the oxide plant, there are two twelve-inch pipelines from the Rio San Pedro, carrying a total of 17,000 metric tons per day of slightly brackish water. This water is now used mainly for leaching and for hygienic purposes.

For the present and future needs of the sulphide plant, it was calculated that at least 32,000 metric tons per day of make-up water would be required. For this purpose, a pipeline forty-four miles in length was constructed to bring in the entire flow of the Arroyo Salado, one of the eastern tributaries of the Loa. The Chilean government had been studying projects to separate these waters from others of the Loa system in order to improve agricultural conditions in the fertile valley of Calama. It so happened that the government was willing to award rights to the Arroyo Salado waters under agreement whereby the company removes waters from the Rio Loa system above Calama for all time. The outlet of these waters, after serving their purpose at the new concentrator and leaving the plant in tailings, is the Salar de Talabre, an old salt lake which presents fully ten square miles of surface to serve as an evaporating pan, the outlets having now been blocked by dams. Here the dry climate of Chuquicamata is a favorable factor, evaporation averaging slightly above one-quarter inch per day.

The Toconce and San Pedro pipelines have been functioning from twenty-six to thirty years. Through the use of special cleaning tools which were developed at the plant, as well as deaeration of the more active Toconce water, these pipes are now maintained at capacities which do not diminish as years go on.

A period of great expansion followed the acquisition of the Chile property by Anaconda. It included development of the mineral ground, enlargement of plant and increase of property holdings. By January 1941, there were 22,830 acres of mining claims, easements and concessions including plant sites, tailing disposal space, town sites, and ground for other operating requirements. There were also concessions for pipelines for additional industrial and potable water and company railroads.

Under the stimulus of skillful management and the increased facilities, production increased. By 1937 output had gone from 212,000,000 pounds of copper a year to 400,000,-000 pounds. Four years later it had been brought to 480,000,000 pounds. With our entry into World War II, facilities were again increased in conjunction with the Defense Plant Corporation of the United States Government. Now began a period of output that recorded a massive achievement. During the years of American participation in the war the mine produced 2,556,000,000 pounds of copper. From the start of operations in May 1915 to the end of 1955, Chuquicamata has turned out 11,529,129,904 pounds of copper.

The copper, blister for refining and electrolytic refined for the consumer, is transported to the port of Antofagasta, 165 miles distant. Here it is loaded into ocean-going ships. Formerly the Chile Steamship Company, a subsidiary of Chile Exploration, operated two large sea-going freight vessels and five fuel tankers. All this craft has been sold. Freight is now shipped over established steamship lines except fuel oil which is delivered in chartered vessels.

With history and development out of the way and the conquest of the desert assured, we can now have a close-up of Chuquicamata. One more preliminary, however, is necessary. It is the open pit operation. The rise of open pit mining depended on two major technological developments—mechanical methods of handling large volumes of materials and improvement in ore-dressing techniques. Open pit mining with power shovels and other large scale mechanical equipment was borrowed from the iron mining

industry. It has made for the commercially possible recovery of copper from low-grade ores that fifty years ago
would have been considered worthless by most engineers.
Chuquicamata is ideally situated for this type of operation.

The approach to Chuquicamata is unprepossessing
despite the grim grandeur that lies beyond the end of the
journey. You make the trip from Antofagasta through
barren pampa with its low rolling hills and pass the town
of Calama. Looking ahead, the monotony of the landscape
is relieved by the first view of the battlement of the Andean
Cordilleras with their snowclad peaks sharp against the
skyline. The foreground is matched by the geological
stretch of gray rock that surrounds the mining district.
The ascent over the paved road is so gradual that it is
difficult to realize that when you reach Chuquicamata and
its well-ordered community bursts upon your view, you
have climbed more than nine thousand feet.

One contrast is immediately evident once you reach the
mining area. In underground mining camps in western
United States such as Butte, color-stained hills, prospect
cuts and shafts with hoists and headframes feature the landscape. At Chuquicamata there is no such detail. Nature
and man have resorted to no spectacular window dressing,
so to speak, with the environment. You have the town, the
plants and the super spectacle of the mine.

I have seen all the great open pit mines from the Belgian
Congo to Utah. Nowhere is there such an impressive picture as is revealed in Chuquicamata. The eliptical amphi-
theater is a gargantuan man-made crater in the mountain
side, one and eight-tenths miles in length and seven-tenths
of a mile wide. To view its massive proportions is to recall
instinctively Kipling's words: "They shall splash on a ten-
league canvas with brushes of comet's hair." For such is
Chuquicamata with its muted coloring, gray, green and
brown, that make it the Grand Canyon of Chile, full mate
to the Arizona wonder.

On each side of the crater rise the tiers of benches, 100 feet wide and 40 to 90 feet high. Everywhere is movement and sound—the roar of the shovels, the rattle of the endless trains rushing off to the crushers, the boom of explosives. It is ceaseless movement but orderly action. From the rim the workers appear to be pygmies and the shovels and trucks, toys. The pit is completely electrified so that all shovels, locomotives and churn drills are power-operated. Each day over 110,000 tons of material are taken out. Of this, 38,000 tons are waste and the remainder, ore.

By day the pit is an eye-filling spectacle with its soft gleam of color and incessant movement. Nor does it lose its glamour at night. When shadows shroud the peak, as someone wrote, it is "a glittering pendant of lights on a gown of darkness."

One site at Chuquicamata rates attention for, like the huge mine, it has an interest all its own. It is the place where Protestant services are held at dawn on Easter Sunday. Here the minister stands near the edge of a flat ledge with a large wooden cross behind him. His altar is of Nature's making for it is granite. To the south loom the giant peaks of Mt. Pedro and Mt. Publo while all around stretch the great open spaces. It is an inspiring and unforgettable spot when the rising sun paints those tremendous stretches with crimson and gold.

At Chuquicamata is one of the most striking contrasts in any mining area. Just beyond the rim of the pit is a small, hand-operated, Chilean-owned copper mine. The few workers use hammers to knock off the ore, while just below them huge electric shovels gouge out eleven cubic feet of material with every bite.

When I first visited Chuquicamata in the early years of Anaconda ownership, it was a camp sheltering 15,000 people. Today it has emerged as a town with a population of 25,000 of which 5,000 are workers. It is a sort of League of Nations with fifty-five different nationalities represented.

Every possible facility is afforded the workers. They pay nothing for rent, electricity and water, and purchase their food and clothing at three company stores at 1932 prices— a miracle of present day living.

Housing for the workers is being constantly modernized and increased. Two hundred new units are built every year. One group of new houses, named Campamento O'Higgins after Chile's great patriot, was constructed at a cost of $7,000,000.

Medical attention is free. The existing general and maternity hospitals will be superceded by a new six-storey building with 208 beds. The thirteen doctors on the staff are sent in relays to Europe or the United States every three years for refresher courses and to keep abreast with medical advance.

The 3,000 children have roomy schools with playgrounds. English and Spanish are included in the courses. Additional school facilities are under way. They include more grade schools and a vocational school. The company finances four scholarships for Chilean citizens who have graduated from college and desire to take up graduate work in the United States. Each scholarship winner is permitted to select his or her college and is given sufficient funds to pay tuition and living expenses. A large number of other scholarships are given to the children of workers to enable them to attend trade and technical schools in Chile after they have completed their courses in primary schools.

There is no lack of diversion. Two motion picture theaters show the latest American films. Transportation is adequate for there is now a good road to Calama and Antofagasta. A fleet of busses travels daily to and from the port. Two daily newspapers in Spanish provide news of the day.

The welfare program for the workers enlists the efforts of the Help Chuqui Club for better sanitation in the homes and medical attention for both parents and children. Four sanitary nurses are in constant service.

An experience of mine will indicate the growth of culture. I went to a Sunday afternoon concert in the large auditorium of the staff club. Every member of the orchestra was an employee in one of the company activities. A program including Bach, Haydn, Mozart, Schubert, Grieg and Mendelssohn compositions was played admirably. The orchestra was assisted by the Chuqui Polyphonic Choir, also recruited from employees, which sang Negro spirituals, parts of Handel's oratorio *The Messiah*, and other numbers.

One interesting change in conditions among the workers is worthy of note. In 1948 forty-five per cent of the workers were single and fifty-five per cent married. Today the number of single men has decreased to thirty-seven per cent which means that sixty-three per cent are married. This is an evidence of stability in the community. The sons and daughters are staying in Chuquicamata instead of leaving as they formerly did.

The staff, which includes 150 Chileans, 80 Europeans and 70 Americans, has its golf course, tennis courts, swimming pool and a magazine, *The Chilex Weekly*. There is a Chile Copper Society with monthly meetings when mining problems are discussed and threshed out.

Plant development has kept pace with town growth. A new power plant at Tocopilla is under construction in three stages to replace the old one. Technical changes within the concentrator will permit a twenty-five per cent increase in over-all copper production. A plant for the recovery of molybdenum sulphide will be built in 1957. Plans for additional potable water and electric consumption in the town, due to the introduction of electric kitchen gadgets, have been made.

Men notable in mining operations have directed the course of Chuquicamata from the earliest period of development. They have included Herman C. Bellinger, Fred Hellman, Burr Wheeler, Thomas A. Campbell and Douglas M. Dunbar. Today Charles M. Brinckerhoff is not only

General Manager of Chuquicamata and General Manager in charge of operations in South America but also Vice President of Chile Exploration and the Andes Copper Mining Company. A graduate of Columbia University in metallurgy, he served at Inspiration, Potrerillos, and as Manager of Operations of the Andes Copper Mining Company before taking over the Chuquicamata post. He is an able executive embodying the highest tradition of Anaconda service. In June 1956, the Chilean Government awarded him the Order of Merit in recognition of his services to the republic.

Campbell, who began as chemist and metallurgist for Chile Exploration in 1925, has also made a notable contribution to Anaconda operation. He became Executive Vice President of Chile Exploration and Andes Copper Mining Company in 1952 and a Vice President of The Anaconda Company in 1956. Campbell combines business acumen with high technical ability.

As Vice President and Resident Director of Chile Exploration and Andes Copper, Don Rodolfo Michels has an important role in Anaconda operations in Chile. Born in Santiago, he first studied at the School of Mines in his native city. He obtained his degree as Mining Engineer at the Institute of Engineering and Science in Chicago, later receiving an Honorary LL.D. from Lehigh University and a Doctorate in Foreign Service from the University of Southern California. While engaged in private mining and business interests he performed a notable public service for his country, serving as member of the Chamber of Deputies and the Senate, and later as Chilean Ambassador to the United States. In 1944 he became associated with Anaconda. As Vice President and resident director of Chilean operations he has been active in the new developments in the republic. With his agreeable personality, his mature wisdom, good judgment and his wide and influential acquaintance in Chile, Don Rodolfo is an invaluable executive.

Anaconda investment in Chuquicamata led Kelley to say on one occasion:

"If you should put five billion dollars tomorrow in South America, you could not duplicate what American pioneering and research have done down there."

II

Although overshadowed by Chuquicamata, Potrerillos has played an important part in Anaconda operations in Chile. To get the beginning it is necessary to turn to William Braden, called "The Father of the Andes." Braden was an alert and capable mining man. In 1905 he acquired a mining property at Sewell in Chile and after overcoming great difficulties in transport and supplies, developed the mine which bears his name into a highly successful operation. In 1908 he sold the Braden mine to the Guggenheims who later turned it over to Kennecott.

Braden was now at a loose end. Being a man of action, he looked about for a new mining field to conquer. He had become widely known and respected in Chile. It followed that many mining propositions were offered to him. In 1913, Anaconda made an alliance with Braden who, for all practical purposes, became the company's South American representative. He now began to scout for a desirable property. Anaconda needed copper and in Braden they had the man who could find it.

Braden studied many prospects. At long last he found what turned out to be a desirable acquisition. It was located in a valley near the southern end of the Atacama Desert in the western range of the Andes ninety-six miles from the port of Chanaral. Since 1875 individual Chileans and later, a Chilean company, had mined stringers of rich copper in the area and had named the camp Potrerillos, which means "little fields" from the solitary patch of grass and brush that grew nearby.

After his engineers had explored the area and found it worth developing, Braden acquired options on the property covering 3,532 acres. In 1916, the Andes Copper Mining Company was incorporated by Anaconda as a subsidiary and took over the Braden options. The original capital was 500,000 shares par value $100 a share. Subsequently the number of shares was increased to 3,600,000 par value $20. The Anaconda Company now owns 98.83 per cent of the Andes Copper Mining Company. Dr. L. D. Ricketts became President. William Wraith, Sr., was placed in charge while construction was entrusted to Wilbur Jurden.

In Wraith, Anaconda has had another stalwart whose skill has been demonstrated in many important undertakings. A graduate of the Michigan College of Mines, his first job was as underground surveyor for the Santa Fe Railroad. His initial contact with mining was as transit man for the engineer in charge of construction at the Boston & Butte and the Butte & Boston properties, later becoming Chief Engineer. With the absorption of these companies by the then Anaconda Copper Mining Company, he moved up fast. He built the flue system and the huge stack at Anaconda. He then took charge, as Vice President of the Andes Copper Mining Company, of the development of the Potrerillos undertaking.

Potrerillos took full measure of Wraith's ability. His task included the laying out of a mining and transportation system to handle 30,000 tons of ore from an underground mine, to coordinate the treatment of both oxide and sulphide ores, and to provide the necessary water. It was tribute to Wraith's competency that this immense and difficult task was achieved, and copper produced, the day before the estimated date. He was Executive Vice President of The Greene Cananea Copper Company, and of Chile Exploration, Chile Copper and Andes Copper when he retired in 1945. Wraith died October 11, 1956.

Jurden is Anaconda's master builder. After his university training in engineering in Utah, California and Wisconsin he worked at miscellaneous construction and engineering jobs until 1917 when he became associated with The Anaconda Copper Mining Company at Anaconda. Subsequently he was Construction Superintendent and chief draftsman for the company and its subsidiaries. His present post is head of the Anaconda Engineering Department which touches every company activity.

Among the projects engineered and constructed under Jurden's supervision are: The smelting and refining plant at Potrerillos; the improvement of plants of the Chile Exploration Company at Chuquicamata; the construction of the electrolytic zinc plant and the new copper ore crushing plant at Anaconda; the zinc fuming plants at East Helena; the reorganization and completion of the construction of the plant of Basic Magnesium, Incorporated during World War II; the new copper production plant at Greene Cananea; the engineering, design and construction of the completion of the chromium mining and reduction plant at Columbus, Montana, during World War II; the sulphide crushing mill and smelting plants at Chuquicamata; the company's open pit copper mines and plants at Yerington; the original uranium ore reduction plant at Grants, and the aluminum plant at Columbia Falls.

More than $45,000,000 was spent in equipping and developing the Potrerillos property before the first ton of blister copper was produced. The delay in getting under way was due to the low price of copper. It was not until the end of 1924 that operations got under full swing. Because of a thick overburden of waste, open pit mining could not be practiced. The ore body is mined by block caving. At the outset both oxide and sulphide ores were mined. The average copper content over the years has been 1.50 per cent. The oxide ore became exhausted, leaving only the sulphide.

As at Chuquicamata, immense difficulties of terrain, supply and transport had to be overcome. The camp is at an altitude of nearly 10,000 feet and the region arid for most of the year. There was no adjacent water. This necessitated the building of a pipeline thirty-five miles in length. It was also necessary to construct a sixty-mile railroad, a power plant, wharves and warehouses at the seaport of Barquito and, of course, adequate reduction plants at the mine.

With every obstacle removed, mining began with a favorable output. In 1929 the production was 162,000,000 pounds of copper. The depression years witnessed a sharp decline in output, the production in 1932 having dropped to 23,237,111 pounds. By 1937 there was an increase. In 1941 production had reached 208,000,000 pounds. From the start of operations in January 1927, to the end of 1955, the total output was 3,243,498,940 pounds.

In 1949 production began to decline with the decrease becoming more manifest each year. Potrerillos was doomed. The end was in sight before another decade passed.

With Potrerillos on the way to depletion, it was necessary for the Andes Copper Mining Company to find a replacement. Happily that replacement was found in what is known as the Indio Muerto district fifteen miles by airline from Potrerillos. It not only insures a future supply of copper but saves Potrerillos from extinction because the ores will be processed there.

Like Chuquicamata, the Indio Muerto area has a picturesque background. There is evidence of shallow primitive turquoise mining by the Indians centuries ago in the pre-Inca period. The prominent Indio Muerto Mountain, which rises more than 3,000 feet above the surrounding pampa, was a landmark for the inhabitants long before the white man came, as the historic Inca trail passes by the foot of the peak. Evidences of old Indian encampments and burial grounds abound.

Early Chilean prospectors were attracted to the area by the green copper-stained outcrops. Their early mining attempts were uneconomic because of the low grade character of the ores which were exploited in shallow pits and shafts. The district was abandoned for many years.

In 1944 the Andes Copper Mining Company purchased seven old mining claims in the northern part of the Indio Muerto area. Early preliminary geological studies were made, but the district was not considered to have important economic possibilities until 1950, when a thorough geological study was made at the request of Vincent D. Perry, head of the Anaconda Geological Department.

As the investigations advanced from preliminary mapping to an actual drilling program, development of a water source became important. On studying old trails, camp sites and burial grounds of the early Indian inhabitants, some of their original water holes were discovered. These were cleaned out and exploited by means of shallow shafts and small gasoline-driven pumping units. They have provided sufficient water for the initial drilling program. As prospecting and development work continue to increase in proportions, additional water sources are being prospected and pipelines of considerable lengths are contemplated. The prospecting program to date has indicated several centers of low grade copper mineralization, associated with several porphyry intrusions, aligned along a northerly belt for a distance of several kilometers.

This relatively recent geological study led to new discoveries in the southern part of the district, several kilometers to the south of the old mining claims, which exhibited enough possibilities to justify additional prospecting by diamond drilling.

As a result of these studies, title to the Inca group of 302 mining claims was perfected through surveying. Several

hundred additional mining claims were denounced to pro-
tect the possibility of lateral extensions. A preliminary
prospect diamond drilling program was initiated in February 1952. Initial drilling results were sufficiently favorable to warrant continuation and expansion of the drilling
program to its present state. At this writing there are nine
drills and two churn drills operating and five prospect
tunnels in progress. The exploration drilling and tunneling
have raised the estimate of ore reserves from 78,000,000
tons to 200,000,000 tons and probably more, averaging 1.6
per cent copper.

The ores are sulphides with an estimated copper content
of 1.6 per cent. They will be mined from what is termed
a secondary enrichment blanket, approximately 350 feet
thick, the top of which is from 300 to 500 feet below the
surface.

The complete program will mean an expenditure of
$80,150,000. Plans provide for the development of the de-
posit in the Turquoise Gulch area as an underground mine.
Into this mine there will be driven a main haulage tunnel
which will be electrified for the haulage of the ore to the
concentrator. Two adits will be driven on mining levels
to facilitate mine development.

The surface installations proposed will consist of transmission lines and water lines into the property, the construction of primary and secondary crushing plants near
the main tunnel portal as well as the construction of a concentrator including ore bins, fine grinding equipment and
the most modern flotation installations. Copper concentrates will be pumped through a pipeline to Pastos Cerrados,
a point on the Potrerillos Railway. Here they will be
filtered, and then transported by railway to the Potrerillos
smelter.

At El Salvador the plans provide for the construction of a
town near the mine embodying the various features required for a modern village. Besides up-to-date dwellings

the plans contemplate a well equipped theater, an employees club, schools, hospital, church, stores and various other welfare projects such as playgrounds and athletic fields.

Originally the new property was named Indio Muerto, which means Dead Indian. This was deemed a somewhat morbid title for a new mine with a bright future. While Indio Muerto will still apply to the mountain, the mine will henceforth be called El Salvador—the Saviour. The reason is obvious since it saved the situation so far as a replacement for Potrerillos and the company's future supply of copper in southern Chile are concerned.

Another comparatively recent development is the reopening of the Africana mine, located twelve miles from the city of Santiago. The Anaconda Company owns 99.25 per cent of the Santiago Mining Company which operates the mine.

The original Africana claims were denounced on December 11, 1896, by J. A. Pinochet. They were later sold to Guillermo Acuna who perfected title to the claims on March 7, 1910. The Andes Exploration Company of Maine bought Acuna's interests in the Africana claims on December 24, 1914, consolidated the group and transferred the titles to the Santiago Mining Company on November 14, 1917. From June 1917 until January 1918, William Braden contracted for the delivery of a small quantity of ore to the Naltagua Smelter, near Santiago. This ore came from a shallow working serviced by a small incline shaft.

A three-compartment, vertical development shaft and a tunnel level were started by the Santiago Mining Company in 1917. Prospect levels were driven at four horizons to a depth of 1,000 feet, together with cross-cuts through the vein for sampling purposes. The workings total 12,000 feet. Although a small tonnage of ore was developed, economic conditions did not permit profitable exploitation of the ore body at that time and operations were suspended in 1924.

The property remained idle until 1955 when a resurvey inspired resumption of work on the property.

Work is being actively pushed. Construction will comprise a concentrator for sulphide ores, power plant, shops, warehouses, housing and a restaurant for workers, potable water works and a clubhouse for both staff and workers.

The Africana mine and the nearby Lo Aguirre property cover a large mineralized area. The company also owns 17,000 acres of ranch land which is being utilized for agriculture and stock-breeding. It is being converted into a model farm for scientific farming.

One new feature at Africana is the handsomely appointed guest house completed late in 1955. It is named Parque Lo Aguirre, which means Lo Aguirre Park. It is really a group of three houses, one for company directors and the two others for guests. On the tree-dotted terrace in front is a swimming pool, one of the largest in Chile.

The Anaconda operations in Chile are highly organized. In the belief that all personnel be acquainted with company progress, a weekly publication called *Oasis* is published in Santiago for distribution, free of charge, to all members of the organization, both workmen and staff. It contains material on social events, sports, plant progress and any other items that may interest the community as a whole. The issue is abundantly illustrated. The company has another means of communication to the personnel in the form of letters from the management, sent out once a month. The recipient's name and address are on both the envelope and the letter. Progress reports are included in all the communications which are signed by Brinckerhoff.

As at Santiago, a publication in Spanish is put out at intervals by the Potrerillos management. It is entitled *Andino* and is an effective medium for communication with all the employees, whether workers or staff. Like the Santiago publication it contains items of social and industrial news and any other news of interest to the working community. The management also sends personally addressed letters to staff and workers commending them when the occasion warrants it.

Such is the Anaconda domain in Chile. The operations have enhanced company prestige and production and fortified the economic stability of the republic.

⚴ 10

THROUGH WAR AND DEPRESSION

WITH the properties in Chile functioning and The American Brass Company now an honored unit in the Anaconda domain, the end of the Twenties loomed ahead with the prospect of a period of unprecedented prosperity. Ryan and Kelley had demonstrated their faith in the future of America by committing themselves to a program of mine development and the acquisition of new properties to meet the demands for copper which they felt certain would develop in the future. As the decade neared its end, they had launched Anaconda Wire & Cable and were now fabricators on a huge scale.

Came 1929, destined to be the year of economic wrath. It found Anaconda in the full swing of its expanding program. To all America that fateful year seemed filled with golden promise. There were unprecedented peacetime requirements for the metals which the company produced and for the products of its subsidiary fabricating concerns. These concerns and the Chilean properties were prepared to meet the new and higher business cycle then shaping.

The American people were enjoying a measure of prosperity hitherto unknown. The stock market boomed. Maids, bootblacks, clerks, in fact a considerable portion of the population, owned securities, most of them bought on margin, and were rich on paper. Wages had soared. Politicians were demanding "a chicken in every pot and two automobiles in every garage."

Then the bubble burst in late 1929 followed by the recession of the following year, ushering in the most disastrous depression not only in America's economic history but the world's as well. Business everywhere was forced to make arbitrary and summary retrenchments. Production slumped. Increase in the popular demand for staple goods was cancelled. Even normal requirements began to shrink. Gloom was dominant.

Anaconda had built its world structure on a firm foundation. Its commitments had been courageously but carefully made in view of the general expectation in business that a period of greater demand lay ahead. It was to be more than a decade before the country realized fully the wisdom of the plans which had been laid down by Ryan and Kelley in the 1920's.

When depression gripped the country the copper industry, as a whole, was slow to contract its operations. There was a general opposition to closing down the plants which meant throwing thousands of employees out of work. The government, with false optimism, let it be known that it expected the worst of the depression to end shortly and that it looked with concern upon any proposal to suspend industrial operation with its consequent idleness.

Some producers continued to throw their metal on the market in large volume and the result was a complete price collapse. Copper sold far below the operating cost of the lowest-cost producers. The price of the metal touched its lowest at 4.7 cents a pound during the winter of 1932–3. The United States Tariff Commission had found the average cost of copper in this country for the three years, 1928–30, to be 13.41 cents a pound, including depreciation, depletion, interest and overhead after deducting the value of by-product precious metals.

The time inevitably came when employees in the copper mines were working only part time. Production had to be curtailed below the now reduced demand if the industry was to be restored to a basis where surplus stocks could be liquidated and future operations put on a sound basis. Stringent economies were imperative. Some copper producers proposed that the industry cut wages.

It was during this time of stress that Kelley demonstrated his concern and that of the Anaconda Company for the welfare of their employees. He held that a proposal to cut wages was unjust, pointing out that the miners were working only two weeks out of six and that with these reduced wages, they were obliged to support their families. He indicated that it was the conviction of the Anaconda management that the employees had first call at such a distressful period, even before the stockholders. Kelley's stand was at a time when Anaconda's cost of production was several cents a pound higher than the boasted costs of some of the other producers, and when the company had a large and growing indebtedness. Following his dictum there was no further talk of cutting the wages of Anaconda employees during the emergency.

Now followed the six years of the depression. They witnessed Anaconda dividends wiped out, the necessity for the company to borrow money to pay operating expenses, with many mines and plants idle. These properties had to be maintained at a cost of millions to keep them in good physical condition.

During this period of economic woe Ryan and Kelley were required to spend much time in Washington as a result of governmental investigation of the copper industry, which was charged with manipulation of prices. The charge was wholly unfounded and subsequently proved to be without a basis of fact. Early in 1931 Ryan made an informal public statement informing stockholders that the current quotations for Anaconda stock, about $35 a share, did not then represent the book value of the plants and equipment, without any consideration of the value of the mining properties. Like Kelley, his faith in the company never wavered.

In 1933 there came to Kelley, to the company and to a large and devoted circle of friends, the shock of Ryan's death. The strain of the depression travail and the unwarranted attacks on leaders in the copper industry, had weakened his heart. On February 9 he had been served with a subpoena to appear before a Washington investigation committee. Notwithstanding Kelley's earnest plea that he go instead, Ryan persisted in his determination to appear.

Ryan was a devout Catholic but few knew that he went to mass every morning before going to his office. On February 10 he went to morning mass as usual, collapsed in church, and died the next day at his home. The Catholic Church accorded Ryan the highest honors it could bestow on a layman. Pope Pius XI had made him a Knight of St. Gregory the Great. High pontifical mass was celebrated at the Church of St. Ignatius Loyola in New York by the Rev. John Gregory Murray, Archbishop of St. Paul, Minnesota. Two thousand mourners filled the church or stood with bared heads on the street outside. During the funeral all Anaconda properties were closed. Requiem masses were celebrated in all the Butte Catholic Churches. A wave of sorrow swept over all Montana.

With the death of Ryan a dominant figure in industry passed from the scene. Sincerity, courtesy, simplicity and kindliness were among his major qualities. He was modest, retiring and soft-spoken with a love of things of the mind and the spirit that ripened with the years. The gifts of leadership and organization were part of his heritage and were impressed upon every productive activity he touched.

The year 1933 was fatal to high Anaconda executives for, before it passed into history, death claimed B. B. Thayer,

former President of Anaconda. Ryan had succeeded him in
that post in 1915 when Thayer became Vice President.

The death of Ryan left the main burden of directing the
colossal business on Kelley's shoulders. He and Ryan had
worked as a team. Now the task was his alone.

In 1933 when desperate efforts were being made at Washington to revive industry, Kelley was called upon to act in
an advisory capacity for the copper industry. He cooperated
with government agencies and officials. His advice and
judgment were almost invariably heeded. He suggested to
the federal agencies that the government start a stockpile of
copper at a time when producers had half a million tons of
refined copper on hand with the price five cents a pound
and were seeking to keep their technical staffs together and
their help employed. If that had been done, there probably
would have been no shortage of the metal when the United
States was again plunged into war in 1941.

In 1933 Kelley, with other copper executives, was called
to Washington to aid in drafting the N.R.A. Code. During
the following year the life of the Anaconda corporation was
legally extended to 1975. The business and accounts of the
subsidiaries were consolidated.

The depression dragged on. Production of copper was
held to only a fraction of the capacity of the mines and
plants. More and more time and effort were demanded by
the various government hearings, investigations and reports. Kelley was frequently called to testify to correct mis-
apprehensions about the company. Reports and figures had
to be prepared.

Hobbins was called to New York from Butte in 1936 to
become Executive Vice President and to ease the burden on
Kelley's shoulders. He had played a vital part in meeting
the shock of the economic collapse and the depression in
Butte. He was succeeded at Butte by Daniel M. Kelly, former Western General Counsel, who had been a member of
the legal staff since 1915. He was succeeded as Western

General Counsel by W. H. Hoover who later became president.

Hoover, a graduate of Harvard and the Montana School of Mines, was admitted to the Montana Bar in 1914 and engaged in general practice in Great Falls until 1933 when he became president of the First National Bank in that city, holding that post for three years. His association with Anaconda began in 1936 when he became Western General Counsel. In succession he capably filled the posts of General Counsel, Vice President and General Counsel, and ultimately President in 1949. His legal and financial experience were effectively capitalized in the service of Anaconda. He died June 6, 1952.

Operations had been placed upon the most economical basis possible in the company's history. Methods had been devised for parcelling out what employment was available so that the procedure would benefit the greatest possible number of employees. Men who had been laid off by necessity were still regarded as company employees and given consideration whenever it could be done.

Gradually the copper metal surplus disappeared and the price rose to 11 cents a pound in December 1936. The trend continued through March 1937 when the price reached 16.-775 cents a pound. Employment increased throughout the industry and production schedules were enlarged. Then came a sudden reaction of government sentiment which affected public morale and impaired confidence. The country fell into another decline. The budding demand for copper was wiped out. Buying all but ceased. Buyers refused to commit themselves for more than a few days' supply at a time. The demand for copper on the domestic market in March 1937 approximated 100,000 tons. This condition was confined entirely to the United States since foreign consumption of copper in 1937 amounted to 1,604,000 tons. Domestic deliveries, on the other hand, were 689,053 tons, only 80.3 per cent of the 1929 consumption. The price dropped to 9.9 cents a pound and once more there was an over-supply of the metal for the market needs. Production had to be curtailed. Until 1939, when war clouds again gathered, the price fluctuated between 9.77 and 11 cents a pound. With the outbreak of war in Europe in 1939 the demand for copper became heavy and continued to increase.

In 1926 Anaconda and its subsidiaries, together with Chile Copper, had outstanding a total bonded debt of $249,000,000. The liquidation of this debt began at once. It had been greatly reduced when the depression year dawned. The company, by the exigencies of the times, was required to make bank loans which, in 1932, aggregated $70,500,000. At the end of 1932 the debt, including bonds and the bank loans, was $105,815,000. By the end of 1933, this had been reduced to $102,561,000.

During this period there occurred an interesting episode. Anaconda had $109,000,000 in bank loans and needed $6,000,000 to carry on. Kelley went to see William C. Potter of the Guaranty Trust Company and James H. Perkins of the National City Bank at Potter's office. He made his request for the additional loan and then said:

"If we do not get this money, you will be in the copper business tomorrow."

Kelley not only got the loan but Potter soon after joined the Board of Directors of Anaconda.

At the end of December 1941, the debt, under Kelley's guidance, had been reduced to $20,935,000. In nine and a half years the company had decreased its indebtedness by $88,437,000. As of December 31, 1942, all indebtedness of the company and its subsidiaries, other than current liabilities consisting principally of accounts, wages payable and accrued taxes, had been paid. During that nine and a half year period the financial condition of the company and its subsidiaries, through increase in its net current position and discharge of indebtedness, was improved by $140,116,-

649.89, or $16.15 per share, after payment of $101,923,-471.50 in dividends.

Here was demonstrated the recuperation and recovery of a great American industrial enterprise as a result of courageous, prudent policies in operation and financing. It won the admiration of the country's most prominent financial and industrial figures. Anaconda had wrought what many regarded as a miracle in liquidating all its heavy debt and bringing its current net current assets to unprecedented heights. At the end of 1942, it had no debt and its financial position was excellent. With a vision that seemed to penetrate the future needs of the nation, Anaconda had perfected an organization upon which an embattled America was soon to make unprecedented demands for its vast military establishment.

II

As the clouds of World War II closed in on the American horizon, Anaconda was prepared to meet the necessities of national security. Its highest officials remembered the tremendous demands which had been made on the non-ferrous industry in World War I and realized that the needs of that war would be dwarfed by the requirements of the gigantic struggle that now threatened the world. Many years previous, the statement had been made that civilization was built on metals. Now the world was soon to learn that civilization could be destroyed by the misuse of metals and could only be saved by a colossal production of metals for war which must far surpass the output of those who challenged peace and security.

Throughout the preparatory stages and the war, Anaconda devoted itself and all its resources and personnel to the service of the nation. Its officials consulted continuously with government agencies in supplying the armed forces with their vast needs of strategic and vital non-ferrous metals. Its entire production of metals and products was directed exclusively to filling these requirements. Its technical staff assisted in solving the many and difficult problems of military supply.

On April 30, 1940, Kelley became Chairman of the Board. The onetime dollar and a half a day water boy in Butte had risen to the highest post in the bestowal of the company. There had been no Board Chairman since Ryan's death in 1933. Kelley, as President, had met the responsibilities of both posts. He had piloted the farflung concern through the dark years of operating losses to bring it debt-free to the travail of World War II. Hobbins succeeded him as President.

Kelley defined a program of capacity production of vital and strategic metals and minerals and their fabrication by The Anaconda Company, its subsidiaries and affiliates, aligning the entire organization with the National Defense Program. This program was to record one of the most dramatic periods of service in the history of the company.

During the early part of 1940 there had been no great increase in the demand for copper although the European phase of the war had been in progress for nearly a year. At that time the industry was operating at a normal rate of about 166,000,000 pounds of copper a month of which about 13,000,000 pounds was secondary or reclaimed copper. The Anaconda Company and its affiliates were producing 33,500,000 pounds a month of which 3,000,000 pounds was secondary. Anaconda's foreign properties were able to supply the overseas demands. Foreign markets had been greatly reduced by the British blockade and the only substantial market abroad consisted of the requirements of the French government. With the collapse of the French military effort, the unexpired French contracts were cancelled and the Latin-American producers left practically without a market. By August of 1940 the foreign properties of Anaconda were producing at the rate of about 20,000,000 pounds a month.

Six months earlier, the National Defense authorities instructed all production officials of the company mines and plants and those of the subsidiaries to increase output as rapidly as possible. A comprehensive program of plant facility enlargement and mine facilities was now launched. The acute shortage of copper was not visualized by the Office of Production Management until the spring of 1941, although it had been forecast the previous year. Early in 1941, Office of Production Management officials were exercised over the zinc situation and the threatened shortage of manganese. More than 400 men at Butte were then moved from copper production and put on zinc and manganese. The zinc output from the Butte mines was increased from 5,000,000 pounds a month to 7,700,000 pounds.

The Butte mines and the company's plants in Montana which had been producing 240,000,000 pounds a year increased production to 274,000,000 pounds in 1943. A year later it reached 285,000,000 pounds. The mines had been placed on a seven-day basis with the men working six days a week.

Throughout the Anaconda domain production grew apace. The Mountain City Copper Company with properties in Mountain City, Nevada, produced 25,000,000 pounds a year. The Copper Canyon Mining Company at Battle Mountain, Nevada, was brought into production during 1942 to turn out 3,000,000 pounds a year. So it went.

The Anaconda group of properties had answered the nation's need for copper metal. From 774,000,000 pounds in 1940 the output expanded to 994,000,000 pounds in 1942. In the two following years the production was 1,300,000,-000 pounds and 1,200,000,000 pounds respectively. A total of 8,313,000,000 pounds of copper was taken from all its sources by Anaconda during the war years.

The mines of The Anaconda Company and its subsidiaries produced approximately one-third of the total amount
of new copper available in the United States for the prosecution of the war. Putting it another way, Anaconda contributed 51.26 per cent of the total copper increase for the
national emergency, or 3,744 tons more than all the other
producers combined.

The government's emergency requirements for zinc were
no less urgent than the need for copper. This need was adequately answered by Anaconda. A new plant was constructed in Tooele, Utah, to recover zinc from slag. New
electrolytic tanks were installed at Great Falls and Anaconda. The figures tell the story. In 1940 Anaconda produced 303,952,760 pounds of zinc. In 1943 the output was
514,624,000 pounds. Anaconda's total zinc production from
1940 to 1945 resulted in an average annual increase in output of 100 per cent over the prewar years. The total Montana production of zinc for this period was 1,193,642 short
tons. Very little Anaconda ore was used in the operations.
Most of the concentrate was supplied by Metals Reserve
Company from Mexican ore because this ore was unsuited
for treatment in other plants but could be treated in Anaconda properties. This plan released zinc miners to other
labor-short operations.

With American-Japanese relations moving toward a
crisis and with Lend Lease assistance to Great Britain and
Russia developing on a tremendous scale, government officials were warned of an impending critical situation in non-
ferrous metals in this country. Priority regulations for all
essential commodities likely to be scarce were being formulated. Officials of the Office of Price Adminstration and
Civilian Supply and the Office of Production Management
called a meeting on July 17, 1941, of the copper producers of
America to devise ways and means of getting still more copper into the defense program.

The price of copper had been frozen at 12 cents. Discus-

sion evolved about how much increased production could
be secured at that price and what might be added to the
available supply if the price were increased. Early in December 1941, a few days before the sneak attack on Pearl
Harbor, the Anaconda Company, at the request of William
L. Batt of the Office of Production Management, sent to
Chester C. Davis, Chairman of the O.P.A., a statement of
the increased copper production effective and planned by
the company. This statement showed that Anaconda had,
within a year and upon its own judgment, increased its production of copper from 767,000,000 pounds to 1,139,000,-
000 pounds a year, and was planning still further increases
in 1942.

During the early discussions with government representatives over the availability of larger quantities of copper for
the defense program, Anaconda officials were in frequent
consultation with Batt, R. C. Allen and Dr. Andrew K.
Leith, all government advisers and later associated with the
Metals Division of the Office of Production Management,
which later became the War Production Board.

At one of these conferences it was stated by government
officials that large quantities of manganese would be required for the defense program. With 12.5 pounds of manganese needed to desulphurize and deoxidize every ton of
steel produced, the need of this metal is evident. Prior to the
war 97 per cent of all manganese ore used in the United
States was imported. Foreign sources of supply had been almost completely cut off by the German submarine campaign. Once more, Anaconda heeded a call for metal. The
company drew on its experience in World War I and its
subsequent technical knowledge acquired in the development of manganese ores and their treatment. A contract was
negotiated under which Anaconda was to deliver to the
Metals Reserve Company, a government agency, over a
period of three years after the completion of a plant, 240,-
000 long tons of manganese ore of certain specifications. De-

velopment at the Emma and Travona mines in Butte for the production of manganese ore and the construction of a concentrator and nodulizing plant at Anaconda were begun in August 1940. The plant started operations in June 1941. The mines were producing more than 1,000 tons of ore a day to the end of the emergency. The reduction plant produced at the rate of 100,000 long tons of 60 per cent manganese nodules a year. At the conclusion of the original contract a second agreement was made for the production of 80,000 tons of manganese for the ensuing year. This manganese plant was constructed by the company at its own expense. The production represented in excess of 98 per cent of the total manganese produced in the United States.

In the mid-Forties the Northern Pacific Railroad published an advertisement in leading newspapers and magazines stating that capture or destruction of Butte and its surrounding area by enemy forces in 1941 might have crippled United States war production for the reason that at the outbreak of war "mines in Butte and vicinity worked a miracle of manganese production, using 'pink ore,' a former waste material. This manganese has been a mainstay of America's armament industries."

The German submarine campaign brought about another metal shortage. We imported nearly all the chrome used in the United States. It was an essential metal since it is used as an alloy in steel production.

The Office of Production Management queried Anaconda about the chrome deposits in Stillwater County, Montana. Company officials replied that the deposits had been thoroughly explored many years before and that it had been determined they were not of commercial value. The Washington officials proposed that Anaconda develop a method of mining and treating the Montana deposits for government account. This involved geological, mining and metallurgical investigations. Anaconda engineers were directed to begin surveys. All this, and other preliminary work, was undertaken at the company's expense.

In November 1940 Anaconda entered into a contract with the Metals Reserve Company under which the company was to develop the chrome mines, construct a plant for the treatment of ores, and carry on as operator for the government agencies. The Metals Reserve Company took over control of the properties under a lease and option from the owners. Development started in the Benbow and Monatt-Sampson properties in Stillwater County, Montana.

The development of the chrome properties and the construction of the plants involved many metallurgical problems as well as the conquest of natural obstacles in an almost inaccessible Montana country where roads had to be blasted out of the mountain side before machinery could be brought in. Within nine months production was under way at the rate of 75,000 tons of chromium concentrate a month. A second installation was planned.

In September 1943, representatives of the Metals Reserve Company served notice on the Anaconda Company that, at the request of the War Production Board and in view of the improved chrome situation and the current manpower shortage in other fields, the chrome program should be curtailed. The property was then shut down. It was held by the government as a stand-by protection to be put into operation should the necessity arise.

Copper, manganese, zinc and chrome were not the only vital metals poured by Anaconda into the giant maw of war needs. The company produced large quantities of lead, vanadium, bismuth, cadmium, arsenic, superphosphate, sulphuric acid, white lead, zinc oxide and molybdenum, all essential to the war effort, at rates which had previously been maintained and, in some instances, increased.

Up to the attack on Pearl Harbor, through the Preparedness Program and on into the War Production schedules, the astounding increases in the production of Anaconda mines and its subsidiaries and affiliates had all been achieved through the company's own efforts and expense. These increases amounted to an addition to the available supply of copper of approximately 400,000,000 pounds a year. In all the mines and plants the objective had been set for capacity production, regardless of the price which the government would pay for metals.

For the purpose of bringing about the expanded output of all vital non-ferrous metals and their fabrication, Anaconda and its subsidiaries authorized the expenditure of $27,346,562, of which $21,401,637 had been expended in the two-year period ending June 30, 1942. The remainder was employed for further projects in the following year. All these expenditures were made by the company and its subsidiaries upon their own facilities and were in no way connected with any projects undertaken with the government, nor did they involve the use of government funds.

The additions and improvements in mines and plants made by the company were practically all completed, with increased production achieved during 1943. With expansion marched salvage. Many thousands of tons of old tailings and mine dump material from the company's settling ponds in Deer Lodge Valley and dumps from the Butte mines, produced sizable quantities of copper which added to the available supply of metal for war at the rate of from 25,000,000 to 30,000,000 pounds of copper annually. At the slag treatment plant at East Helena 700 tons of hot slag, formerly regarded as waste, were treated for the recovery of zinc and lead.

A remarkable feature of Anaconda operations during the war period was the production of the Butte mines. In World War I the mines produced in 1916, 1917 and 1918, a total of 721,139,610 pounds of copper. In World War II, with the mines 1,300 feet deeper, they produced 917,757,849 pounds. This was accomplished in the face of a serious labor shortage and with the necessity of overcoming numerous difficult engineering problems which included hoisting ore from increased depth, higher temperature in the mines, pumping and ventilation.

During the war emergency period the company was frequently beset with manpower problems. At times big production could not be reached in various mining areas because of insufficient labor. This problem was accentuated when many of the younger employees were called up for military service. The situation was temporarily relieved when the military authorities, recognizing the vital requirements for non-ferrous metals, assigned many men, then in uniform who had been engaged in mining, to the mines of the company. These soldier-miners were afterward withdrawn. The induction of all young men from the mines into military service had a serious effect on production. Where output declined from peak figures the cause was almost invariably due to lack of sufficient manpower to operate at capacity schedule.

When Hitler invaded Poland in 1939 and set off a global war, the United States was war-wise in that it could make planes, guns, explosives, tanks, ships and could train men to be soldiers and sailors. It knew very little, however, about a metal which was to play a decisive part in the conduct and outcome of hostilities. That metal was magnesium out of which was fabricated the aerial incendiary bombs that rained terror and destruction upon hapless cities. One of Germany's first major advantages in the war was the ruthless employment of these bombs. By a kink of fate, they were the agency which brought about her defeat.

No chapter in Anaconda's history was more impressive than the production of magnesium for which it assumed responsibility. A detailed approach to this outstanding achievement is therefore necessary for an understanding of what was accomplished.

Although our knowledge and use of magnesium was meager when World War II started, the metal had been produced in small quantities in this country. The year 1915 saw the first commercial production by a well-known chemical company. Only a few tons were produced in that year. The cost of producing was $5 a pound. Under pressure of World War I needs the output reached 142 tons. After the end of the war production was curtailed and it was not until ten years later under the stimulus of a high level industrial activity, that the peak of the war years was surpassed. In 1929 the price of magnesium dropped to 55 cents a pound. With the advent of 1940 when Germany began her aerial warfare it had dropped to 25 cents a pound.

The first large scale anhydrous magnesium chloride plant ever constructed was built by the I. G. Farbenindustrie in Germany and was in operation prior to World War I. It later became one of the principal sources of supply for Hitler's *Luftwaffe*. The I. G. Farbenindustrie held the basic patents for the manufacture of the deadly bombs.

The British had made some progress in the production of magnesium. Magnesium Elektron, Limited, had built a thirty ton plant at Clifton Junction, England, after the close of World War I.

Magnesium Elektron, Limited, had been operating before the war in cooperation with the I. G. Farbenindustrie and the Imperial Chemical Industries, Limited, of England as a production concern for British military needs. When war was declared the German interest in the company was taken over by the British Custodian of Alien Property. During the early part of 1941 the British Government needed more magnesium to counteract the German hail of death but did not deem it safe to expand production because the enemy was bombing nearly everything in sight. With the consent of the government, representatives of Magnesium Elektron, Limited, were sent to Canada with plans to interest the Dominion authorities in the production of magnesium using the German process. The Canadian Government was not receptive. At this juncture the United States entered the magnesium picture.

It had become increasingly apparent to those responsible for the preparedness program in this country that large quantities of magnesium must be provided for the War Department. Imperial Chemical Industries informed representatives of the United States that they were producing some of the material that we needed. Washington then sent an agent to England to inspect the British production. British interests agreed to make their patents and processes available provided a suitable location and the necessary raw materials could be provided. They specified, however, that they would not operate such an undertaking in the United States. It was now up to Washington to translate the offer into action.

The first step was to locate a source of supply. The Bureau of Mines discovered that Basic Refractories, a small Cleveland concern, had been making refractories for some years but had never undertaken large scale operations. Basic Refractories was interested in some mining claims at Gabbs, Nevada, which were held by Basic Ores, Inc., a subsidiary. It was possible to obtain suitable ores from these claims. Defense Plant Corporation, a government agency, decided to locate a metallurgical plant between Las Vegas and Boulder Dam and to use these ores.

Basic Refractories had little knowledge of the processes necessary for the manufacture of magnesium. Imperial Chemical Industries supplied the know-how as well as the technical knowledge necessary for the building of a metallurgical plant. A new concern was incorporated under the name of Basic Magnesium, Incorporated in which British interests, through Magnesium Elektron, Limited held a 45 per cent stock interest and Basic Refractories, 55 per cent. The Defense Plant Corporation entered into a contract with the company to finance the construction of a magnesium plant and the development of the mines. Basic Magnesium was to manage and operate the entire project. The agreement was signed April 1, 1941.

The original estimate of the cost of the undertaking was fixed at $63,000,000. Within a year the Defense Plant Corporation had put more than $90,000,000 into the project. The specifications called for a maximum capacity of 112,-000,000 pounds of magnesium metal a year, with production to be in full swing by February 1943. British interests provided not only the design of the plant but sent representatives to the site, which was Henderson, Nevada, to assure the proper setting up of equipment and machinery. The American concern that took over management was beset with many difficulties. It was a case of a small company with a limited technical staff undertaking a colossal project. It did not work out.

Officials of the War Production Board and its Aluminum-Magnesium Branch realized the necessity of enlisting a concern experienced in large scale mining and metallurgical operations. President Husbands of the Defense Plant Corporation made a proposal to Anaconda to take over management of the project because of the company's demonstrated record and ability in the field of electrometallurgy. The proposal was made August 5, 1942, to Hobbins, then President of Anaconda.

While the Anaconda Company was not particularly impressed with the set-up of the magnesium project Kelley, as Chairman of the Board, directed that an investigation of the situation should be made by representatives of the technical staff as part of its policy to aid the national war effort in every way possible. A group of the highest technicians in the company, led by Laist, Vice President in charge of metallurgy, Clyde Weed, then Vice President in charge of mining, and Reno H. Sales, Chief Geologist, was despatched to the property in August 1942, to examine the plant and the mines and to study the processes which were being installed.

The magnitude of the project is gained from the fact that

the works under construction covered an area of four square miles in the desert and that 1,500,000,000 kilowatt hours of electricity a year would be required. It was in a location where this amount of power was available but had not been employed. It was more power than was used for all purposes in the states of Arizona, Colorado, Wyoming and New Mexico. More than 12,000 men were engaged on the construction job while 5,000 were later required for plant operation. A small city of 1,000 homes with hospitals, schools, stores and movie theaters had to be built.

The contract by the Defense Plant Corporation with Basic Magnesium, Incorporated, provided that The Anaconda Company should be paid a royalty of one-fourth cent per pound of magnesium metal produced. Basic Magnesium, Incorporated, was to be compensated for its management and operation of the property with a payment of one-half cent per pound on magnesium produced. It also received a fee of $300,000 for supervising construction of the plant. Anaconda had the benefit of an agreement with Defense Plant Corporation under which it might negotiate with the government for the purchase of the plant after the war emergency. This right was never exercised.

The Anaconda Company insisted that if the necessary agreements could be reached, it would undertake the management and operation of the plant on condition that it should not be held responsible in any way for the acts of omission and commission by the prior management, and that it would have no responsibility for the design of the plant then within nine months of completion.

These conditions were accepted by the government and a basis for taking over the interest of Basic Refractories was worked out. The Defense Plant Corporation purchased the mining claims of Basic Refractories for $450,000. Anaconda bought from Basic Magnesium, Incorporated, a 52½ per cent interest in the Cleveland company. These transactions occurred simultaneously. Anaconda now became manager and operator of the great government plant. A historic chapter in the annals of the company was now to unfold. All rights, patent uses and other privileges which Basic Magnesium, Incorporated, had obtained from the British concerns were continued in the company under Anaconda management.

Two of Anaconda's most efficient executives took over direction. F. O. Case, a distinguished chemical engineer who had been in the company organization since 1921, was named Manager of the plant. H. G. Satterthwaite, another outstanding chemical engineer, was appointed Assistant Manager. He joined Anaconda in 1916 and had done much of the experimental work in the electrolytic treatment of zinc and in the development of the leaching process.

The magnesium operation marked the entry of C. Jay Parkinson into the service of The Anaconda Company. He had been a highly successful attorney in his native Salt Lake City and had capably represented many important Western mining concerns. When the magnesium operation was undertaken by Anaconda, Parkinson was engaged as Counsel and became Assistant Secretary of Basic Magnesium, Incorporated. He became General Counsel in 1957.

In October 1942, the Board of Directors of Basic Magnesium, Incorporated, elected Hobbins President of the company. Laist became Vice President. Together with Kelley they became members of the Board. Major C. J. P. Ball, Chairman of Magnesium Elektron, Limited, and Edward Barnsley, Chairman of Imperial Chemical Industries, also became directors representing the British interests.

When all these arrangements had been completed and the Anaconda management installed, Hobbins received the following letter from A. H. Bunker, Chief of the Aluminum and Magnesium Branch of the War Production Board:

"May I take this opportunity to thank you for your willingness to assume responsibility for the management of Basic Magnesium, Incorporated, and for the expedition with which you have carried the negotiations through to completion. We invited the Anaconda Company to undertake this task for the government in view of your outstanding record of accomplishment in the fields of mining, electrometallurgy and efficient management, and your wide, varied and successful experience with large scale operations.

"In your assumption of the responsibility of managing and operating this enterprise, you may rest assured that you will have the full cooperation of the War Production Board and I feel confident that I may speak for the War Department and the Defense Plant Corporation in stating that they will furnish you and your organization with all possible help and support in your future work with Basic Magnesium, Incorporated."

H. P. Eells, Jr., head of Basic Refractories, issued a statement in which he expressed gratification that Anaconda had agreed to step into the management of Basic Magnesium, Incorporated. He added that "the fact that the interest of The Anaconda Company was developed by government agencies made no less welcome the prospect of its active participation in the Basic Magnesium, Incorporated, management." Barnsley, expressing the British view, wrote stating his company's satisfaction in the fact that Anaconda had agreed to take over the management of the project.

Basic Magnesium, Incorporated, made its first metal production on August 31, 1942. The peak of production was reached in September 1943, when output was at the rate of 120,000,000 pounds a year, substantially more than the original estimated capacity of the plant. Production of magnesium at the Nevada plant alone increased to eighty times the prewar level for the entire industry. When Anaconda engineers took over management and operation, they at once set out to simplify the operation and to reduce the pound cost of producing the metal. It was found that peat, difficult to obtain and brought from Canada, could be eliminated from the process without retarding chlorination. A substitute was devised for this operation, and equipment

similar to that used in the manufacture of phosphate fertilizer at Anaconda was installed and proved successful. It not
only saved the cost of the peat but it involved 85 per cent
less labor than was required in the preparation plant. The
cost of producing a pound of magnesium was substantially
reduced. This operation was typical of the economy and
efficiency that Anaconda know-how achieved. They included improvements in the electrical system, labor saving,
improved material handling which made production possible at one-third the original cost.

Ninety-five per cent of all the magnesium produced between 1941 and 1945 was made into bomb alloy or powder
which was later converted into incendiary bombs or tracer
flares. These were the bombs that beat the Nazis at their
own game of destruction.

Early in 1944 it became apparent that an overproduction
of magnesium metal had been reached. Great Britain
changed the construction of her bombs from magnesium to
phosphorous and other materials. The United States did
likewise and the great use of magnesium was discontinued.
Late in World War II oil bombs proved to be cheaper and
more destructive than those made from magnesium. Magnesium did not pass out of the picture, however, since it
came into use as an alloy and in the construction of air-
planes and other equipment where light metals are required.

Late in 1944 production at Basic Magnesium, Incorporated, was entirely cut off by government order and the vast
plant, which had hummed with activity, was idle. It had
well served its purpose for, from its confines had come the
raw material out of which had been shaped the agency of
destruction that brought Nazi Germany to her knees. Here,
too, the genius of Anaconda organization and efficiency had
laid its impress. A few years after the end of the war the
plant was sold by the government to the State of Nevada for
one dollar. It now houses a number of small industries.

While the Basic Magnesium plant was in production, the Defense Plant Corporation called upon The Anaconda Company to prepare engineering designs for an aluminum and magnesium plant to be constructed on a government site near Columbus, Nebraska. The design had been completed by the company engineers in 1943 when Washington announced that similar facilities, already installed, would be adequate to meet military requirements. The construction of this, and two other similar plants, was then suspended by government order.

During the period of the government's urgent request for the exploration of every possible avenue for increased copper production, officials of the Federal Loan Agency and the Office of Production Management asked the copper producers to submit for their consideration any known deposits of copper ores whether considered to be commercially feasible or not. On October 24, 1941, Kelley wrote W. L. Clayton, Deputy Administrator of the Federal Loan Agency, outlining all possibilities within the scope of The Anaconda Company's operations for increased production. The company had already put into effect its own program for capacity output.

Kelley described six possible projects involving five properties, either owned by Anaconda or by concerns associated with it. Three were selected by the Washington authorities as most likely to provide a quick and substantial increase in the government's copper supply. Two involved property of the Chile Exploration Company and one of the Cananea Consolidated Copper Company in Mexico. Kelley and Hobbins were asked to go to Washington for conferences with regard to these possible projects. The conferences resulted in the submission to the government of engineering plans and estimates for their development. The company notified government officials that it had found these proposals to be not feasible in the normal course of business. War needs, however, overrode this decision.

The first of the projects involved the production of 50,-000,000 pounds of copper a year at the Chuquicamata mine, in addition to the then regular capacity production there of 480,000,000 pounds annually. The second project related to the mining of a low grade ore body of unknown extent which, it was estimated, could produce approximately 300,000,000 pounds of copper by open pit mining. It was located on the property of the Cananea Company. The third project, also located at Chuquicamata, involved a tremendous production through the expenditure of a large sum for entirely new plant facilities to treat sulphide and oxide ores. This project was not carried through because of the length of time involved before production could be attained, and also the reluctance of the government to permit shipments of machinery and scarce materials abroad.

While negotiations on the first two projects were being carried on between the government and the company's engineering representatives, Kelley felt that the emergency need for copper was growing acute. On February 8, 1942, he wrote Clayton that he had determined, in view of the copper situation, that orders should be placed at once for the materials and equipment necessary at Chuquicamata and Cananea even though contracts with the government had not been negotiated or the terms agreed upon.

On February 14, 1942 Hobbins accepted the government terms on behalf of the Chile Company for the initiation of the first project which involved expansion of facilities at Chuquicamata. The contract was signed with the Defense Plant Corporation April 16, 1942. Despite difficulties of priorities and other obstacles, the project was vigorously pushed to completion. In January 1944, a statement of the company's production showed that 43,895,000 pounds of copper had been produced in excess of the Chile Company's base production of 400,000,000 pounds.

The second project which involved the undeveloped low grade ore body at Cananea encountered some difficulties before it got under way. Before definite agreement could be reached with the Washington authorities, it was necessary to ascertain the attitude of the Mexican Government with regard to the admission into the country of skilled labor, technicians and supervisory staff. No difficulty was encountered in this respect. From President down, the Mexican Government gave every assistance.

It was estimated that it would take two years to complete the construction of the project. This fact, in addition to the difficulty in getting the steel usually used in such construction, caused the project to be frozen by the War Production Board on February 25, 1942. In the meantime the Anaconda Engineering Department overcame the difficulty in obtaining steel by substituting reinforced concrete, the materials for which were available in Mexico. The project was reinstated in July 1942, after which a contract was signed by Metals Reserve Company and Greene Cananea Copper Company. Cananea Consolidated Copper then entered into a contract with Cananea Consolidated Copper Company, S. A., the Mexican subsidiary.

Development of the ore body by means of churn and diamond drilling indicated sufficient tonnage available for open pit mining to furnish feed for a concentrator having a capacity of 12,000 tons a day and capable of producing 54,-000,000 pounds of copper a year. In this project Cananea Consolidated Copper Company, S. A. undertook to assist in meeting the American Government's emergency requirements for copper without realizing any profit from the plant or from the ores while the contract was in operation. The preliminary engineering and design of the plant and part of the development of the ore body were carried on by the company at its own expense.

Despite the extraordinary demands of all these wartime requirements and the capacity operations on its own properties and those of affiliated concerns, the company did not depart from its custom of making its mining and engineering talent and knowledge available to others in the industry. Before the war emergency the Phelps Dodge Corporation had projected a large metallurgical plant at Morenci, Arizona. Anaconda engineers headed by Jurden assisted in making the plans for the plant and in the process under which it was to operate. Later, when the government called for expansion of the Morenci plant, Anaconda engineers continued to assist in the project.

Throughout Anaconda's far-flung organization there had been created a consciousness of the great need brought on by the war emergency that extended from top executives down to the lowliest laborer, and with it a determination to meet the challenge. Kelley and Hobbins had girded the company and all its subsidiaries and affiliates with the will to achieve what at times seemed to be the impossible, yet it invariably became possible.

The tremendous production of copper, zinc, manganese and other non-ferrous metals comprised only one phase of the company's war effort. These metals all had to be fabricated into the implements of war. The needs of the armed forces were almost endless. They included cartridges for small arms, shells for big guns, machine gun parts, assault and field wire, Signal Corps supplies, copper tubing for ship boilers, condensers, radio equipment, radar material and marine and other types of cables. The vast expansion of the Navy and the Liberty and Victory ship programs had to be met.

These demands did not come upon most manufacturers gradually, permitting them to build up facilities. They broke with all the suddenness and urgency of war. Happily, American Brass and Anaconda Wire & Cable had been preparing for the emergency. Both concerns performed prodigies of service for both Army and Navy. From 1940 to 1941 their production increased 69 per cent with all output under government control. This increase of 69 per cent in the output of fabricated, semi-fabricated and manufactured materials for war purposes was but the beginning of a vast production by American Brass. In 1941 the company shipped a total of 956,000,000 pounds of materials while in the next year it shipped 1,487,000,000 pounds. Shipments for 1943 were 1,768,000,000 pounds. So it went with each succeeding year, rolling up a record volume. The American Brass Company's peak of employment was reached in June 1943, when 19,933 persons were employed in the United States and 1,745 in the Canadian subsidiary.

At Kenosha, Wisconsin, the Defense Plant Corporation erected a plant for the Kenosha Brass Company, a subsidiary of American Brass, which increased production of brass cups and discs for cartridge cases from 126,000,000 pounds to 265,600,000 pounds a year. So great was the demand for small arms cartridges that another plant was fitted for production of ammunition cups and bullet jackets at the Buffalo branch of American Brass. Anaconda American Brass, Ltd. of Canada and Stripkill, Ltd., both subsidiaries of American Brass, contributed their full share of output of brass strip and discs. To accomplish the vast production of fabricated materials for both governments, American Brass and its subsidiaries used 767,000,000 pounds of copper in 1944. By 1942, 99.7 per cent of all the company production was for direct or indirect war purposes.

By far the greater part of the American Brass war production, and in peacetime as well, became raw material including alloys for other manufacturers. Only a small part and a slight fraction of its facilities were, and are, devoted to finished goods. The changes in company business as a result of the war needs of the government may be gained from the facts that production of sheet brass increased from 341,913,-000 pounds in 1941 to 700,659,000 in 1943. During the five years prior to the war, the average annual output of castings was 359,421,000 pounds while during the four war years it rose to 1,167,616,000 pounds. The increase in production of brass rods was on the same scale.

Vastly increased production schedules were the least of the many difficulties that beset Anaconda Wire & Cable as the demands of mechanized warfare broadened to include practically all the ingenuities developed by mankind down the years. The concern found itself plunged into an intricate and complex series of chemical and engineering problems which taxed the resource of the staff and forced it to adopt new principles and formulas for the production of commodities that had never been made before with materials entirely strange to the industry. Anaconda ingenuity overcame all these obstacles with the result that many wartime hazards were reduced and, in some instances, eliminated.

Anaconda Wire & Cable had been a peacetime leader in the field of insulating all types of wire and cable for use on land, under the earth and sea, and in the air. In a previous chapter the innovations in the manufacture of cables that searched out and detonated magnetic mines were disclosed. Under government order the wartime cables had to be insulated without rubber which had been the principal insulatory material of the industry. Anaconda found a wood pulp substitute and other synthetics. It was also necessary to find substitutes for tin, fats and practically all the materials that had previously been imported. The Anaconda Wire & Cable laboratory at Hastings-on-Hudson served the technical personnel of the Army and Navy as well as of the industry. At the request of the government the trade secrets and formulas which had been developed in years of study and research were divulged and made common property.

At the Hastings laboratory, company engineers developed a substitute for tin which enabled Anaconda alone to save annually 600,000 pounds of what had become a scarce and vital metal. This substitute—Anacondaloy—was so successful that the War Production Board requested the formula so that other concerns might make use of it. The process of applying lead alloy to copper wire for electrical conductors, another Anaconda innovation, was divulged so as to speed up the work of the entire industry for war.

All this research and investigation, and only a few striking results have been chronicled, constituted Anaconda Wire & Cable's vital contribution to the war effort. This contribution was made at the company's own expense. Its engineers engaged not only in laboratory work but in field trials as well. They witnessed the explosion of mines by the use of the new complicated cables, studied the possibility of erecting radio antennas of hitherto unparalleled dimensions and specifications on mountain tops and in remote places from which signals could be sent to the most distant points. This study was made to save steel towers. Some antennas, 600 feet high, more than a mile long and a fourth of a mile wide, were made by the company and proved to be successful.

The war demands made on the company necessitated the use of additional plant facilities. At the suggestion of the government, two plants were established and financed with Defense Plant Corporation funds. At Marion, Indiana, a plant produced field and assault wire in immense quantities for the Army Signal Corps. Company engineers devised an extruded type of synthetic resin for insulating. The plant at Sycamore, Illinois, produced Army field wire. Here Buna S was employed for insulation.

At all the principal plants of American Brass and Anaconda Wire & Cable, as well as at the great metallurgical works of The Anaconda Company at Anaconda, Great Falls, East Helena and the International Company's plants at Miami, flew the proud pennants of the Army and Navy, indicating that the "E" award for excellence in war production had been conferred upon them. They attested to the quality of the products turned out in the plants and the efficiency of their operations. The thousands of employees were cited for their skill and devotion to their tasks. A distinctive lapel insignia was awarded to each worker. Management was also recognized and extolled.

Besides the Army and Navy "E" awards, Anaconda Wire & Cable was the recipient of the Naval Ordnance Award "for exceptional service to Naval Ordnance research and development." The distinction was bestowed after the close of the war by Rear Admiral G. F. Hussey, Jr., as a result of the development of a secret device used in connection with magnetic underwater ordnance which represented long study, research and experimentation by the company's laboratory staff and engineers.

Throughout its far-reaching organization Anaconda had perfected plans formulated before Japanese bombs crashed on Pearl Harbor. Production had been increased beyond the expectations and estimates of the engineers. Vital materials, without which global war could not have been waged and won, were produced in quantities that have seemed fantastic to the peoples of other lands. The statement made by Marcus Daly in 1895, that the Anaconda structure was being built with thought for the public welfare as well as for profit, had been demonstrated during the period of the nation's peril.

♦ 11

WELDING THE EMPIRE

FROM that fabulous hole in the richest hill on earth at Butte where the foundation of The Anaconda Company was laid, stemmed mining properties that welded an empire of production. None of these annexations had so vivid a background in many respects as the Cananea group in Mexico in which the company crossed the border for the first time. Chuquicamata, Potrerillos and their sister mines in Chile had brought Anaconda into the international field. The entry into Mexico rounded out the world operations.

Cananea did more than add a jewel to the diadem of Anaconda properties. It projected the most picturesque character, perhaps, in all the history of mining whose career has become a legend. That character was Colonel William C. Greene. Father of Cananea, swashbuckler, gambler, extrovert, he became, for a time, the Industrial Czar of the Border in a story of spectacular success and ultimate failure that reads more like fiction than fact. His career may well form the prelude to the drama of Cananea in which for years he played the leading part.

Greene was born in Hornellsville in New York. When he was in his mid-forties he tired of the quiet life in his home town and went west. For a few years he drove ox teams in

Kansas, punched cows and fought Indians in Arizona and became part and parcel of frontier life. In 1890 he took a job at Tombstone, then in its most flourishing day. It was there that the smell of copper first permeated his system to remain for the rest of his life. For the first and only time in his life he practiced thrift and saved enough money to buy a small ranch near Hereford in Arizona four miles from the Mexican border. Here he accumulated a herd of cattle, married and started to raise a family.

Now came the incident that launched him in copper. One day some of his cattle wandered across the border into the grassy lands on the Mexican side. Greene mounted his horse and rode over after them. It was necessary for him to travel forty miles to reach his stock. When he caught up with them night had fallen so he decided to remain in Ronquillo settlement at the foot of the Cananea Mountains until the next morning. He put up at the house of an intelligent Mexican woman, the widow of General Ignacio Pesquiera. The general had come to Northern Sonora with a detachment of five hundred soldiers to clean out the hostile Apaches. While camped near the Cananea Mountains some prospectors brought him chunks of rich copper ore left by the Spaniards many years before. Like the Anaconda properties at Chuquicamata and Potrerillos, the area had been worked as early as 1784, perhaps earlier, and was part of an old royal Spanish grant. The Jesuit fathers worked the Cobre Grande mine in the eighteenth century. When the district was opened up in 1899 a mile of old workings was found in it.

The name Cananea has intrigued many people. For years it was generally supposed by Americans to be the Spanish equivalent of Canaan. Historical research refuted this impression. The name actually signifies an inhabitant of Canaan or a Canaanite, literally the scriptural appellation of "The Canaanitish Woman." Such a woman was supposed to live in the neighborhood several centuries ago.

Pesquiera, who later became Governor of Sonora, had

done some mining in various parts of Mexico. He realized that the district was worth developing so he acquired most of the mineral area and opened up seven mines. He built a small adobe furnace at nearby Ronquillo to melt down the ore. When his soldiers were not fighting Indians they sorted out the high grade ore and packed it down to the smelter on burros. Pesquiera melted down the ore with charcoal and sent the matte by mule train three hundred miles to Guaymas on the Gulf of California to be shipped around the Horn to Swansea in Wales where Daly had sent the first ore from the Anaconda mine. It was a long-drawn procedure but the ore was so high grade that it brought riches to the general. When he died in 1880 the mining operations at Cananea ceased.

Señora Pesquiera lived on at Ronquillo. She had tired of paying taxes on the mining properties so, when Greene turned up, she told him her troubles. Meanwhile, her visitor had cast an appraising eye over the district and noted that the stained hills resembled the area around Bisbee, which he had visited after his Tombstone days. The upshot of the talk with the widow was that Greene obtained an option from her on the Cobre Grande claim for $47,000. This transaction marked Greene's entry upon the Cananea scene which, before many years passed, was to make him rich and famous.

Greene then incorporated the Cobre Grande Copper Company, S. A., in Arizona in 1899 and also the Cananea Consolidated Copper Company, S. A., in Mexico the same year. He brought down two mining pals, Jim Kirk and Ed Massie, from Tombstone to help him launch the enterprise. Greene then went to New York to sell stock in his companies. He took an elaborate suite at the old Waldorf-Astoria Hotel and began to spend money lavishly, which was instinct with him. By this time he had become known as "Colonel Greene of Cananea." No one ever knew where or how he got the military title but it clung to him until his death. With his ingratiating, if blustering, personality, he gained access to the money kings of Wall Street, among them Henry H. Rogers and William Rockefeller who had started Amalgamated on its way at Butte. Greene made no headway with them. He kept on spending the money that came up from the Cananea property until his outlay far exceeded his intake. The story has often been told that when he was down to his last few hundred dollars he went to Canfield's gambling house, resort of New York's elite, to stake all he had left on the turn of the cards. Luck was with him for he came away with $20,000.

Lady Luck did not forsake him because a few days later he met Thomas W. Lawson. Greene and Lawson had much in common. They were both plungers, willing to take chances. Greene sold Lawson on the idea that Cananea meant millions. Lawson agreed to honor Greene's drafts up to a million dollars in return for short term notes and an option on control of 600,000 shares of Cananea Consolidated Copper at a third of its ten dollar par value.

Greene was now well heeled. Back at Cananea he started operations on his usual lavish scale. He planned a thousand ton smelter, a six hundred ton concentrator and started to build a railroad to Naco in Arizona forty miles away. He developed the Overnight and Capote mines. Greene was making the money fly spending, as was reported at the time, "two dollars for every dollar's worth of copper the smelter turned out." Lawson now reneged on the million he had promised Greene. This put Greene on a hot spot. He hurried to New York, interested John W. "I Bet a Million" Gates and his associates in the Cananea properties which now included Veta Grande, Cananea-Duluth and Elisa. Gates and his associates helped him sell his stock at $10 a share. Once more Greene was in the money.

Money, however, frittered through Greene's hands. In 1906 he was unable to meet his payrolls. He had spent $6,-000,000 and failed to complete plant extensions. The uncompleted railroad to Naco was sold to E. H. Harriman for the Southern Pacific in Mexico and finished by the new owners.

The year 1906 was momentous for Cananea for it marked the first steps that led to Anaconda's eventual acquisition of the properties. John D. Ryan and Thomas F. Cole had eyed the district with interest for some time. They knew the inherent value of the ore bodies and decided to investigate. In the summer of 1906 they visited Cananea and bought the America and Bonanza mines. They then organized the Cananea Central Copper Company and provided the $6,000,-000 necessary to clean up Greene's financial situation. They took the various Greene companies and merged them in Greene Cananea Copper Company. A substantial stock interest was provided for Greene. On February 18, 1907, he and his board of directors resigned from the various Greene corporations. The two concerns not merged in Greene Cananea Copper were devoted to stock raising and irrigation. In his grandiose days Greene had acquired a 500,000 acre ranch extending to the border where at times 40,000 head of cattle grazed. This property he retained to his death and passed into the possession of his heirs.

The Cananea mine continued to produce copper in large quantities. The Kirk, Veta Grande, Sierra de Cobre, Henrietta and Puertocitos mines were developed. Greene's vision and courage found ample justification.

In 1926 came the discovery that put Cananea on the map in a big way. It was the opening of the Colorado, one of the bonanza mines of all time. Its discovery was the result of one of the many chance episodes that give mining history a touch of the unreal and the fantastic.

A mine superintendent named William Catron was engaged in churn drilling near the known Veta Grande ore body. Sixty-three holes had been drilled without result. He then started on the sixty-fourth. At 900 feet where there was still no ore, he received instructions one afternoon to stop the work. Without leaving any instructions to his men, he quit work and went to a motion picture show in Bisbee. When he got back on the job the next morning he found that his men, having received no orders to quit, had continued drilling and had encountered an ore body assaying 7.5 per cent copper. This became the famous Colorado mine rivaling some of the great strikes at Butte in richness. When news of the Colorado reached New York the stock of Greene Cananea jumped from $10 a share to $170.

By 1928 the Colorado, of which there had been no surface indication, was proved, by the addition of several additional drill holes, to be a breccia pipe and was not only rich but extensive. Mining of the ore body was begun on October 15, 1928. The great mine earned dividends until 1944 when exhaustion ended its fabulous production. It had mined out 701,339,583 pounds of copper and was the largest high grade ore body on the North American continent.

Some years previous to the opening up of the Colorado, there had arrived in Cananea the man who was to make the camp a monument to high technical skill and outstanding management. He was Dr. Louis D. Ricketts whose name and achievements are preeminent in the Mining Hall of Fame, and rank him among the mining greats.

Ricketts graduated from Princeton as chemical engineer. His first instinct was to take on a professorial career. A friend, who sensed his talents, gave him the famous Horace Greeley injunction, "Go West, young man." Ricketts heeded it to become a premier factor in the mining development of the Southwest. He was a protégé and friend of the famed Dr. James Douglas and, like Douglas, enriched mining tradition. Between them they were responsible for the major part of the mining history of Arizona. No one ever rivaled him in the number of large and successful plants for the reduction of copper ore he built, or surpassed him in the flair for organization and in the selection and training of his associates and assistants. He was a constant ideal and inspiration for the men who worked with him. Nor is it surprising that he was chosen as "Arizona's most useful citizen."

Ricketts made many notable contributions to mining and processing. At Ajo he developed a process for leaching low grade copper oxide. In the Clifton smelter, which he built, he employed belt conveyors for the first time. While in charge at Cananea he first used a spreading bed for mixing the smelting furnace charge. All these innovations, and others, have become standard practice. It was Ricketts, together with William Wraith, Sr., and Frederick Laist, who made the survey that induced Anaconda to proceed with the development of Potrerillos. This was only one of the many important mining operations which invoked his rare judgment. Calumet & Arizona, Miami, Old Dominion, New Cornelia, Detroit Copper and many other properties bear, or felt, his constructive impress.

Ricketts' attire and general personal appearance belied the genius that reposed within him. He was tall, spectacled, lanky and lean. He wore a soiled slouch hat, soft shirt and khaki trousers that were never pressed. His pants always seemed to be falling down, for his belt seemed in constant danger of coming apart. The Mexicans called him "*Mal Cintado*," which means "Badly Belted."

Many stories were told of the mistaken impressions evoked by Ricketts' rough and unconventional appearance. On one occasion he was the guest of Ryan on his private railroad car. The train stopped at a station in Arizona and Ricketts got off to buy a newspaper. When he went back to the car the porter, who had taken over from the man who had started out on the trip, refused to let him get on, saying: "Move on. We don't haul tramps in this car." It was not until Ryan appeared that the great mining engineer was allowed to enter.

Such was the man whom Greene called to Cananea in 1903. The colonel was in dire need of skilled direction. He had come to the realization that his Tombstone associates lacked the technical training and experience equal to planning and building the smelter. Ricketts filled the bill. He built the plant and put the camp on a sound production basis. After he took over, as someone wrote, "efficiency knocked romance out of the window." Order was now to be the keynote. The fact that Ricketts was in command undoubtedly influenced Ryan and Cole to make the first investment in the district.

Up to the time of the Ryan-Cole entry into Cananea, Anaconda had no association with Cananea. Kelley had visited the camp in 1907 and was favorably impressed. In 1929 Anaconda named Ricketts, Wraith, Thayer and Robert E. Dwyer, who later became President of the company, to make a survey of the property. As a result, Anaconda decided to take over the property on the basis of one and one-half shares of Anaconda for one share of Greene Cananea Copper. This gave Anaconda what became a 99.40 per cent interest.

Colonel Greene passed from the picture. Despite his bizarre methods and his complicated financial operations that often involved him in desperate situations, he had vision and courage. He will live in mining history as the creator of an enterprise that gave opportunity for American skill and enterprise.

W. D. Thornton served for a considerable period as President of Greene Consolidated Copper Company, the predecessor of Cananea Consolidated. His father, Col. J. J. C. Thornton, had settled in Montana after the Civil War and amassed a fortune. W. D. Thornton graduated from the Mines School at Columbia and early displayed a keen flair for business. He became interested in the Great Falls Power Company and was associated with Ryan in the formation of the Montana Power Company. When Montana Power was sold to American Light and Power, Thornton turned to mining.

Ricketts had established a tradition of high service at Cananea. It was ably maintained by Clyde E. Weed who took over as President and Manager in 1929. A native of Moorestown, Michigan, he graduated from the Michigan College of Mines at Houghton. His first mine work was as surveyor for the Victoria mine in Ontonagon County, Michigan. This did not appeal to him so he transferred to the Superior mine of Calumet & Hecla, first as mucker, then as miner and later as shift boss. In 1913 he became mine superintendent of the Victoria mines. Up to that time all mine superintendents in the Michigan copper district were practical miners who had worked their way up through various supervisory posts. This was the first time this post was given to a college graduate and it was watched closely by all the mine operators in the Lake Superior copper region.

After two years at Victoria, Weed became superintendent of the Lake Copper Company in Ontonagon County, Michigan. Two years later he was made manager of the Hancock Consolidated Copper Company in the Houghton area. This mine was controlled by Ryan, then Chairman of Anaconda. When this property was closed down in 1920, Weed went to the Inspiration Consolidated Copper Company at Inspiration in Arizona as shift foreman. Now began the progressive ascent to high place. His next step up was as Assistant Manager. During his stay at Inspiration the underground caving system was revised. With slight modification this method is used in all the mining caves of the world.

During Weed's stay at Cananea the metallurgical plant was completely modernized. He developed the mining methods by which the Colorado output could be developed. There was considerable molybdenum in the Colorado area. Weed devised a process for the extraction of the metal from the copper ore. It was the first time that this had been achieved. The method became standard in all the copper mines that produce molybdenum from their copper ores.

Weed produced the first 200 tons of "molly," as molybdenum is called for short.

In January 1938, Weed was named General Manager of Mines with headquarters in New York. The post was established by the company to bring its mining practices up to date, and to consolidate all the mining functions. Four years later he was advanced to the position of Vice President in charge of Mining Operations. In 1949 he was made a director of the company.

During World War II much of Weed's time was devoted to service as liaison man between The Anaconda Company and the various copper departments in Washington in the effort to obtain more copper for the needs of the armed forces. In this he succeeded, for Anaconda's output in the war years was little short of phenomenal.

It had been known for some time that there were large low grade ore bodies in the Butte area not susceptible to mining by selective methods. Weed and Richard S. Newlin, his assistant, originated the idea of block caving in the district. The results will be indicated in a subsequent chapter on the Greater Butte Project.

The year 1952 brought fresh advancement for Weed. He became Vice President in charge of all operations. Considering the extent of the Anaconda empire, it is the biggest of all administrative mining posts. He became a Field Marshal, so to speak, in charge of vast operations that extended from Montana to Chile. His subordinate commanders were the managers of more than half a hundred properties; his field army the miners who delve above and below ground, and the men who operate the myriad plants. It is up to that army to produce the life blood of the company which is copper.

Weed has been the recipient of many honors. One of the most cherished is the degree of Doctor of Engineering from Michigan College of Mines and Technology. The William Lawrence Saunders Medal for achievements in mining was bestowed on him in 1951 by the American Institute of Mining and Metallurgical Engineers. In 1955 he received the citation for achievements in mining, employee relations and public relations from Michigan State University.

On May 24, 1956, Weed was elected President of Anaconda, a signal recognition of his eminent service. He is the first engineer since 1915 to occupy the post. All the Presidents had been lawyers or financial executives.

Weed took over from Robert E. Dwyer who had been President since 1952. When he retired Dwyer had rounded out fifty-three years of meritorious service in Anaconda employ. Born in Anaconda where his father, Daniel J. Dwyer, was a mason contractor, he first went on the Anaconda payroll as an employee in the blacksmith shop in the Reduction Works. The elder Dwyer was a partner in the contracting firm of Dwyer & Cosgrove. The firm put down the stonework for the foundation of the large hoisting engine at the Anaconda mine which was considered to have been one of the finest pieces of masonry in Montana.

Young Dwyer did not remain long in the blacksmith shop. He displayed a great aptitude for figures and his advancement began. During the following years he served in various capacities in the Accounting and Auditing Departments at Anaconda and Butte before being transferred to New York in 1918. He was appointed General Auditor of the company in 1922, elected Vice President in 1926 and Vice President and Treasurer in 1932. He was elected a director of the company in 1933, Executive Vice President in 1940, and President in June 1952. He was at the same time elected President of the Chile Copper Company, Chile Exploration Company and Andes Copper Mining Company.

During Dwyer's more than half a century of service in the company, there were many manifestations of the esteem and affection which he inspired among his associates and the concerns with whom he did business. One of the most notable occurred on September 17, 1953, the date of his fiftieth anniversary with Anaconda. He was presented with a parchment sheet on which was fastened a circle of fifty-one pennies, with the number 50 in the center. Below was this sentence:

"May these 51 little coppers symbolize a notable career with a big copper company, and express to you the felicitations of your friends in the Chase National Bank."

After the word "coppers" on the sheet was an asterisk to denote the following explanation: "Sorry one is steel. Anaconda was far too busy helping to win the war in 1943 to bother with pennies."

Although retired from the post of President, Dwyer remains in the company service to continue his wise counsel and to contribute the benefit of his long and rich experience. He is a member of the Executive Committee and a director in many of the Anaconda-owned companies.

Coincident with the retirement of Dwyer was the retirement of E. O. Sowerwine which ended a notable career of service for Anaconda covering a span of forty-nine years. Like so many of his associates in the company, he rose from humble job to high post.

Born in Cicero, Indiana, his early ambition was to study law. By working at odd jobs during the summer he earned his way through Wabash College. He then decided to teach school long enough to pay for a law course. He was attracted to Anaconda where he taught Latin and German in the high school. After school closed for the summer of 1907 he went to work for the vacation period in the Anaconda smelter office. When the employee for whom he substituted did not return in the autumn Sowerwine was given his job. The law, however, still beckoned to him. He hoped that by 1908 he would have sufficient resources to start in law school. Instead, he remained with the company beginning as Metallurgical Clerk. Later he became Chief Clerk and Cashier in the Tooele office. In 1919 he was transferred to the Executive Offices in New York. Now began a succession of advances that demanded financial skill and executive ability. Sowerwine met these requirements in exceptional fashion. His knowledge of company finance and operations became little short of uncanny. The year 1937 saw him Assistant to the President. Nine years later he was named a Vice President. He became a company stalwart, on call for services that required delicate and diplomatic negotiations. Two of them will serve to indicate what he accomplished.

When Anaconda decided to enter the fabrication field Sowerwine was selected by Ryan and Kelley to make a confidential appraisal of the value of The American Brass Company. At their direction he hired a suite of rooms at the Belmont Hotel in New York where he met with Brooker, Chairman of American Brass, John A. Coe, Sr., President of the company, and various other officers and accountants. The entire survey was conducted so secretly and confidentially that not a single rumor reached Wall Street until the transaction was ready for consummation.

The second outstanding service related to the Anaconda operation in Poland. A few years after World War I, Kelley's attention was directed to the opportunity to produce lead, zinc and coal in Silesia. Sowerwine accompanied Kelley to Europe in 1925. The negotiations for the properties had just begun. When Kelley returned to New York Sowerwine took over the negotiations which were delicate and difficult. Both the German and Polish governments were involved. He brought the transaction off and Anaconda set up massive operations with signal success. A Little America sprang up within Polish confines. Anaconda was now in full swing on three continents. The German invasion of Poland in World War II put a stop to operations. With the complete domination of the country by the Russians after the second global conflict the Iron Curtain was clamped down and the Polish operation became a war casualty.

On the day that marked Weed's elevation to the Presidency of Anaconda and the retirement of Dwyer and Sowerwine, W. Kenneth Daly was elected a Vice President of the company. He had been Comptroller of Anaconda and its subsidiaries since 1940. With only a high school education, he had entered the Anaconda employ in 1907 as an accountant. Later he became General Auditor. His rise to Comptroller followed. He is a Vice President or director in many of the Anaconda subsidiaries.

Daly's fiscal colleague, C. Earle Moran, Secretary and Treasurer of Anaconda, opened the books for the Guggenheims in 1914 when Chile Exploration and Chile Copper were formed. When Anaconda acquired control of the Chile Copper Company in 1923 Moran was Assistant Secretary and Assistant Treasurer of the company. He continued in these capacities until 1937 when he became Treasurer of the Chile companies. In 1945 he was elected Secretary of the parent organization and its subsidiaries. Upon the death of James Woodward, the Treasurer, in 1947, he was named Secretary and Treasurer of Anaconda and its subsidiaries.

When Weed left Cananea to assume his post in New York he was succeeded by Albert Mendelsohn, his onetime work associate in Michigan, who became Manager and President of the company. He has maintained the high standard of direction and operation set by his predecessor. His principal associates are Carroll P. Donohoe, Vice President and Assistant Manager of Cananea, and Robert C. Weed, the General Superintendent.

As is customary with non-Mexican operations in the so-called Prohibitive Zone of Mexico, which extends 100 kilometers wide along the border, the Cananea Consolidated Copper Company, being an American corporation and owning all the shares except directors' shares in the Mexican company, was obliged to form the Cananea Consolidated Copper Company, S. A., a Mexican subsidiary. This company owns, subject to the laws of Mexico, all the property and is the operating concern.

Today three mines are in operation at Cananea. They are Sonora Hill and East Pit, both open pit, and the extension of Republica C, which is underground. The blister copper is shipped to Mexico City to the Cobre de Mexico refinery in which Anaconda has a twenty-five per cent interest.

Production at Cananea has increased steadily. In 1954 the output was 59,760,149 pounds of copper while in 1955 it was 66,062,280 pounds. Every day 15,000 tons of sulphide ore are taken out. The mining area covers 60,000 acres and prospecting still goes on. Cananea also buys ore from small mines.

Adjacent to the mines is the town of Cananea with its population of 17,000 and its background of the Cananea Mountains, which were originally named El Cobre Grande and El Pinal. Like most Mexican communities it has the baseball fever. The town team won the pennant in 1955 in the Arizona-Mexican League. The Cananea Company subsidized the well-organized local hospital, which provides all facilities for residents as well as workers, and furnishes light and water.

Cananea not only contributed the most picturesque character in the category of mining magnates but has enhanced the enterprise and prestige of Anaconda in an alien land.

II

Another jewel in the Anaconda diadem is the Yerington mine in Nevada, the first copper mine of major proportions to be brought into production since the end of World War II. Starting literally from scratch and developed in two years, it represents an achievement unique in mine initiation and operation. The youngest full-fledged unit in the Anaconda empire of copper output, it has a string of innovations to its credit that rival those of many of its older sister mines.

The area of Nevada in which Yerington reposes is not new copper country. The red metal was found in the region a century ago. Prospectors and their burros ranged the area for years. In the Sixties when the bonanzas at Virginia City were disgorging fortunes, a considerable quantity of copper ore from the Yerington hills was sent by wagon to Virginia City. This operation put the town of Yerington, seat of Lyon County, on the map. Desultory work was carried on until 1930 when the Mason Valley Mines Company smelter at Wabuska, Nevada, was forced to shut down due to the low price of copper. The early mining was both glory hole and underground. Production almost petered out and the adjacent Smith and Mason Valleys turned back to farming.

Copper, however, was not dead. It was merely sleeping underground. In the late Thirties the General Development Company drilled five holes and found some copper ore. It was not considered of commercial value, however, and the operation came to an end. Judge Guild of the Yerington Circuit Court acquired the claims.

At this juncture the veteran William Braden, who had secured Potrerillos for Anaconda, once more appeared in the company picture. He had gone into retirement but retirement had no place in the Braden make-up. Aggressive, and with copper in his system, he yearned to get back into the mining game. Anaconda gave him the opportunity. He was engaged to look into the situation at Yerington. His report was favorable. He was therefore instructed to obtain a lease and option on the area and succeeded in making the deal.

Recognizing that the somewhat limited reserves and low-grade ores would not justify large capital investment in normal circumstances, Anaconda did not begin exploration and development until 1942 with the aim of augmenting the wartime copper supply, for World War II was in full swing.

The War Production Board decreed that the Yerington

output could not be ready in time to justify diverting scarce material for development and the project was shelved. On instructions from Weed, however, the Anaconda Geological Department went into action. An extensive exploration was begun under the capable direction of Alexander M. McDonald, an Anaconda geologist.

A thorough prospecting program was launched with diamond and churn drilling. An intensive study of the geology of the deposit started. Underground exploration was begun and a 400 foot shaft sunk, with lateral development on two levels. The ore body was then blocked out. Estimates of the grade and tonnage were made. Due to the existing economic conditions the decision was reached not to begin mining operations.

Early in 1950, and at the request of the government, Anaconda began actively to consider mining the deposit. All available exploration data was re-evaluated. The government also requested the company to develop, if possible, its own sulfur supply for leaching the oxide ore because of the acute shortage of elemental sulphur at that time.

Anaconda engineers studied all available sources of sulfur. The most likely find was 58 miles from Yerington at Leviathan in Alpine County, California. An option on this property was obtained from the Texas Gulf Sulphur Company, owners of the deposit.

Events in far-off Asia that were to project Yerington into a valuable producing property, were shaping. On June 25, 1950, the Communists invaded South Korea and the United States went to war again.

The government called for a stepped-up copper production. Again Anaconda heeded the call. The company reached the decision to mine the Yerington ore body. Although the development would cost $35,000,000 Kelley decreed that the company wanted no federal money.

Now developed an illuminating example of government cooperation with industry. A Certificate of Necessity was granted Anaconda by the government, which permitted the company to amortize for tax purposes 75 per cent of the eligible part of the cash outlay for construction, this amortizing to come within five years. The government furthermore agreed to buy up to 256,000,000 pounds of copper for at least 25½ cents a pound for the first six years of operation provided Anaconda could not sell this copper to industry at that price. Up to this writing copper has not dropped to the minimum price. Industry is taking all the copper it can get.

The exploration program showed between 35,000,000 and 40,000,000 tons of oxide copper. Below it was at least 15,000,000 tons of sulphide ore. As a result of further exploration and development, present ore reserves exceed the original estimate. Yerington's annual output is 65,000,000 pounds of copper.

When the decision to go ahead was made in November 1951, Albert E. Millar was placed in charge of the project. He had been with Anaconda since 1924. A graduate of the Mining Branch of the University of Texas, he had devoted the greater part of his career to open pit mining notably at Chuquicamata, where he was in charge of engineering and development. He was the ideal chief to take over and he amply justified the company's confidence in him.

Everything was now set to add Yerington to the mine map of Nevada. The first step was to select a town site. Appropriately it was named Weed Heights in honor of the man who, from the inception, had fathered the project and given it the benefit of his rare executive direction.

The first shovel dug into a blasted bank in June 1952; the first cement copper was hauled away in November 1954. In the space of two years Anaconda had brought the pit into production, developed the sulfur supply, built a town, offices, shops, warehouses and essential plants. Every piece of lumber, machinery, and all supplies had to be hauled in from the railroad twelve miles away. A miracle in a desert area had been wrought.

The mine was formally dedicated on November 10, 1953 with appropriate ceremonies and in the presence of a distinguished assemblage. Three hundred people were present. Millar was master of ceremonies. The speakers were Charles Russell, Governor of Nevada, Senators Pat McCarran and George W. Malone, Dwyer, and Weed. Among the guests were Congressman Cliff Young, Chester H. Steele, Vice President in charge of Western Operations, Colonel Floyd Rutherford, Chief of the Nevada Military District, and Commander Mayer of the Hawthorne Naval Base.

It has been said that "from the beginning of mining, water was both a blessing and a problem." The problem is nowhere more pressing than at Chuquicamata. In Western mining camps water is often difficult to obtain for plant use and other operations. Yerington has no such problem. The pit area to the southeast is rimmed with wells. The water supplies mine, plant and the town of Weed Heights.

Yerington is a triumph of planning because the ore body is so variable in grade. The mining, acid preparation, leaching and cementation flowsheet must be, and are, operated as one close-knit, coordinated unit. In short, from the time a truck load of ore leaves the shovel its entire course through the plant process has been planned and provided for. One of the significant factors in the operation of the mine is the demonstration of how effective engineering, blasting, and processing can profitably recover low content ores. The plant design at Yerington was created by Jurden, who worked in consultation with Laist and Frederick F. Frick, then in charge of research at Anaconda.

The copper precipitates are hauled twelve miles to the railhead of the Southern Pacific Railroad at Wabuska, Nevada, whence it goes by rail to the smelter at Anaconda. This is the longest haul of any precipitates for it covers 800 miles. Like most open pit mines, Yerington is an animated sight. The electric shovels steadily scoop up the ore, load it on trucks which, with their 25-ton loads, roar to the primary crusher a mile away. Day and night the vehicles maintain their thundering way. The crushed ore is moved on a feed belt for processing. Yerington's agglomeration process, which originated there, prevents segregation in the crushed ore.

The two sulfur operations, one at the Leviathan mine and the other at Yerington, rate special mention since they reveal some unusual features. First, the sulfur mine near Markleeville. Anaconda bought it in 1951. Leviathan had only been partially explored by underground work and diamond drilling before Anaconda took possession. It was decided to make it an open pit operation. An immense stripping operation was necessary before the mine could be opened. Since the mine was at an elevation of 7,200 feet it was difficult to get equipment in. An access road twelve miles in length had to be built from U. S. Highway 395 through virgin region. All difficulties were surmounted, however, and in less than a year the sulfur ore, at the rate of 1,600 tons a day, was rolling by truck to Yerington 58 miles away. Because of weather conditions the mine is operated only six months a year. Enough ore is trucked in during the favorable season, however, to insure a twelve months' supply. Six hundred tons of sulfur ore are used at Yerington every day.

Once at Yerington the ore is processed and the sulfur released. It is then processed again, the final operation producing sulphuric acid. The plant turns out 450 tons of the acid every twenty-four hours.

The Yerington mine is unusual for a variety of reasons. It began from the sagebrush; it was supplied and now operates entirely by truck since the nearest rail connection is twelve miles away. It is the largest copper mine ever planned from the start to recover all its output by iron cementation and to ship precipitates for treatment 800 miles to Anaconda. Its method of agglomerating ore fed to the leaching vats is original, unique and effective. In short, Yerington is a balanced job from shovel to copper precipitation.

Yerington has registered a number of notable mining and metallurgical firsts. It was the first to use rotary drilling exclusively for blast hole drilling in a porphyry copper open pit mine, the first to develop and operate on a large scale a low grade sulfur mine in the United States, the first to use agglomeration on coarse particles so as to make the costly erection and operation of a separate slime leaching plant unnecessary, the first to use trucks for transportation of tailing to the disposal area, and the first to make sulphuric acid on a commercial basis.

The capstone on the Yerington story may well be placed with a close-up of the town of Weed Heights. Here, to an even greater degree than in the mine, can the miracle of development be visualized. Like the mine operation, it is perfectly planned. As you walk through the well-planned streets named after Nevada cities, you see block after block of one to three bedroom houses, most of them with gay gardens; yet, within easy hearing distance, are the roar of trucks and the throb of machinery. All the 250 houses are company-built. There are also quarters for the bachelors. The rent to employees is low. Water is furnished without charge and electricity at cost. All the houses have the latest electrical gadgets, electric stoves and refrigerators. Weed Heights has its own post office. The wife of the General Mine Foreman is postmistress.

There are ample recreation facilities. Weed Heights has a swimming pool, tennis courts, a nine-hole golf course, community center and soft ball diamond. Nothing is left undone to provide healthy living, diversion, and the best working conditions.

All in all, Yerington provides a model demonstration of mine planning and operation. The transition of a waste area into a productive community was another evidence of Anaconda resource and enterprise.

♠ 12

THE GREATER BUTTE PROJECT

FOR considerably more than half a century Butte has loomed large in mining annals as the setting of the richest hill on earth, glorified in story and legend. The saga of American mining is written across the scarred elevation that looks down upon the bustling city. On Butte Hill delved the founders of Anaconda, leaving the impress and the measure of their vision and courage upon its sand and rock. They made Butte the Copper Capital. Here Daly made his bow to fame and fortune and laid the foundation of an empire; here Kelley embarked upon the long and distinguished service that stamped him as Mr. Copper; here Ryan demonstrated his genius of organization that projected him to the heights of the industrial great.

Since the first crude shaft was sunk in the flank of the Hill, a fantastic output of 21,674,000,000 pounds of copper, zinc, lead and manganese has been wrested from its stony depths, metals more precious today than ever before for the vital needs of war and peace. In the years that have intervened since Daly's day, Anaconda has extended its operations from the Rockies to the Andes. Impressive properties dot the company map. Chuquicamata is a prize exhibit. Yet, a particular sentiment has always attached to Butte Hill with its rich and opulent tradition.

Down the years only high grade ore was produced. All the while a vast and untapped treasure of 180,000,000 tons of ore lay deep in the depths of the Hill. It was so low in copper content that the cost of mining it by conventional underground methods was prohibitive. Here were 3,500,-000,000 pounds of copper for a metal-hungry America.

That untapped treasure of copper is now being mined through the operation of the Greater Butte Project, an undertaking involving an outlay of $27,000,000, which underwrites an impressive future for Anaconda in the place of its birth. To achieve it, Anaconda engineers have employed an adaptation of block caving, the low-cost method of mining already in use by the company in other properties. Thus has come about the resurgence of Butte and the continuation of its long and honored tradition. It writes a new chapter in the history of the richest hill on earth.

The first public announcement of the Greater Butte Project was made by Kelley at a civic dinner given in his honor on September 10, 1947, in the Silver Bow ballroom of the Finlen Hotel in Butte attended by 500 persons. Some extracts from it will disclose a preview of the historic undertaking. After reviewing the past history of operations on the Hill, Kelley said in part:

"It is always a pleasure to speak of successful past accomplishments and to predict success for the future. I have enjoyed tonight recalling the great industrial years of this community, but it is with the future that all of us are most concerned, and I propose now to speak to you of what will be the greatest period in the history of Butte, its future as affected by what I shall designate as 'The Greater Butte Project.'

"I have so designated it because to my mind it ushers in the greatest period of the long and exciting history of the richest hill on earth. It is an entirely new project through which will be recovered billions of pounds of metals which under existing methods would be lost to a needy world.

"The mining of the higher grade ores through many years had revealed large areas of lower grade copper-bearing material in and around the larger veins. As the mining of these veins proceeded downward, increasingly greater tonnages of this lower grade material were indicated in the pillars between them and in the surrounding ground. In these areas the copper occurs in a multitude of small veins and veinlets forming a 'horsetail pattern' and in the old gobs where the larger veins have been mined and filled. Experimental operations recently completed and still under way on this type of material in one of the Butte mines, have clearly demonstrated that the proposed method of mining will be successful.

"These low grade ore bodies have been accurately delineated by intensive studies. Exploratory openings totaling 20,848 feet of drifts and cross-cuts on nine different horizons were driven in and through the various zones. The material excavated from these openings was carefully sampled and subjected to exhaustive laboratory testing. A 500-ton test mill was put into operation at Anaconda, and 111,760 tons of the accumulated stockpiles of the excavated material were treated in it. The result is the assurance of more than 180,000,000 tons of this material available for mining by the proposed methods above the 3,400 level; that it can be successfully mined and treated and will return at least 20 pounds of fine copper per ton, together with substantial precious metal credits. This is the equivalent of 3,500,000,000 new pounds of copper which may be confidently expected from The Greater Butte Project above the 3,400 level, all of which are additional to Butte's copper resources as measured in the light of the present mining methods.

"It is also known that large tonnages of ore with similar grade and characteristics exist below the 3,400 level, but sufficient work has not yet been done to delimit these potential reserves. In addition, there are probably many more million tons of low grade ore in the Butte Hill, which may become commercial in the future as experience is gained through the operation of The Greater Butte Project.

"For the first time, through The Greater Butte Project, with the carefully estimated tonnages known to be available for the production of copper from low grade ore, there is now the assurance of a longer period of activity than it has been possible to state positively at any preceding time. With its high grade northwestern veins and extensive reserves of both copper and zinc and its reserves of manganese, it is now possible to visualize many years of a more varied and flexible mining operation than in the past."

It was Weed, with his discerning vision and Richard S. Newlin, his able assistant, who, in 1943, first sensed the potentialities of what became The Greater Butte Project. Serious problems confronted them. Since the key unit would include old workings there was a fire hazard. This was eliminated by filling the fire area with tailings. It was necessary to remove masses of old timbers and find a solution for dust accumulation. All these difficulties were surmounted.

Work was begun on April 17, 1948, after more than four years of exploration and research; the first ore was yielded April 26, 1952. Within the space of four years a mammoth undertaking that was to add a significant chapter to Anaconda history was under way. It was peculiarly fitting that the key unit should have been called the Kelley mine to commemorate the man whose name is so indelibly impressed upon the company advance.

The Kelley mine has been called a "monument to a bountiful natural treasure, a well-spring of technical progress." Such it is, for it is unique and distinct among mining properties, a triumph of new ideas and mechanical progress. In every phase of its construction and operation it has set a standard evoking the admiration of the world of mining. Furthermore, the Greater Butte Project has meant a Greater Butte as well.

To begin with, the Kelley mine is the first block caving mine in the Butte district. In view of the important part this type of operation plays in The Greater Butte Project, it may be well to trace its history. Back in the Nineties operators at Pewabie, Michigan, had, for some years, mined large blocks of ore by a procedure which made use of the available earth's gravitational forces for crushing the ore to a size suitable for handling. This was the concept of block caving in operation for the first time. Since then the concept has made possible the mining of large low grade ore bodies previously considered economically unsuitable for development, at greatly reduced mining costs and in serious competition with the open pit. Hence, its employment in the Kelley mine. In the Kelley mine block caving is used for the first time in old workings.

The area in which the Kelley mine is located is the Dublin Gulch on the eastern part of the famous Hill between the historic Anaconda and the Leonard shafts in the largest multi-fractured granite section of the Butte district. The actual site of the Kelley mine was selected because geological cross-section through this area indicated that it was free from faults, veins or other geologic structure that might cause ground movement in the shaft. It is also far enough from the mining area to insure safety from subsidence damage.

The Kelley mine embodies features that make it a model. The steel headframes are 178 feet high and stand out impressively amid the forest of frames that cap the Hill. The low-grade development demanded a shaft capable of producing from 10,000 to 15,000 tons of ore every twenty-four hours instead of the ordinary 2,000 tons. It was imperative that it be fireproof. The shaft, which has the largest cross-sectional area of any in the Western Hemisphere, is thirty-eight by nine feet and is finished in concrete. The mine is also partly concreted.

The mine has two shafts. What is called Kelley Number One has four compartments for ore while Kelley Number Two is for the workers and supplies not taken by One.

The Kelley mine taps a group of old mines that are rich in history and output. They are the ever-faithful Anaconda, Mountain View, St. Lawrence, East Colusa, West Colusa,

Tramway, and parts of Never Sweat, Leonard and Rarus. The ore occurs in two structural types, horsetail and wide vein zones. It averages twenty pounds of copper to the ton. At this writing it is down to the 1,300 foot level. It is proposed to go to 3,800 feet.

Two features of the Kelley mine stand out in any appraisal of the property. Dust is always a danger in a mine. In a coal mine it can produce explosions; in a metal mine it is a hazard to health, producing silicosis. In the Kelley mine this hazard has been eliminated so far as human ingenuity can accomplish it.

There is an electrostatic dust control, or rather collector—a Web Impact so-called—by which the dust is forced by suction on to plates and then washed off. Dust collecting units are installed at points where large tonnages are dumped into transfer raises, ore storage pockets, skip loading pockets and, on the surface, at the primary crushing plant and ore loading bins. The dust collector is an Anaconda innovation devised by John W. Warren and is made available to the industry. It is part of the elaborate ventilation system which is also a model of its kind.

The second outstanding feature is the electric railway system, another model of its kind, operated with almost uncanny efficiency. There is a central station manned by a dispatcher who has a battery of radio telephones. He knows the location and movement of every ore train. Haulage operations are directed by telephone. The dispatcher has a loud speaker and microphone in addition to his telephones. Before him is a 100 scale map of the entire haulage level upon which he can chart the movement of ore trains by inserting pegs at points indicated by the locomotive operator. The trolley wire serves both as a source of power and carrier for the speaker units on the locomotives and dispatch station. The installation enables the dispatcher to communicate at will with motormen. No train movement is made without specific clearance from him.

Development of The Greater Butte Project necessitated a reorientation of the company operations in Butte. All available manpower, which has been increased by 2,500 workers, is engaged for mining copper ore, working the zinc mines to the fullest extent and continuing manganese production on the largest possible scale. Production of copper from the low grade ore reserves embraced in The Greater Butte Project supplements the output from the regular ore of the higher grade ore reserves. This combined production of copper from both classes of reserve results in a more flexible and advantageous use of available manpower, lowered over-all costs and finally, assurance of a lengthened and more profitable life for Butte copper. In Kelley's words: "This is the most conclusive answer that can be given of Anaconda's faith in Butte and its confidence in the future."

The Kelley mine is not only an example of outstanding development but has become a showplace as well. Every day the Butte Chamber of Commerce arranges for a tour of the property by visitors who come from far and near.

The entrance of the Kelley mine into the field of low grade operation by no means reflected the passing of Butte's high grade resources. It is definitely an addition to them. The high grade ores are contained in a complex pattern of mineral veins which cross Butte Hill in several directions. For many years development procedure in these veins has succeeded in replacing every ton of ore mined with a new ton. The tonnage available for mining each year, therefore, has shown no decline. This is known as the Ton for Ton development procedure. Geologic evidence is that it can continue for many years to come. The mining of the high grade materials must necessarily be confined within the walls of the veins which contain them. The mining practice is by highly developed conventional methods in relatively small individual units distributed on several levels in several mines. However, fifty years of this kind of mining and the precise geologic mapping that has long been carried on, have revealed the immense importance of Butte's low grade resources.

In most of the district the vein pattern is widely spaced, that is, the individual veins may be from a hundred to several hundred feet apart, separated by wholly unmineralized granite. In the eastern part of the district, however, the geologic maps show that the fracturing and alteration of the country rock is much more intense. The pattern of the larger veins remains the same. In the spaces between them there are innumerable small veins and veinlets, far too narrow to be mined individually, although they contain the same high grade copper minerals as their larger minable counterparts. The areas which include this type of mineralization are so extensive that they are known to contain almost unlimited quantities of low-grade material which can be mined profitably by block caving.

The Kelley mine is part of the huge development that makes for a resurgent Butte. Second in the program is the Berkeley Pit project by which another large tonnage of low-grade copper is mined directly from the surface by large scale open pit methods. During the development of block caving the ore bodies of The Greater Butte Project for the Kelley mine, certain members of the Anaconda Geological Department, always alert along research lines, found indications that a thick layer of copper-bearing material, resulting from a process known as secondary enrichment, might exist in a large area to the east and southeast of the area outlined for block caving, and that it might be available for mining from the surface after the removal of the waste overburden. Accordingly, certain underground exploration into this area was undertaken. When this work proved encouraging, an extensive drilling program was inaugurated with the result that a relatively large open pit resource was outlined. It is known to contain in excess of 100,000,000 tons of minable low-grade ore. This is a copper content of 1,600,000,000 pounds. The area of the Berkeley Pit occupies the whole southeasterly slope of Butte Hill. It is quite separate from the area outlined for the block caving ore of the Kelley mine and is a separate project.

The drilling program started during 1954. In the southeast corner of the large area which was outlined, a preliminary pit was opened in 1955. After sufficient overburden had been removed, the first ore was shipped in December, 1955. The pit is being rapidly expanded and is shipping in the range of 5,000 tons of ore per day. This was increased to 10,000 tons at the end of 1956 and will reach 17,500 tons by the middle of 1957.

It had long been recognized that a large area in the northwest segment of the Butte district could not be properly explored and developed from existing operating shafts because the distances have become too great. Furthermore, it was known that large important veins, which have been highly productive in the adjoining mines, extend into this area. There was no shaft from which they could be developed. It was also recognized for some time that the present operating shafts have reached the point where they cannot efficiently mine, develop, and hoist the ore and waste from their own deep levels which, in some cases, have reached 4,500 feet. Certain underground developments from the present shafts indicate that additional low grade ores, both zinc and copper, would require additional hoisting facilities in the future. These were the circumstances that suggested the Ryan Shaft, named for John D. Ryan, which will be large like the Kelley, together with a somewhat smaller auxiliary one to be known as the Missoula Shaft near the present mining area and a short distance from Centerville.

The site selected for the Ryan Shaft is at a considerable distance from Butte Hill. It is located nearly a mile northeast of Big Butte, not because of any large new ore discoveries in that vicinity, but rather because of the lack of them. Its chief purpose is to provide adequate large scale underground haulage and hoisting facilities for the mining of the increased production of both copper and zinc ores which will be developed in this part of the Butte district. It will also provide relief for deep level hoisting at several of the older producing shafts for many years to come. It was essential, therefore, that it be located so that it will never be disturbed by adjacent mining operations. In order that it may fully accomplish these purposes, the auxiliary Missoula Shaft will provide facilities for service and supplies. It is suitably located for the development and mining in the northwest area. The ores will be hoisted through the Ryan Shaft.

The development is known as the Northwest Project. The Ryan and Missoula Shafts are only a part of it. It has nothing to do with The Greater Butte Project, the block caving operation at the Kelley mine, or with the Berkeley Pit.

The Special Development Program is not another project in the same sense as the Northwest Project, the Kelley mine or the Berkeley Pit since there is no construction in connection with it. Development procedure in the vein mines has long been the Ton for Ton Program. With the extensive hoisting facilities which the Ryan Shaft will provide, together with the addition in the future of certain secondary hoisting from deep levels, the production of vein type ore can be much greater than it is now. The Ton for Ton development will be accelerated to provide the additional ore to keep pace with the increased mining rate. This is what the Special Development Program is doing.

The program is exploring well-known veins, chiefly in the copper area, by advancing more drifts and cross-cuts from several of the existing mine shafts. It was started in March 1955, and has met with much success in adding substantially to the available copper ore reserves in the vein mines. Incidentally, it has also given important information regarding the potentialities of additional low grade ore resources which will eventually go into production when the facilities of the Ryan Shaft are available.

With the Kelley mine, the Ryan Shaft, the Berkeley Pit,

the Special Development Plan and the Northwest Project, there is projected a massive program of immense significance for the future of The Anaconda Company. It means increasing tonnage and, with it, a new prestige for the richest hill on earth. The tradition of Butte as a great ore producer is enhanced. Furthermore, in the Kelley and Ryan Shafts, the names of the two Titans of the organization are fittingly commemorated.

As Kelley put it: "Butte Hill will not only be digging copper for another fifty years, but will be digging copper when, with one exception, no other producing mine in the United States will be digging the metal."

At the head of all Western operations is Chester H. Steele, who is also a Vice President of the company. A native of Portland, Oregon, he graduated from the Montana School of Mines where he received his Engineer of Mines degree. He was also a graduate in Geological Engineering. He has been associated with Anaconda since 1916, beginning in the company's Geological Department and rising to be Chief Geologist. He became General Manager of Western Operations in 1952. His domain includes all the Montana properties, Yerington, the uranium operation at Grants in New Mexico, the Darwin and Tecopa properties in California, and the phosphate mine at Conda, Idaho. He has been intimately associated with the development of The Greater Butte Project and the kindred operations, contributing his rare judgment, keen sense of diplomacy, and rich experience.

This seems to be the appropriate place to detail some of the big facts about Butte operations. There are 2,422 miles of underground passage ways including 41 miles of vertical shafts. Every day 25,000 tons of copper, zinc and manganese ore are shipped from Butte. This tops the record of the old peak period. Butte Hill has produced more copper and silver continuously than any other district in the world. All this means that Butte is still the richest hill on earth.

Butte has not only produced a vast amount of metal but has also produced men of big caliber for Anaconda service. In 1924 a highly personable young man, who had graduated as mining engineer from the Colorado School of Mines, applied for a job with the company. His name was Edward S. McGlone. His first work was as mucker in the Tramway mine. Soon he was a sampler. Next came the advance to shift boss and later to mine foreman. From this point McGlone went onward and upward serving successively as General Superintendent of Mines, General Manager of Montana Mining and Metallurgy, and Vice President in charge of Montana operations. In 1952 he was named Executive Vice President.

Once in a commanding possition at Butte, McGlone displayed rare qualities as negotiator. He was particularly successful in labor relations. In this activity he was associated with Daniel M. Kelly, then Western General Counsel and later Vice President in charge of Montana operations, Roy H. Glover and Hoover. In 1944, McGlone received the Medal for Meritorious Service awarded by the Colorado School of Mines. He is President or Vice President of more than a dozen Anaconda corporations and a director of American Brass and Anaconda Wire and Cable.

To return to development in Butte, improvement in mine transportation has been achieved. Formerly the ore cars held only three-quarters of a ton and were hauled by mules and men. Today the cars each hold five tons with twenty cars in a train. The electrically driven trains in the Kelley mine carry a 100-ton load.

An important advance has been brought about in ventilation under Warren, who devised the dust collector. Ventilation is the life blood of a mine. In former days dust drifted in and out the apertures. Anaconda was the first operator to start wet drilling as opposed to the old dust-raising dry drilling. In the Kelley mine a 10,000 horsepower air ventilator sufficient to serve as utility for a city the size of Helena is in operation. The Mountain Con mine is completely air conditioned.

The Anaconda Bureau of Safety is highly efficient. Anaconda was the first metal mining concern to make an organized effort to prevent accidents, taking a leaf from medical prevention. Anaconda also was the pioneer to provide oxygen breathing apparatus for the protection of miners fighting underground fires. There is a Rescue House equipped with ambulance and staff to meet all emergencies.

One final detail is well worth mentioning. It is the School for Supervisors. Here mining methods, costs, efficiency, new equipment, ventilation, geology and maintenance of equipment are studied. There are also refresher courses for postgraduate supervisors. Supervisor conferences are held regularly to keep them up to date on all mine and company developments and new equipment.

II

The giant smokestack that towers over the town of Anaconda is the symbol of industrial might for, in this community, are located the greatest and most diversified reduction works in all the realm of metal. Here the clanking ore trains from Butte disgorge their freight for the chain of operations that process it into copper, zinc and manganese. The massive plants comprise a world of production that is a bulwark of The Anaconda Company's prestige. As is the case at Yerington, the town is the plants and the plants, the town.

Like Butte Hill, a sentimental interest attaches to Anaconda for it was the first outpost of what became the far-reaching Anaconda domain. Within its confines Daly launched his initial processing operation, built his famed Montana Hotel and his race track. The town was close to his heart for, you will recall, he spent a fortune in the unsuccessful effort to make it the capital of Montana. Thus it is something of a monument to the gallant Irishman who blazed the way for all that Anaconda signifies today.

In Anaconda all the company's ore in Montana is concentrated and smelted. There is no need to go into the intricate technical operations that transform ore into metal save to say that from bin it goes to the central crushing plant, then on through concentrator, roasting, reverberatory and converter installations. The product from the final reverberatory operation is blister copper, approximately 99 per cent pure but not yet pure enough for commercial use. It is cast into anodes used in the production of electrolytic copper at Great Falls. The zinc plant is divided into five main divisions—concentrating, roasting, leaching, electrolyzing and casting. In Anaconda there are manganese, phosphate, ferromanganese, sulphuric acid and arsenic plants.

Aside from being the greatest and most diversified reduction works in the world another distinction attaches to Anaconda. It was the first place where the flotation process was used in the United States. Flotation was an epochal process since it recorded the most revolutionary of all developments in metallurgy. As was the case in many kindred events, there are various versions concerning its discovery.

According to the story that persists, the discovery was made at Central City, Colorado by Mrs. Carrie Elverson, wife of a doctor whose hobby was prospecting. While washing out some ore sacks in a tub, she noticed a peculiar phenomenon—heavy mineral particles floated on the surface of the water instead of sinking to the bottom, as they would ordinarily. Being inquisitive, she started an investigation as to what caused the heavy mineral particles to float while the much lighter portions of the ore sank. The reason soon became apparent. In some manner the ore sack had accidentally come in contact with some oil, causing the mineral particles to become coated or filmed with oil. Mrs. Elverson reasoned that the oil coating or filming caused the mineral particles to float rather than sink, as their heavy gravity would cause them to do. The discovery led her to take out the original patent on the flotation process. After many years of bitter litigation, since Mrs. Elverson's claim to the first discovery was challenged, flotation came into its own, to change the entire process of ore concentration.

Four thousand men are engaged in the operation of the Anaconda plants which handle over 20,000 tons of ore a day. Eventually the capacity will be increased from 26,000 tons to 40,000 tons daily. In 1955 the Anaconda Reduction Department produced 252,255,787 pounds of copper, 153,-571,951 pounds of zinc, 145,274 tons of sulphuric acid, 89,-642 tons of superphosphate, 73,813 tons of manganese nodules, and large quantities of arsenic.

Among the many noteworthy features of Anaconda is the smokestack, largest in the world, erected in 1918–19. The first brick was laid by Ryan. It is 530 feet high, built of 7,-000,000 locally made acidproof bricks and can withstand a 100 mile an hour gale. The inside diameter of the stack at the top is 60 feet and 76 feet at the bottom. The walls are 22½ inches thick at the top and 64 inches at the base. The entire weight above foundation is 23,700 tons. You could place the Washington Monument in the nation's capital inside the stack and have room to spare.

As in every other community where it operates, Anaconda has bestowed many benefactions upon the town of Anaconda. The company built the local hospital, sold the plot for the Mormon church for one dollar, built the Mitchell Stadium, sold lots on the old Daly race course to workers at less than cost, and endowed and operates the Washoe Gardens.

Metallurgical processes of far-reaching importance have stemmed from the Research Department at Anaconda. In 1914 a research program was undertaken to develop a process for recovery of zinc and associated metals from the complex ores of the Butte district. This work resulted in the first successful commercial application of the electrolytic zinc process in the United States, and the building of a plant at Great Falls in 1916 to produce 100 tons of high-purity zinc per day. This was followed by successive enlargements of the Great Falls plant and the building of another plant at Anaconda, until now the combined productive capacity is 20,-000 tons of slab zinc per month, or approximately 25 per cent of the total zinc-producing capacity of the United States, and the greatest for any single company in the world.

Development of the electrolytic zinc process has made possible, and economically feasible, the treatment of vast tonnages of otherwise valueless ores throughout the world and has added tremendously to the mineral resources of Montana. Considerable quantities of lead and cadmium are recovered as by-products. Indirectly, it has added to the economic growth of the United States and to our ability to defend ourselves through making available large tonnages of zinc of higher purity than ever known before.

Another phase of The Anaconda Company's zinc production development is a process for recovery of zinc from lead blast furnace slags, developed in 1927 and first applied at East Helena, Montana, in 1928. The process has since been adopted by many lead smelting plants. The total zinc so recovered from what was formerly a waste product, now exceeds that from any of our states.

The establishment of a Research Department at Anaconda made it possible to investigate many other metallurgical problems. One was a process for the treatment of old mill tailings. The first commercial copper leaching plant was put into operation about 1914. Recently a plant using similar methods was constructed at Weed Heights for the treatment of low grade oxidized ore. Processes for concentrating and leaching copper ores which occur at Potrerillos were developed and subsequently embodied in plants constructed about 1925. The so-called "L.P.F. Process" for the treatment of partially oxidized ores from the Kelley mine is a recent major achievement of the Research Department and substantially increases the recovery of copper from such ores.

One of the problems at the Yerington property was the production of sulphuric acid from an ore containing native sulphur. This problem was solved by burning the ore in FluoSolids reactors which were first experimented with on a pilot plant scale at Anaconda. Such reactors are now also used for the production of acid from zinc concentrates. In order to utilize the acid which was being produced as a by-product from various concentrates, a process was developed for the manufacture of high grade treble superphosphate from phosphate rock mined in Idaho.

About 1940, the concentration of manganese ore was brought to a successful conclusion and the resulting concentrate was nodulized in a rotary kiln. The 56 per cent kiln product was sold under a contract to the United States government as well as to private concerns. It was an important contribution to the war effort since very little high grade manganese was being produced within the borders of the United States. Anaconda produces approximately 90 per cent of the domestic production of such ores. A part of the nodulized concentrate is smelted in electric furnaces to ferromanganese which is sold to the steel plant at Geneva, Utah, and elsewhere.

Obviously the post of General Manager at Anaconda demands ripe experience and high technical ability. Willard E. Mitchell fills these requirements. He, too, started from the ground up; his first job, after having graduated in mining from Washington State College, was as laborer in the Anaconda Reduction Department. Since then he has filled many important company positions, including Superintendent of the zinc plant at Great Falls, General Superintendent of the Great Falls and Anaconda Reduction Departments, and finally Manager at Anaconda.

Great Falls, Montana, is linked with Anaconda in a community of industrial interests. One supplements the other in many respects. Together, they comprise Twin Cities of Production.

Where Anaconda started from the bare prairie under Daly's stimulation, Great Falls was a going concern when Anaconda entered upon the scene. Early in 1891 the Boston & Montana Consolidated Copper and Silver Mining Company broke ground for the construction of a copper reduction works on the north bank of the Missouri River across the river from the east end of the town of Great Falls and about two miles from the business district. These works were built to treat ore from the company's mines at Butte. The ore produced copper and a relatively small amount of silver and gold.

During the summer of 1909 a new flue system including the present Big Stack, then the largest and tallest chimney in the world, was built. Although surpassed in size by the stack at Anaconda, it is a landmark for the Great Falls community and the nearby countryside.

In March 1892, the concentrator, roasting furnaces, reverberatory smelting furnaces and converters were ready to begin operations. A year later the blast furnace was completed, thus rounding out plant construction necessary for a chain of operations for the production of blister copper. An electrolytic copper refinery and a furnace refinery were installed. All these plants were enlarged in 1925. A few years previous, a plant for the production of electrolytic zinc was erected and enlarged until it is now the largest installation of its kind in the United States. A plant for casting copper billets for the manufacture of copper pipe and tubing was included. Thus, sufficient capacity became available to handle maximum Butte copper output through to finished shapes for the fabricating plants.

During 1910 the properties of the Boston & Montana Consolidated were taken over by the then Anaconda Copper Mining Company, now The Anaconda Company. The metallurgical plants at Great Falls became known as the Great Falls Reduction Department of The Anaconda Company.

In 1918 a mill was completed for the manufacture of copper rods, wire and cable made from copper produced at the refinery. The completion of this mill brought the industry at Great Falls to the point of producing a product ready for the consumer. In 1929 this mill was transferred to The Anaconda Wire & Cable Company which was formed in that year.

In 1955 a new modern mill, a model of its kind and the most mechanized mill in this country, was put in operation for the production of aluminum rods, wire and cable. A feature of this plant is the highly intricate mill of Swedish manufacture, the only one in the United States, for the production of aluminum rods. This mill, designed to roll 88,-200 pounds of aluminum rods each day, today produces 100,000 pounds. The aluminum comes from the Anaconda plant at Columbia Falls.

The Great Falls Reduction Department has the capacity to produce these amounts each month: 25,000,000 pounds of high grade zinc, 23,000,000 pounds of refined copper, and 150,000 pounds of cadmium metal as a by-product of zinc operations.

The Great Falls area of 7,500 acres is the only highly landscaped group of metal plants anywhere. The beds of tulips, geraniums and petunias and the lily pond form a lovely contrast with the huge stack with its streaming banner of smoke and the great buildings pulsing with machinery. Many of the walls of the plants are ivy covered. The former Plant Manager, A. E. Wiggin, was responsible for the landscaping. There is a nine hole golf course open to management and employee alike.

At the head of operations at Great Falls is Floyd S. Weimer, graduate of Purdue University in chemical engineering. His first work for Anaconda was in the Research Department at Great Falls. From research he went to operations as foreman in the zinc plant. Henceforth, he went steadily up the ladder efficiently filling various important posts until his elevation to be Manager at Great Falls.

Operated as a part of the Great Falls Reduction Department is the slag treatment plant at East Helena, Montana. Lead blast furnace slag is purchased from the adjacent lead smelting plant of the American Smelting & Refining Company. The zinc oxide fume is recovered and sent to Great Falls for the recovery of high grade metallic zinc. The East Helena plant rounds out the company processing operations in Montana.

The International Smelting and Refining Company, with its various plants, is an important factor in Anaconda operations. The copper smelter at Miami in Arizona and the Raritan Copper Refinery at Perth Amboy, New Jersey are impressive properties. At Salt Lake City, where F. A. Wardlaw is in charge, are the headquarters of what is known as the Intermountain area which includes half a dozen states.

The Tooele smelter, first constructed in 1909, is located thirty-five miles west of Salt Lake City. In conjunction is a concentrator where, under selective flotation, lead and zinc concentrates are produced. These concentrates go to the lead plant where the lead bullion is produced. The bullion is then shipped to Omaha, refined into lead and bismuth and returned to Anaconda for sale. Zinc concentrate is shipped by rail to Great Falls where it is converted into sheets of zinc metal. In connection with the operations at Tooele is a Geological Department which works in connection with the Anaconda Geological Department, particularly in the Intermountain area.

Diversified interests stem from the Salt Lake City office. Anaconda, for example, owns 56.97 per cent of the North Lily Mining Company. It also has a part interest in other properties in the Intermountain area and owns the Shoshone Group of zinc and lead mines at Tecopa, California, and the Darwin Group of zinc and lead mines at Darwin, California.

From the mines at Butte to Anaconda, Great Falls, East Helena, Tooele and Perth Amboy, extends a chain of operations below and above ground that produces a wealth of ore and metal that comprises a bulwark for The Anaconda Company.

♤ 13

GEARED TO THE ATOMIC AGE

IN WORLD WAR II the atomic bomb was an instrument of terror and destruction. Its unleashed fury not only wrought unprecedented havoc but literally shattered the Nazi dream of world domination. Few realized, after the horror of Hiroshima, that the deadly power which had created such vast devastation could be harnessed for constructive purpose. Awe and fear of what it embodied for the future were paramount. Yet, out of war's pitiless need, there has emerged an agency for the benefit of all mankind. "Atoms for Peace" is the most beneficent by-product of monster conflict and with it a whole new world of science dedicated to the advancement of industry, agriculture and medicine.

Nuclear energy, as nearly everyone knows by this time, is derived from uranium, today the metal of the hour. From it is extracted the power that will provide an increasing supply of energy for an energy-hungry universe.

History is alive with strange surprises that confute the prophets. In a well known American dictionary, published in 1936, appeared this definition of uranium: "A rare, heavy, white metallic element. It is never found native and has no important uses." Based on prevailing knowledge at that time, the definition was accurate. In view of what later developed with uranium, it was one of the prize understatements on record. In exactly two years nuclear energy was derived.

The sequence of discoveries that led to nuclear energy may well be summarized. In 1895, Roentgen in Germany discovered the X-rays that pierce solid matter. During the following year Becquerel, in France, discovered rays coming from uranium and its minerals. The year 1898 was noteworthy from the fact that Pierre and Marie Curie found a powerful source of radiation in radium. The final approach to nuclear energy was the discovery in 1911 that the atom had a nucleus. The break-up of the uranium nucleus followed and with it, the creation of tremendous energy. It remained for World War II to capitalize the use of that energy. With its adaptation to peaceful activities the atomic age was launched, defined by Sir Winston Churchill as "a turning point in our destiny"—the destiny of mankind.

The eyes of the world were now focused on uranium and the hunt for it got under way. The Curies had obtained their radium from the Belgian Congo which became a source of the much-sought metal. Other sources are Canada, Australia, Portugal, South Africa and the United States.

Nowhere has the search for uranium been so widespread as in this country. A uranium madness developed enlisting men, women, even children. What might be called the March of the Geiger Counter has enlisted a small army recruited from nearly every walk of life. We have had many rushes in the United States, the most notable having been the historic trek to California following the gold discovery there in 1849 and the no less frantic hegira to the Klondike.

The uranium rush has far exceeded those two adventures in fortune hunting in the number of people involved and the territory covered. It is history's greatest metal hunt. The Atomic Energy Commission has estimated that more man hours have been spent in the quest for uranium than were spent seeking all other metals in history.

Most of the prospectors are without any previous mining experience. So great is the fever for uranium that colleges are giving classes in prospecting for amateurs. Some of the novice prospectors have made bonanza finds and amassed fortunes. Towns have sprung up in prospecting areas. A new industry has developed to outfit the horde of hunters. At first, uranium gear moved through traditional mining equipment channels but the vast amateur turnout has changed it. Mail order houses, in particular, now list Geiger counters in their catalogs and sales have skyrocketed.

The amateur prospectors have been found in great numbers in the Colorado Plateau where a large amount of uranium is being mined. The quest, however, has spread rapidly to New Mexico, the Dakotas, Wyoming, Florida, Tennessee and Idaho. Canada has become one of the greatest magnets since some of the largest uranium mines now being worked have been located there. Thanks to huge uranium fields nearby, the onetime sleepy seasonal lumbering hamlet of Blind River, as someone observed, "has changed as if touched by a magic wand and hit by a steamroller." The place throbs with a Klondike fever and bustles with expanding life, action and business. It is one of the many results of the hectic uranium rush.

It was natural for Anaconda to become an important factor in uranium development. For well over half a century the company had pioneered in every phase of mining development with copper as its outstanding product. The advent into uranium meant that Anaconda, following its invariable policy, was keeping pace with progress.

Many important developments, particularly in mining, have resulted from chance meetings or casual remarks. Daly's unexpected encounter with Michael Hickey on Butte Hill, for example, led to the opening up of the Anaconda mine. So it was, with Anaconda's entry into uranium.

One day in 1950, Kelley attended a meeting of the Executive Committee of the Guaranty Trust Company in New York of which he is a director. As the members filed out of the Board room Luther Cleveland, Chairman of the Board and a director of the Santa Fe Railroad, remarked to Kelley that the Santa Fe had a uranium property in New Mexico. Kelley, always alert to any new aspect of mining, had already received reports from the Anaconda Geological Department concerning its uranium exploration on the Colorado Plateau.

Kelley, immediately interested in Cleveland's remark, asked him to arrange a meeting with his friend, Frederick Gurley, President of the Santa Fe, who was in Chicago, which he did. Kelley left that afternoon for Chicago. From Gurley he learned that the Santa Fe had made a uranium strike on Section 19 in the desert eighty-five miles from Albuquerque. This information was sufficient to speed Kelley into action.

First, however, the detailed approach to the Anaconda operation with its picturesque Indian background. The initial discovery of uranium in the Grants, New Mexico, area was in late 1947 although no public announcement was made until July 1950, when Paddy Martinez, a Navajo Indian, found some ore on mineral lands owned by the Santa Fe. The discovery was made in the Todilto limestone formation at Haystack butte, approximately fifteen miles west of the town of Grants, New Mexico.

Santa Fe immediately began to develop this discovery by surface drilling. By November 1950, it became apparent that the Haystack ore body was of sufficient size to justify the erection of ore processing facilities in the district.

Anaconda's entry into the Grants picture dates from early December 1950, following the talk between Kelley and Gurley in Chicago. A discussion between Kelley, Hoover, then President of the Anaconda, and Gurley, regarding the possible participation by Anaconda in the

Grants uranium development, followed. Subsequently, under authorization from Hoover, Richard S. Newlin met with Gurley and his Santa Fe associate, R. G. Rydin, Executive Vice President, in Chicago and was advised that Santa Fe would welcome erection and operation by Anaconda of a mill to process the Haystack ore, and that the railroad would aid the company in its prospecting and exploratory activities and its property acquisitions.

Prior to the Haystack ore discovery the Atomic Energy Commission had repeatedly requested Anaconda to undertake exploration and development in the Colorado Plateau and particularly in New Mexico and Arizona. In response to these requests several field investigations were conducted by Anaconda geologists. They indicated that, while uranium mineralization was widespread throughout these areas, actual ore occurrences were too small to permit sustained mining and milling operations.

The Haystack discovery, coupled with Santa Fe's desire to have Anaconda erect a mill near Grants, gave new impetus to the company's participation in the uranium field. Accordingly, in February 1951, Hoover informally discussed the situation with Jesse Johnson, Director of the Raw Materials Branch of the Atomic Energy Commission, in Washington. He affirmed Anaconda's willingness to aid the government's efforts to expand the uranium supply, then in critical shortage. Johnson assured Hoover that the Commission was not only anxious to have Anaconda's participation but that, by contractual agreements, the Commission would designate the company as its ore-buying agency at Grants. He further agreed to facilitate the erection and operation of an ore-processing plant by Anaconda under terms by which the company would finance all plant construction, and that the Commission would purchase all so-called U_3O_8 concentrates produced at a price to insure Anaconda's recovery of its plant investment, plus a reasonable operating profit.

Following the Hoover-Johnson discussion, an Anaconda policy decision was made for the purchase and the eventual processing of Haystack ore. An agreement was made with the Atomic Energy Commission for the construction of an ore processing plant near Grants. This decision was due to the vision, courage and leadership of Kelley and Hoover.

Once the decision was made, Anaconda geologists, under the direction of Vincent D. Perry, were sent to Grants and the adjacent areas to initiate an extensive program of prospecting and exploration. Newlin was authorized to undertake contract negotiations with Santa Fe and the Atomic Energy Commission.

To J. B. Knaebel was entrusted the entire supervision of operations. No executive in Anaconda service has had such a far-flung experience. He has operated properties in the Philippines, Mexico, Salvador, Nicaragua and our Western states. He joined Anaconda in 1946 and conducted intensive exploration and mine development in British Guiana and Brazil. The assignment to New Mexico took toll of his wide experience and proved ability. In June 1955, Knaebel was appointed Assistant to Vice President Newlin, who is in charge of mining operations with headquarters in New York. Albert J. Fitch, formerly Assistant Manager at Grants, was named Manager of the New Mexico operations, while E. C. Petersen, who had been General Mill Superintendent, was moved up to Assistant Manager.

During the spring and summer of 1951, while contract negotiations were in progress, aerial and ground reconnaissance by Anaconda geologists verified the widespread distribution of uranium mineralization in the Grants area although, except for the Haystack deposits, no important ore bodies were discovered at that time. This work, however, indicated the likely occurrence of small ore bodies on land owned by individual ranchers within a radius of some fifteen to twenty miles from the Santa Fe Haystack ore deposit. Uranium leases were thereupon negotiated by Knaebel for Anaconda, notably on the Andrews and Elkins ranchlands in Valencia and McKinley counties. Other early land acquisitions by Anaconda involved leasehold of large tracts owned and controlled by the New Mexico and Arizona Land Development Company. Programs of exploration and development by drilling and trenching were immediately started on these acquisitions. The Elkins and Andrews properties are the present site of the company-owned limestone production.

The manner in which Anaconda has carried on regional exploration in the Grants area is unique in ore-finding. In view of the tremendous areal distribution of uranium throughout the entire district, it was at once found that geological investigations could be undertaken most successfully by airborne prospecting. A few of the participants in the uranium rush, especially in Colorado, have used helicopters. In no area, however, have planes been employed to such an extent as at Grants.

The company uses planes suitable for low level flying. They are equipped with a scintillometer, that is, a Geiger counter which detects the radioactive emanations given off by surface, or close to surface, concentrations of uranium. Small plane exploration has been supplemented by use of a company-owned helicopter. A geologist usually accompanies the aviator. The observer has a tape recorder to record his observations. After these have been registered, the ground crews take over. The grizzled prospector of yester-year, with his burro, pick, shovel and pan, would rub his eyes and think he was dreaming if he saw an ore-seeking plane soaring over his onetime domain.

The most dramatic aerial discovery in the Grants area was the finding of the now fabulous Jackpile mine, which is located on the Laguna Reservation approximately sixty miles east of the Bluewater townsite. On November 8, 1951, Woodrow B. House, the aviator at Grants, took off in a Piper cruiser equipped with a scintillometer. He flew alone.

Before setting out Knaebel said to him, "Start flying over the outcrop of Morrison sandstone at the northern end of the reservation."

House then took off. In the area suggested by Knaebel he flew down an arroyo at ten feet above ground. Just over a float, that is, loose pieces of rock brought down by rain or erosion, the needle on his instrument began to go wild. House knew that he had struck it rich. He flew back to Bluewater and returned with Knaebel. They took some ore for assay at the company laboratory. It was found to be high grade. The Jackpile mine, largest in the United States and named for Knaebel, who is familiarly known as Jack, had been discovered.

The Jackpile mine is shaped like an hourglass. The upper part, called the North Jackpile, is larger in area with a low-grade ore while the lower part is smaller in area but with richer ore. The slot between the two areas is also rich in ore. The mine went into full scale production early in 1956 with the completion of the processing units.

The Jackpile is an open pit operation and is located in a uranium area comprising 115 acres. When you look at the grayish white and yellow ore it is difficult to realize that, within the piece of rock held in your hand, lies an element capable of releasing tremendous energy.

Rail connections have been established from Jackpile to the main line of the Santa Fe railroad whereby ore is rail-hauled from Jackpile to Bluewater and introduced directly for plant treatment and production of high grade uranium concentrates.

The discovery of Jackpile and the intensive exploration by Anaconda have given the town of Grants a big boost. The mile-long Main Street is alive with business and new construction. Already the natives call the place "The Uranium Capital of the World."

Early in the summer of 1951 the aerial investigations indicated the likelihood of important uranium occurrences within the Laguna Indian Reservation in an area sixty miles east of Anaconda's plant site at Bluewater. On the basis of the Laguna ore indications, Knaebel immediately began negotiations with the Laguna Tribal Council and local representatives of the United States Bureau of Indian Affairs in August 1951 to secure prospecting permits and leaseholds on the reservation. By an agreement dated October 18, 1951, Anaconda acquired prospecting permits on 410,587 acres of Laguna tribal lands for exclusive permission to prospect for, and to lease, under a sliding royalty scale, all uranium deposits discovered.

It was fortunate for Knaebel that his negotiations were carried on with a tribe of the high character of the Lagunas. They are a pastoral people, abhorring war, and have only fought, in bygone years, in self-defense. The tribe in New Mexico, which numbers 2,500, originally lived in what is now Colorado. A famine drove them southward to New Mexico which has been their habitat ever since.

The Lagunas are sober and industrious. Many of them cultivate large carrot farms. The crop is shipped to many points in the West and Southwest. The most cordial relations exist between Anaconda and the Indians. Virtually all the men employed at the Jackpile Mine are Lagunas. They are excellent workmen and possessed of quick intelligence. With proper training, they make skillful shovel, bulldozer and other machine operators. A considerable number of Lagunas are also employed at the Bluewater plant.

All the Lagunas have not concentrated on mine working or farming. Some have achieved reputations in the outside world. One of the most notable was Willie Surracino, a graduate of Carlisle, who became a crack pitcher for the old Philadelphia team. He won fame as both a right and left hand pitcher. He is now employed as a prospector for the company.

In Oklahoma the Indians, on whose reservations rich oil

wells have been brought in, have squandered their wealth. The Lagunas are the exact reverse. The Pueblo of Laguna has already received substantial money payments from advance rentals and royalties on ores mined on the reservation. The money is deposited in a bank in Albuquerque and draws interest. In time it will be employed in conservative investments.

Once the agreement with the Laguna Tribal Council was reached, a detailed program of exploration and development by surface drilling and trenching was started on the reservation. In light of later events, the Laguna uranium deposits were of tremendous significance, inasmuch as they led to the development of the Jackpile ore bodies which have proved to be the largest ore concentrations discovered to date within the entire Colorado Plateau.

It was necessary to make two other agreements for ore production at Grants. The second was with the Santa Fe, concluded November 29, 1951. Under it Santa Fe gave exclusive permission to Anaconda to purchase the Haystack ores. Anaconda, in turn, agreed to erect a processing plant to treat these ores. The agreement insured for Anaconda an adequate supply of ore feed to warrant construction of a plant at the Bluewater site. At that time the Haystack ore body was the only major concentration of discovered uranium ore in the Grants-Bluewater area. This fact, coupled with the availability of an adequate water supply, controlled the choice of the Bluewater location.

The third agreement, also negotiated in 1951, was with the Atomic Energy Commission whereby Anaconda contracted to become an ore-buying agent of the Commission and would erect the processing plant. With the three agreements all signed, Anaconda was ready to begin an operation of tremendous importance not only to the company but to the United States government as well.

In January 1952, Anaconda began the construction of temporary ore crushing and sampling facilities to fulfill its contract obligation as an ore-buying agent of the Commission. These temporary facilities were completed in May 1952, and were designated by public AEC announcement in June 1952, as the Anaconda Bluewater Receiving Station. Concurrently, Anaconda began construction of a Carbonate Leaching Plant for the processing of uranium ores and the production of a high grade uranium concentrate in accordance with contractual agreements with AEC. Since June 1952, numerous independent ore producers in the Grants area have been provided a ready market for their ores at the Bluewater Receiving Station.

The first processing of ores for high grade concentrate production began in October 1953, and since that time several enlargements of the processing facilities at Bluewater have been undertaken. An Acid Leaching Plant, designed and erected by Anaconda, has become an important unit of the Bluewater ore processing facilities. In December 1955, all plant construction at Bluewater was completed. The effective capacity of processing facilities was increased tenfold over those originally planned and designed in mid-1952. This fact is testimony to the aggressive planning and successful completion of Anaconda's contribution to the expansion of domestic uranium ore production for the benefit of the United States government.

The concentrate product is called "yellow cake" and comprises an aggregation of complex uranium compounds brilliantly yellow in color. Grants' "yellow cake" is sold and delivered to the Atomic Energy Commission's Raw Materials Depot at Grand Junction, Colorado. The AEC, at its Feed Materials centers, processes the uranium ore concentrates, that is, the "yellow cake," by complex chemical methods of refining into various forms of uranium fluorides and finally, the refining of these fluorides to uranium metal. The uranium metal is transferred to the Fissionable Materials centers of AEC where fissionable uranium—235—is recovered from the uranium fluorides. Fissionable plutonium is produced from uranium metal by neutron bombardment in reactors. A nuclear reactor is a furnace which releases the tremendous heat energy essential for industrial power development.

In addition to the ore-processing facilities, the construction program at Grants also includes the completion of a modern hospital clinic building comprising X-ray and dental facilities, electro-therapy, drug dispensary, surgical requirements adequate for first aid and emergency treatment, a four-bed ward, doctor's office, waiting and examination rooms.

This facility is known as the Bluewater Clinic and is an essential adjunct to Anaconda's New Mexico operations, since the nearest hospital is sixty miles away at Gallup. A full-time doctor is employed by Anaconda at the clinic, together with adequate nursing aid. Periodic visits to the clinic are made by a local dentist. The services of the clinic are available not alone to Anaconda employees but to other residents over a wide area adjacent to Grants.

At the Bluewater plant site more than eighty housing units have been constructed to accommodate Anaconda salaried personnel. These comprise three and two bedroom houses and also include an attractive single women's dormitory. Nearly a hundred families can be housed at the plant site.

All this construction signifies that Anaconda necessarily was required to build a small town, essentially from grass roots. All houses are modern in every respect, equipped with electric stoves, dish washers and natural gas, heating or cooking units. Townsite playgrounds and Community Center buildings are part of this program.

Anaconda's operation at Grants represents the first stages of uranium's journey toward a multitude of practical applications of nuclear energy not envisioned when that vast force was geared to war. Figuratively, the atomic sword has been converted into a plowshare, with benefits for industry, agriculture and medicine.

All the countries of the world are looking anew at their resources of natural energy as embodied principally in coal and oil. In the past, when national balance sheets were redrawn, the motive was often fear of exhaustion. Today that fear is vanishing because nuclear energy will provide replacement for what have been irreplaceable sources of energy. A new industrial revolution and a new economy are in the making of vast aid to all mankind.

The atomic industry, for such it is becoming, has been termed "a young octopus with tentacles that branch out all over the American industrial map." Universities have courses in nuclear engineering. At Oak Ridge there is a five-year-old school for reactor specialists. The atom business today directly supports 135,000 Americans and governs the lives of 700,000 others. It is a major source of income for 350 concerns. About 60,000 men and women are engaged in construction and 75,000 in the operation of nuclear projects. More than $80,000,000 of private funds has been spent on nuclear research. Many industrial firms have atomic departments. Such is the conversion of the atom into an obedient servant of man.

The greatest benefit to be bestowed by nuclear energy is power, especially for electricity. Its potency is obvious when it is stated that one ton of uranium is equal to 3,770,000 tons of coal. That the practicality of nuclear power is assured is evidenced by the fact that the General Electric Company of Schenectady, New York, the Consolidated Edison Company of New York City, the Commonwealth Edison Company of Chicago, and the Yankee Atomic Electric Company of Boston are building nuclear power plants. Already atomic energy is harnessed to practical use. The first American town to get atomic power was Arco, Idaho, which received its entire supply of electricity for more than an hour in July 1955. On October 19, 1956, Britain entered a new epoch in her industrial history when electricity, generated by nuclear fission, was added for the first time to her electrical system. In a historic gesture Queen Elizabeth pulled a lever that diverted power from Calder Hall, the world's first full-scale nuclear power station. A nuclear power driven United States Navy as well as railway trains are among the possibilities of the future. Such is the vista of the practical employment of atomic energy.

Two significant developments are represented in the United States Navy submarines, the *Nautilus* and the *Sea Wolf*, which are stoked by atomic power. A movement has been launched to permit development of nuclear-powered merchant ships to keep the United States in the forefront as a maritime nation.

Power for industry is only one of the beneficent employments of the atom. The frontiers of farm science and land development must be pushed forward at an ever increasing rate to provide for world population growth and improved living standards. World population is increasing at the rate of over 20,000,000 persons each year. Many peoples are underfed. All over the United States agricultural research is being stimulated through the use of radioactive isotopes. The field being covered includes fertilizers, soil fertility, moisture distribution, insect ravages, diseases of bees and disease resistance.

The power of the atom as applied to medicine has already saved lives. The most widespread application is for cancer where the potent rays of radioactive iodine are destructive to thyroid cancer. Heart disease, diabetes and arthritis may also come into the ken of diseases where isotopes can be beneficial. Twenty-two physicians from a dozen states have taken a course of study at Mount Sinai Hospital in New York on how to use radioactive isotopes in modern medicine.

Finally, and immensely significant, is the role that atomic power has begun to play in world peace. President Eisenhower's authorization of the sale or lease of 88,000 pounds of uranium, valued at $1,000,000,000, for peaceful production of atomic power, launched the beginning of an international accord that may have widespread consequences. It means that "Atoms for Peace" has long since ceased to be a phrase. It is being translated into a utility as potent for construction as it was for destruction.

Anaconda's entry in the field of uranium links the company with the activity that is reshaping the world of production and with it a new era in the march of man.

♤ 14

CHANGE AT THE HELM

THE YEAR 1955 was noteworthy in the story of Anaconda. During its passage the company earnings were the largest recorded since 1929. The aluminum plant at Columbia Falls went into production. The Greater Butte Project and adjacent operations insured a vast new reserve of copper ore. Processing facilities in the Grants area were completed. In Chile operations were expanded to replace the failing Potrerillos mine. Throughout the vast Anaconda domain advance in every activity was the watchword.

At this high plateau in company progress there occurred an event that marked an epoch in Anaconda's history. It was the announcement of the proposed retirement of Kelley as Chairman. Kelley made this announcement on May 18 at the annual meeting of stockholders held in the auditorium of the Employees Club at Anaconda. At the outset of his address he said:

"I am particularly happy that so many of you could come today because this meeting is one with a special significance for me and for the company. After having devoted more than a half century to the interest of our company, the time is now here when I wish to retire from my duties as Chairman. I have chosen this occasion to announce my retirement because this meeting affords me the opportunity to express my appreciation for the years I have enjoyed with Anaconda—years filled with friendships and associations that have contributed so much to the growth and success of our company."

With these words Kelley sent a shock through the assemblage. Tears glistened in the eyes of many listeners, company executives and stockholders alike. Just as his name had become synonymous with the name of Anaconda, so had it been linked with the chairmanship which he had held for fifteen years.

As Kelley stood in that crowded room and voiced his retirement as Chairman, memories must have rushed vividly across the tablets of his memory. In retrospect down the years he saw the dollar and a half a day water boy trudging at his task, the enchanted evenings when he heard the stories of mining related by Daly and his father, his underground work as surveyor, the proud day when he graduated as lawyer, his stormy experiences as criminal and mining lawyer, the part he played in the Heinze litigation, his rise in company councils, the close-knit association with Ryan, the entry into fabrication, his envisioning of the Electrical Age—all the milestones in his march to the top.

It was a notable career that passed in mental review on that May day at Anaconda, a career of industrial leadership vouchsafed to few and exceeded by none. There were company veterans in the room who had watched his rise to eminence, who had felt the impact of his dynamic leadership, and who had profited by his wise counsel. As industrial leader he had inspired the loyalty of a team for its captain.

It is not difficult to inventory the qualities that have animated Kelley's leadership. A great philosopher once wrote, "Where there is no vision the people perish." So, too, with a corporation. It was said of Daly that he could look into the ground. Kelley has the ability to look into the future. Throughout his career he has had the vision that foresees the possibilities of tomorrow and the courage to accomplish them. He dreamed great dreams and implemented those dreams. Economic depression never discouraged him. Rather did it become the incentive to expand and the expansion always paid off. He made Anaconda an industrial Gibraltar around which the business storms that dismayed others played in vain. Such was the Kelley who retired from the Anaconda chairmanship.

The retirement, however, did not mean relinquishment of service to the company. While life breathes in Kelley, it breathes for Anaconda.

At the insistence of the new Chairman the bylaws of the company were amended on May 26, 1955, to provide for an Executive Committee to be composed of five directors who should include the Chairman of the Board and the President. In addition to them, the members are McGlone, Kelley and Dwyer. At the request of the new Chairman, Kelley was named Chairman on May 26, 1955, and re-elected on May 24, 1956. Thus the man who stood at the helm of the company for so many years continues in a post of high service and importance.

Another change occurred at the annual meeting in 1955. The name of the corporation was changed to The Anaconda Company. Kelley explained the reasons in this way:

"In looking back over the many annual meetings of stockholders that I have attended, I believe the meeting of May 18, 1955, is the most significant. It is significant because this growing company will be sixty years of age on the 18th of June, 1955, and still is developing more rapidly than at any other time in its long and dynamic history. Growth and diversification of the industries in which it is engaged are so important that the present name of the corporation is no longer appropriate—it is, in fact, a misnomer.

"At the time Anaconda Copper Mining Company was adopted as the name of this corporation it was truly its appropriate name. The company was engaged primarily in the mining, milling, smelting and refining of copper ore. The Electrical Age was just beginning to develop and copper was needed in increasing quantities. Anaconda pioneered in large-scale production of the metal and helped to make available an adequate supply for the new industrial age. The mining and treatment of copper ores to produce metal and the products therefrom have continued to be major factors in the company's operation, but there has also taken place such a diversification of the company's operations that a change of name now seems imperative.

"The company, in its fabricating operations, through The American Brass Company and The Anaconda Wire & Cable Company, has become the largest fabricator of copper products in the world, and its research and development program has contributed much to the development of modern technology in the industry. These two large fabricating subsidiaries form the important manufacturing and marketing division of the company's operations. During World War II and the subsequent Korean conflict, demands were such as to tax the capacity of these units to the limit, and to necessitate postponement of continuing programs of rehabilitation that were followed in normal times. However, great progress has been made and improvements have now been largely completed with the result that these divisions are prepared for full participation in the growing markets for copper, brass and aluminum products.

"Most people think of Anaconda as a copper producer in Butte and are surprised to learn that our company in the Butte District has become the largest producer of zinc in the United States. Our plants at Anaconda and Great Falls, Montana, are the largest zinc-producing plants in the world. They account for 20 per cent of total domestic output. Zinc will continue to be important in Anaconda's operations as the ore reserves of the Butte District are considered the largest in the United States and Montana is now the leading zinc-producing state.

"With further development of the Butte mining area, the company became the largest manganese producer in the United States, accounting for approximately 90 per cent of the total production in this country. The production of ore in Butte and its processing at Anaconda, Montana, into nodules has been followed by the development and operation of ferromanganese plants in Anaconda and Great Falls, Montana. This project has contributed much to the economy of the United States and to the welfare of the company.

"During World War II and subsequently, it became apparent that the growth of the use of aluminum was such that it would be necessary to enter the aluminum business for competitive reasons. Our sales organization could then offer customers a line of nonferrous metal products that could meet the full range of requirements as to quality of product and price. With an adequate supply of aluminum available to us, and with development by our fabricating plants of facilities for fabricating aluminum, our companies will be in the position to recommend to their customers the best product for any particular application.

"Most of us were unaware of the thing commonly known as atomic energy until the bomb explosions which forced Japan to terminate World War II. Since that time the possibility of atomic war and atomic bombings has been in the forefront of newspapers and propaganda. The specter of death and total devastation envisioned with this newest weapon of mass destruction is not unlike the horror conjured up when poison gases were used and bacteriological warfare was threatened in World War I. The horrors and uncertainties of their use, however, were such that great nations went down to humiliating defeat in World War II without resorting to such tactics despite the fact that they were more accessible than the means of atomic warfare will ever be. In this already demonstrated natural fear of mankind of destroying itself, lies our hope for the future.

"Atomic energy, unlike poison gases and bacteria, has within it possibilities of benefit to mankind such as have never been afforded by any other of man's inventions. So great are its potentialities, that to my mind, we stand on the threshold of a new age—The Atomic Age. This new force, rather than annihilating mankind, will make life possible for countless millions on this earth who could not have been supported without this great factor for good. It opens a new vista that challenges the imagination. Industrial development can now be brought to the remotest places. Now areas otherwise rich in resources will have the means of obtaining the cheap and abundant electrical energy and resultant development of potentialities that have for so long been denied them.

"It is with this philosophy that Anaconda has turned to the development and production of uranium. Again the company has pioneered in its large-scale production with the thought and expectation that after military requirements for the defense of our great country have been met, this new source of energy will be available in abundant supply to be used for the welfare and betterment of the conditions of all mankind. These are the major reasons for giving the company a new name."

The chairmanship did not long remain vacant. On May 26, 1955, Roy H. Glover was named to the chief executive office in the company. Aside from his eminent fitness as counsel and executive, his elevation had peculiar significance for Montana, the state of his adoption. Montana is deeply embedded in the Anaconda tradition. Moreover, Glover succeeded to a post held by two distinguished Montanans—Kelley and Ryan. Like these predecessors, he has impregnated the conduct of the company with a typical Western philosophy of life and authority.

The reaction to Glover's appointment was fittingly expressed in Congress by Senator Mike Mansfield of Montana. On June first he addressed the Senate. Among other things he said:

"Another Montanan, Roy H. Glover, has been elected Chairman of the Board of The Anaconda Company. Roy Glover has earned this promotion through hard work, understanding and a keen awareness of the facts of life. A man of broad knowledge *** his great talents and abilities have been recognized in Montana, throughout the United States and overseas. *** It is heartening that in Roy Glover we have a man who is fully aware of his responsibilities and the opportunities for service they represent. He is a great credit and a real asset to Montana and to the United States. I join with thousands of other Montanans in wishing him Godspeed and good luck in the difficult years ahead."

On motion by Senator James E. Murray, also of Montana, his entire speech and many articles, news dispatches and editorials on Glover's elevation to the chairmanship which had appeared in various papers throughout the country, were printed in the Congressional Record.

The rise of Glover is in the tradition of self-made success that has contributed so materially to the upbuilding of America. He was born in Goldendale, Washington, July 15, 1890. His father, a freighter, died when the young Glover was barely fifteen, leaving the son as the sole support of his mother. They thereupon moved to Portland, Oregon, a larger community affording better opportunities of employment and education for a young boy. For the next ten years the young Glover successfully battled to support his family and obtain an education in the state where his ancestors had been pioneers sixty years before.

Those early years of Glover's life were packed with arduous labor. When he left Goldendale he had finished only the second year of high school. His periods in school were interspersed with, and accompanied by, constant employment in earning a livelihood. The fifteen-year-old lad needed desperately to make money. The time was at hand when the inheritance of a strong physique and a rugged constitution stood him in good stead. His work ranged from newsboy through telegraph messenger, farm laborer, steel cable splicer's helper, shipping clerk, cost accountant in a wholesale hardware concern, disbursement accountant for a railway company and cashier for a transfer company.

It was in this early period of his working career that Glover made his first corporate connection as laborer on the unloading dock of the American Steel & Wire Company handling carloads and trainloads of kegs of nails, barbed wire, telephone and telegraph bare wire, 215 pound kegs of steps for telephone and telegraph poles, carloads of reels of steel cables, and such other steel commodities as were manufactured and distributed by the company. It was the very hardest type of physical labor. His hours of work were from seven in the morning until 5:30 in the evening, with a half hour for lunch.

At first Glover was what was known as a casual laborer and received two dollars per day. After a few days when he had demonstrated his ability to do the job, he was placed on the permanent payroll at $50 per month. Having thus obtained economic security he enrolled in night high school classes to continue his education. From this time until his graduation ten years later from the University of Oregon Law School, Glover had two main objectives— work and education. At times he had to interrupt his educational pursuits to concentrate on a particular job and earn enough to make it possible to take another job that would not interfere with his classes. He found employers and school authorities generally cooperative. Whenever he was in school, however, he also had a shift of work either at night or at some time in the twenty-four hours through which he earned money.

Glover now found employment with the Pacific Telephone and Telegraph Company where he was successively clerk, first in the Commercial Department and then in the Plant Department. Shortly after his twenty-first birthday he was made chief clerk to the Division Plant Accountant, an office of more than fifty clerks and accountants, having jurisdiction of all telephone plant expenditures of the company in the States of Oregon, Washington and Idaho. Although in direct control under the Division Plant Accountant, Glover was the youngest person in the office. It was here also that he had his first direct contact with the legal profession in the preparation of statistical and economic data for rate and plant valuation hearings before the Oregon Public Service Commission. This early training was in later years to prove invaluable to his numerous corporate clients, including banks, transcontinental railroads, electrical and communication utilities, and numerous commercial and industrial concerns of which Anaconda was one. His subsequent phenomenal success before courts and juries and as counsellor, probably stems from these early experiences.

In 1910, Glover married Helen Henderson at Portland and both thereafter entered the University of Oregon Law School as classmates. Because of the excellence of their grades they were permitted to take the last two years of the law course in one year, provided they would maintain the same high scholarship standards as theretofore. The saving of a year was vital to the young couple in their economic situation. They graduated in 1915, she scholastically first and he, second in a class of more than one hundred. Her entire law school grades carried the unparalleled average of 96.8 per cent. The same year they were both admitted to the Oregon Bar. Brilliant of mind, with strength of character and a charm that has made her loved both here and abroad, Helen Glover has been the close counsellor and adviser of her husband down through the years.

After graduation and as soon as he could obtain a connection in a law office in that state, Glover moved to Montana. This was in the period of its homestead development. He first went to Havre in the law office of C. R. Stranahan and then to Helena with Wellington Rankin. World War I intervened and Glover enlisted as a private. After service in this country and overseas, he was discharged on May 24, 1919, as a sergeant. This period, from May 24 to June 1, 1919, had been the only period when Glover has not had gainful occupation since he was ten years old.

On June 1st following, he entered the service of the Great Northern Railway Company as a clerk in its legal department at Great Falls, Montana. At the time Glover entered the Great Northern legal department at Great Falls the office handled exclusively the railway company's business. He proposed that he should handle railway business as directed, but also that he should be permitted to develop a satisfactory personal law practice. This was agreed to by the railroad and his associates in the office. It was not long until this practice far exceeded that of the railway company, both in volume and in income. Glover rapidly achieved a statewide reputation as the young lawyer who could win lawsuits before courts and juries for either plaintiffs or defendants.

The law firm of Cooper, Stephenson and Hoover had long represented Anaconda and the Montana Power Company in northern Montana. In 1936, Harold Hoover, the youngest and most active member of the firm, was called to Butte to become Western General Counsel of Anaconda. He asked Glover to take over the law practice, including the representation of Anaconda and the Montana Power Company. This Glover agreed to do under an arrangement whereby Cooper and Stephenson retired from the firm and active practice. Glover became head of the firm which he continued under the firm name of Cooper, Stephenson and Glover. Headquarters for the Great Northern legal department were thereupon transferred to Helena. Glover and his firm were then named as counsel in Great Falls for the Great Northern and the Chicago, Milwaukee & St. Paul Railway Company, thus becoming the first law firm in Montana to represent two competing transcontinental railroads.

Came the war year of 1942. Hobbins and Hoover came to Great Falls in the fall and told Glover they needed his help. They asked him to leave his law practice and devote his entire time to company affairs with headquarters in Butte. Earlier Glover had tried again to enlist in the Army but had been rejected. The idea of a closer participation in the war effort through the production of metals had a great appeal to him. Also, he now had the largest and most lucrative law practice in Montana and the future seemed to lack the challenge of the earlier years. Without even inquiring as to financial arrangements, he agreed to go. He had tried lawsuits in each of Montana's fifty-six counties. During the last six and one-half years of his practice he had won every jury and court case he had handled, and they were myriad. He had by now become a lawyer's lawyer, frequently being called in by other lawyers to help them in their trial work.

This closed the first chapter. Glover chose Art Jardine as his successor in the law firm. Jardine was a lawyer with whom for two years he had been associated as a young man in the county attorney's office and with whom he had prosecuted many criminal cases. On January 1, 1943, he turned over to his junior partners and to this former associate the entire law practice.

Upon entering the practice of law Glover made a promise to himself that he would never refuse his services because of inability of a prospective client to pay, and that he would never take a fee from a person who earned his living with his hands. His early struggles had given him a deep sympathy for, and understanding of, the problems of people. This vow he kept throughout his career, even to the extent of paying court and appeal costs, in addition to donating his services in some cases. Even when he was representing banks and great corporations, union officials would come to him for counsel and advice and would bring members to him for help. This reputation followed him when he left Great Falls and today he numbers among his close friends high officers in the unions with which the company deals, as well as hundreds of workmen.

The year 1943 was eventful for Glover since it marked his first direct association with Anaconda. He became Counsel for the company. Two years after moving to Butte he was named Western General Counsel.

In 1951, Glover became Vice President and General Counsel. His rise to the chairmanship in 1955 recorded an advance rare in American industry. Within the space of twelve years he advanced from Counsel to the chief executive post in a great corporation.

When Glover became a Vice President of the company he began the service that ranks as an outstanding achievement in his career. To understand its significance it is necessary to know the dependence of the Chilean fiscal system upon copper production in the republic. As you have already seen, a change in the price of copper affects the equilibrium of the national budget. The tax from copper production exceeds $100,000,000 a year. It means that the relations between Anaconda, the largest copper producer in Chile, and the government, must be on a basis of mutual understanding.

The Chilean Copper Law required new interpretation and therefore, new legislation. Glover carried on the long negotiations with tact, diplomacy, and an awareness of the government's problems. In consequence he was able to make a constructive contribution to the economy of the republic that received wide approbation.

An illuminating comment on Glover's negotiations was made in an article published May 28, 1955, in *El Mercurio* of Santiago, the most influential newspaper in Chile. It stated in part:

"The fruits of his (Glover's) labor are incorporated in the Copper Law on which he worked enthusiastically and with infinite patience. On many occasions the discussions were suspended and seemed on the verge of crumbling and collapsing. Then one was able to observe his faith and character. He would again consult with his company in search of counterbalances that would permit negotiations to continue. During this entire period his sense of humor never failed him."

Out of Glover's negotiations there developed a friendship with Carlos Ibanez del Campo, President of the republic. It heightened the economic and political kinship between the two countries.

That the government of Chile appreciates the service rendered by Glover as unofficial ambassador of good will and economic relationship, is evidenced by a high honor bestowed upon him. On April 6, 1955, President Ibanez personally awarded Glover the rank of Knight Commander of the Bernardo O'Higgins Order of Merit, one of the highest and oldest in the category of Chilean decorations and rarely awarded to a foreigner. It was the only time the award has ever been personally bestowed by a President of the republic.

The decoration was given to Glover in a colorful ceremony in the Red Room of the Presidential Palace. The President spoke glowingly of Glover's merits, qualifications and services. The ceremony was witnessed by a distinguished assemblage. It included Mrs. Ibanez, the American Ambassador, Willard Beaulac, and other officials of the Embassy, the Ministers of Foreign Affairs, Economics, Agriculture and Mining, the Secretary of the Treasury, the Navy's Commander-in-Chief, the Secretary of the Interior, and Mrs. Glover.

A second honor bestowed on Glover ranks high in academic importance. On February 7, 1956, he became an Associate Member of the Institute of Political and Administrative Sciences of the University of Chile in another interesting ceremony presided over by the Rector of the University. The distinction identifies Glover intimately with the cultural endeavors of Chile and, as he said in his speech of acceptance, "gives me an authorized title to continue in a foreign land my permanent work of voicing the attributes of Chilean life." It is the only time in the history of the university that a foreigner has been so honored.

Glover's fellow citizens also have an awareness of his qualities as industrial executive. In a poll of state radio stations, owners and managers, conducted by the United Press, he was named Montana's "Man of the Year" for 1955. He was chosen from more than a dozen top leaders in the fields of politics, industry, education and social and other activities. The announcement of the award was made on January 2, 1956. Senator Mansfield made a speech in the Senate announcing the award and received permission to have the announcement, which appeared in *The Montana Standard*, incorporated in the Congressional Record.

When Glover became Chairman of the Board he brought to it a genius for getting along with people—plain and in the upper social bracket as well. It is part of his Western heritage. He has demonstrated this ability as company Counsel, as Vice President and as its chief executive. His flair for negotiation was never demonstrated to a greater degree than in the discussions with the Chilean government concerning the Copper Law. Glover knows and understands his fellow man. He is intensely human; his humor is infectious.

Glover's outside interests are hunting, music, reading, golf, trout fishing and horseback riding. The latter is reminiscent of days when he and his partners owned and operated one of the outstanding cattle ranches in Montana. He maintains a hunting and fishing lodge in the Sun River country of Montana, a rugged environment in keeping with one of the qualities that has made for his success. He is a rugged individualist.

Glover is Chairman of the Chile Copper, Chile Exploration and Andes Copper Mining Boards, and also a director in many of the Anaconda subsidiaries. He touches every aspect of the company's far-reaching activities.

With Glover as Board Chairman and Kelley as Chairman of the Executive Committee, the continuation of the policies that have given Anaconda its premier place in the mining and fabricating industry is assured.

⚵ 15

INTO THE ALUMINUM FIELD

ONE of the miracles of contemporary industry is the production and use of aluminum, often hailed as the metal of the future. Its growth has been little short of phenomenal. In 1938 the per capita consumption in the United States was 3 pounds; today it is 24 pounds. Although manufactured commercially for less than seven decades, it is now in universal use in a great variety of products from toys to skyscrapers. It has more than 4,000 uses in the home, on the farm, in the air and in business and industry. Approximately one million people earn their livelihood directly or indirectly through the output of aluminum products.

Aluminum projected one of the most romantic chapters in all metal history. It was so difficult to isolate aluminum that it was not until the early part of the nineteenth century that scientists were able to produce small quantities. The metal became more precious than gold and sold for $545 a pound. In 1825, Hans Christian Orsted, in Denmark, produced aluminum by a chemical process but development was slow. Napoleon III became interested and commissioned Henri Sante-Claire Deville to find a cheaper way so that he could use the new light weight metal for table ware and equipment for his army. No great progress was made, however, for by 1859 the price was $17 a pound which did not rate it commercially useful at that time.

It remained for two young men, working simultaneously and independent of each other, to unlock the secret that made aluminum available to the world. One was Charles Martin Hall who had just graduated from Oberlin College in Ohio. The other was Paul L. T. Heroult in France. By an interesting coincidence both turned to electricity as the most efficient way to obtain aluminum and, by another coincidence, each man in the same month and almost the same day, discovered the electrolytic process which is the basis for the present-day manufacture of the metal.

The background of the labors of Hall and Heroult adds a unique feature to the unusual story. Hall worked in a woodshed in the backyard of his parents' home in Oberlin, while Heroult conducted his experiments in a small tannery in Gentilly near Paris which he had inherited from his father.

Both young men were of limited means and struggled for two years before sufficient financial backing was assured to put the discovery to commercial use. Commercial production began in 1888. Advances in the use of electricity lowered the cost of electrical energy which paralleled the use of aluminum and reduced its cost.

Anaconda's interest in, and eventual entry into, the production of aluminum largely date from the company's endeavor to produce alumina, first from mill tailings and later from clay. At the present writing aluminum is manufactured from bauxite. Four pounds of bauxite make two pounds of alumina which, in turn, produce one pound of aluminum which has 61 per cent of the conductivity of copper. Aluminum is regarded as the most abundant metallic element, being found in rocks, clays and soils. Bauxite derived its name from the village of Les Baux in France where it was first discovered.

The principal sources of bauxite employed in the United

States are Surinam, Haiti, British Guiana and Jamaica. These sources provide 75 per cent of the total consumption in America. Bauxite is also found in Arkansas which produces the remainder of our supply.

Clay, however, may become a vital factor in the production of alumina in this country, thanks to Anaconda research. In 1914, Laist, with Russel B. Caples as an associate, initiated three research programs in a laboratory at the Anaconda Reduction Works at Anaconda. One was the production of electrolytic zinc from the complex lead-zinc ores of the Butte District; the second involved the production of phosphate acid and Treble-Superphosphate from phosphate deposits in Idaho, while the third dealt with the production of alumina from slime flotation tailings from the treatment of Butte copper ores in the Anaconda concentrator.

Shortly after the inauguration of the research program the demands of World War I for high grade zinc necessitated the deferment of the work on the phosphate and the concentration of all efforts on electrolytic zinc. The success of this effort is detailed elsewhere in this narrative. Laboratory work was now resumed on the phosphate problem and this, too, was later carried through to a successful commercial application.

Laboratory results on the production of alumina from concentrator tailings did not promise any degree of commercial application and work on the project was discontinued until it was subsequently decided to attempt the extraction of alumina from clays in the Spokane, Washington, area where they were available in large quantity and of higher alumina content than in the flotation tailings.

Results in the laboratory were sufficiently promising to justify testing of the process on a large pilot plant scale at Anaconda. This work was carried on from 1915 to 1920 and led to the belief that if alumina could be produced at a sufficiently attractive price, electric power could be generated in

Flathead County in Montana to supply an aluminum reduction plant for the treatment of alumina from clay. The consumption of aluminum in the United States at that time, and the availability of bauxite in Arkansas and areas in the southeastern part of the United States, made the Montana aluminum project a doubtful success in competition with established aluminum sources of supply. The project was therefore abandoned indefinitely.

With the establishment of the Anaconda aluminum plant at Columbia Falls, Montana, and its start as producer of the metal in 1955, The Anaconda Company decided again to investigate the possibility of providing its own supply of alumina from the domestic clays available in our Northwest area. It was known that large deposits of clay, having a higher alumina content than clays of the Spokane, Washington, area, existed near Moscow, Idaho. A re-examination of this district by Anaconda geologists and engineers was undertaken and samples of the clay sent to the Research Department at Anaconda. It was found that the Idaho clays were readily amenable to treatment by a process proposed by Laist. A small test plant was built at Anaconda to demonstrate the process on a scale larger than had been possible in the research laboratory. The expanded work was carried on over a period of many months and served as a basis for design of a pilot plant having a capacity for the treatment of approximately 50 dry tons of clay a day.

It was deemed advisable to demonstrate the success of the process on a semicommercial scale before embarking on a program designed to produce a supply of alumina sufficient to satisfy the needs of the Columbia Falls plant and for possible expansion of these production facilities. It had already been determined that there was a quantity of suitable clay available in the Moscow, Idaho, area to supply not only the needs of Columbia Falls but an expansion of equal capacity over an indefinite period of years. With the assured success of the clay treatment process as applied to clays of the

Northwest area where freight rates are a serious item of cost, the same process could be commercially employed in the treatment of clays of even higher alumina content located in other areas of the United States, thus reducing the overhead on transport.

All plans have been laid for the translation of the clay-alumina process into commercial production. In 1957 a large pilot plant will be erected at Anaconda. As commercialization of the formula progresses, the processing plant will be located in the Moscow, Idaho, area.

The development of a successful process for the production of alumina from clay in the United States is of paramount importance to the aluminum industry and to the defense of the nation. With the United States relying on the Caribbean area for 75 per cent of the bauxite required to supply its aluminum plants, and with the vulnerability of ocean lanes over which the bauxite is transported, to submarine and other attack, the freeing of the American aluminum industry from dependence on foreign sources of supply is of inestimable value. Furthermore, from the economic standpoint, continued depletion of the bauxite resources of the Caribbean area, now located advantageously to river and ocean transportation, together with the tremendous expansion of American aluminum production, will undoubtedly make it necessary for the bauxite producers in South America to go farther inland, thus increasing the cost.

The success of the efforts of The Anaconda Company to solve the problem of production of alumina from domestic clays brings to a fruitful conclusion all of the three original research projects initiated in 1914 at Anaconda. Two of them were outstanding. Electrolytic zinc marked an epoch in the advance of metallurgy. The clay-alumina process is likely to match it as a conspicuous achievement.

Always alert to Anaconda diversification of product, Kelley had watched the effort to produce alumina from clay with increasing interest. Back of his mind lay the desire to expand company output to include aluminum. The tremendous production of the metal in World War II which increased from the 300,000,000 pounds of prewar year 1940 to more than 5,000,000,000 pounds during the global conflict, crystallized his intention to go in for production of the metal.

Anaconda's approach to aluminum production was by way of the Harvey family. For some years Leo Harvey and his sons, Lawrence and Homer, conducted The Harvey Machine Company, fabricators of metals at Torrance, California. Leo Harvey had long cherished an ambition to go into aluminum production. He selected a site seven miles from Kalispell in northwest Montana as the site of his plant.

Harvey needed electric power so he obtained an exclusive contract for it from the Bonneville Power Administration which controls six dams in the Columbia River Drainage Basin. One of these projects is the Hungry Horse Dam from which Harvey was to obtain his power. Under existing rate schedules a plant must be located within fifteen miles of the power station in order to get the best power rate. Harvey's site near Kalispell met that requirement.

In view of the important part that the Hungry Horse Dam played in Anaconda's entry into aluminum production, it is important to know its story. It is a key project in the Department of the Interior's long-range program for multiple-purpose development of the water resources of the vast Columbia River Drainage Basin. The dam and power plant, constructed by the Bureau of Reclamation, is on the South Fork of the Flathead River and is a major factor in the control of costly floods on the Columbia River and its tributaries.

Hungry Horse is the fourth largest concrete dam in the world and also the fourth highest. It is 564 feet high and is exceeded in size only by the Grand Coulee Dam in eastern Washington, Shasta Dam in Colorado, and Hoover Dam in Arizona-Nevada. The dam forms a reservoir 34 miles long and 3½ miles wide at the widest point. It was begun in 1948 and completed in 1953.

There are several versions for the name "Hungry Horse." The *Hungry Horse News* published a manuscript obtained from David Prindiville disclosing that in March, 1901, two horses, Tex and Jerry, strayed from a wagon train while crossing the Flathead River's South Fork near Bad Rock canyon. When the two horses were found in belly-deep snow a month later, they were all ribs. A comment was, "That's an awful hungry horse country up there." A creek carries the name Hungry Horse. It then gave its name to a dam.

Leo Harvey had his power contract and the site near Kalispell. He also had a Certificate of Necessity, a document issued by the government at Washington on the assurance that the recipient proposes facilities for the national defense. The certificate was valuable because it made for plant depreciation for tax purposes within five years. Harvey also had a contract with Westinghouse for electrical equipment, likewise a valuable document, since the prices were lower than obtained at the time of the deal with Anaconda. Harvey needed the capital with which to finance his project. After much effort he found that it was impossible for him to swing it. Anaconda then began negotiations for the acquisition of Harvey's site and contracts in 1951. The final agreement was reached on January 25, 1952.

The Anaconda Aluminum Company, a 95 per cent owned subsidiary of Anaconda and representing a $65,000,-000 investment, was formed in 1953 with Caples as President. The directors are Kelley, Glover, Weed, McGlone, Caples and Parkinson. Vice Presidents named are McGlone, Steele, Parkinson and Mord Lewis. The Anaconda Aluminum Company was the first new concern to enter the American aluminum field since 1946.

It was a happy choice to place Caples at the head of the new operation. Like so many Anaconda executives he started literally from the ground up. A graduate of the Missouri School of Mines, his first employment was as mucker in the lead mines in the Coeur d'Alene mining district of Idaho; his second was as brick mason helper in the Brick Mason Department of the Anaconda Reduction Works. Then came his first opportunity in the Testing and Research Departments in the Anaconda Laboratory. He was Manager of the Great Falls Reduction Department when he took over the aluminum post. In 1955, Caples was named Vice President in charge of Metallurgical Operations, a post of distinction and opportunity.

The Anaconda aluminum plant represents another instance of how the company has transformed bare or forested areas into productive communities. The ground on which the plant stands was virgin forest. Today, where once pines, birch and tamarack flourished in sylvan solitude, machinery hums, trucks rattle, hundreds of men work, and ceaseless activity fills the air where, a few years ago, the only sound was the whisper of wind in the trees. Moreover, when Anaconda began its development, Columbia Falls, two miles distant, was a sleepy village of 637 people. Now, the population has passed the 2,000 mark and is growing.

It was immediately realized that the processing formula must embody the last word in operation. The first step was to study every aluminum plant in the United States and Canada to which Anaconda representatives could gain access. Laist supervised and directed many of the plant studies. He reached the conclusion that it would be advisable to study the techniques and plant designs abroad. To this end, in May 1952, Laist sent a group of four Anaconda engineers headed by the Chief Engineer, to Europe to study operations and procedures wherever possible. Subsequently, Satterthwaite and other Anaconda representatives went abroad to look into operations. After much investigation they found that the Pechiney process, used by the Pechiney plant at St. Jean de Maurienne, the largest in France, located at the foot of the Alps, was the most modern and efficient of its kind. The Pechiney process provides the most efficient ventilation yet achieved in the industry, collects fluorine gas precipitate for disposal and turns out a pure grade of metal.

A satisfactory agreement was then negotiated. It enabled Anaconda to make a complete and detailed study of the plant and, if Anaconda decided to go ahead with its project, to furnish the "know-how" with regard to design, plans, construction and, finally, the operation of the plant at Columbia Falls. Pechiney also agreed to send over personnel to assist in launching the enterprise. Upon completion of the contract Anaconda sent a team of men representing various departments to study the Pechiney plant in detail and observe its operation. Laist also made a trip to France to observe the Pechiney operation.

After the operation at the Pechiney plant had been checked again—it had reached 90 per cent efficiency as against 80 to 82 per cent in similar operations in the United States—Anaconda decided to adopt it. Meanwhile, the Anaconda Engineering Department in New York, one of the most efficient organizations of its kind in the world, had been working on portions of the new design. The site at Columbia Falls having been secured, and with adequate power assured, work got under way on June 9, 1952, reaching completion in the summer of 1955 when the first aluminum was produced. The site represented a prodigious task of reclamation. Hundreds of trees were felled in an area of 260 acres. Altogether the company owns 790 acres in the mill area.

The plant was planned by Jurden. Again there was a happy choice, this time in placing Satterthwaite in executive charge. He had ably proved his worth in the Anaconda magnesium enterprise in World War II. He was in charge of the aluminum plant construction and brought to the assignment his years of experience with the Anaconda organization.

The plant embodies the most modern, and therefore, the best in technical design and equipment. Architecture, production facilities and layout represent the culmination of Anaconda's many years of experience in plant design. The moving of material and equipment is a major factor in aluminum plant operation. The layout contributes much to the ease and efficiency with which this task is performed.

The alumina is converted into aluminum metal in two so-called pot lines, each containing 120 pots, and housed in four pot rooms. Altogether there are 240 pots which produce approximately 60,000 tons of aluminum each year. The plant uses 120,000 tons of alumina annually. It is processed from ore mined in Jamaica, British West Indies, and shipped to Columbia Falls from Corpus Christi, Texas, and Hurricane Creek, Arkansas.

Production is divided four ways. The Harvey concern has an option on part of the output. Anaconda's two fabricating concerns, American Brass and Anaconda Wire & Cable, use a considerable portion, while the remainder is sold in the open market in areas where the freight rates are reasonable. Anaconda Wire & Cable has five aluminum fabricating mills scattered throughout the United States. They include the new rod rolling mill at Great Falls. American Brass uses aluminum in its Connecticut division and is building a $25,000,000 aluminum mill at Terre Haute, Indiana.

A well-equipped laboratory is attached to the plant. It contains the most recent equipment available in the fields of analyzing and testing. Typical of the instruments provided is the Production Control Quantometer, a scientific tool capable of analyzing a sample for 16 elements within four minutes. Such instruments make it possible to closely control the raw materials coming in to the plant, the materials in process, and the finished metal. Facilities are also provided for special projects as requested by the various operating departments.

A $250,000 clubhouse has been built for the use of employees. It houses six bowling alleys, lounge and snack bar, as well as a recreation hall equipped with stage and motion picture projecting machine and screen. Lunches, committee meetings, dances, amateur plays, recitals and other forms of entertainment are promoted. The only prerequisite for membership in the club is that the person works in the plant.

The plant was dedicated on August 15, 1955, with appropriate ceremonies. It was an auspicious occasion not only in the advance of the company but also in the industrial annals of Montana. A distinguished assemblage attended the ceremonies over which Caples presided. Heading the list of guests was the Hon. J. Hugo Aronson, Governor of Montana. The roster included men notable in business, industrial and banking circles. Many came from New York to join in the tribute to the vision and courage that made the plant possible. Rarely has such a group been gathered for a kindred dedication.

The opening address was made by Governor Aronson. After detailing the resources of Flathead County he said:

"When The Anaconda Company decided to build this aluminum plant, the timing was excellent. Coming at a period when employment at government dam projects was declining, and when building was leveling off, the construction of this plant has helped to take up the slack in construction employment. Actual construction began the second quarter of 1953 with 11 employees drawing about $13,000 in wages. Then the pace began to quicken and monthly employment increased to approximately 644 in November, the highest month in 1953. The construction payroll for the nine months of 1953 was approximately $1,300,000. During 1954 the largest number of workers on the project was in the month of October with 1,604. The payroll for 1954 was over 4½ million dollars. The total payroll for the 24-month period ending March 31, 1955 was over 7½ million dollars. Because of this construction project, there was an expansion in other industries which created new jobs and additional payrolls. This dedication marks an era of steady new employment for an estimated 450 men and women. This will be a major addition to the economy of the Flathead and most certainly to that of Columbia Falls.

"The Anaconda Aluminum Company is to be congratulated on its foresight and confidence in Montana and in this area. I wish them every success in operation. May the relations between this community, and labor and management continue on a high plane. The unexcelled recreational facilities, invigorating climate, and abundant resources will produce a healthy, prosperous community, which in turn will add to the general well-being of Montana and the nation."

The response to the Governor's address was made by Robert E. Dwyer, then President of The Anaconda Company, who said:

"Governor Aronson, may I say that we of Anaconda are most appreciative of your generous and friendly statements. In the past Montana has been the birthplace of Anaconda's activities in the production of copper, zinc, manganese and other metals, and it is, therefore, peculiarly appropriate that Montana should again be the birthplace of another completely new activity, that of the production of aluminum. As much as any other reason for our determination to enter the aluminum field in Montana is the friendly spirit of cooperation that we find here, and that is evidenced, Your Excellency, by your address of welcome. We know that in expanding our activities in Montana we are developing our industry among good friends and good neighbors.

"I feel particularly privileged to attend the dedication in Montana of this new company enterprise for the reason that not only is Montana the state of my birth, but Anaconda, Montana, is the place of my first employment more than fifty years ago with The Anaconda Company. Also, my father before me participated in the construction of the first reduction plant of the company at Anaconda. Therefore, Governor Aronson, in responding to your warm and cordial address of welcome, I feel that I am doing so as one Montanan to another.

"This is a great day for all of us, bringing as it does to this beautiful Flathead Valley the beginning of the operation of the most modern aluminum plant in the world. It will provide a substantial and stable year-round payroll to this area which should materially benefit these communities and the state as well. The plant is located a distance from markets for its products, but we of Anaconda have confidence that whatever handicap this may imply will be more than offset and overcome by the fine and friendly feeling of cooperation and help that we may expect to encounter in this state of birth of our enterprises, and which has been so eloquently promised to us by Your Excellency.

"The activities of The Anaconda Company have greatly expanded since the days of my early beginnings in Anaconda, particularly in recent years, and it now has many branches in other states, Canada and Latin America. Yet, its roots are firmly implanted in this State of Montana, and this large plant which we are dedicating today, together with the new mining activities coming into being in Butte, make that root structure after seventy-five years of life, all the more firm.

"In these critical days of world affairs it has seemed that the maintenance of our Western civilization and the security of our country have required the greatest possible expansion in the metals industry. This demand has occurred during a period of economic as well as political uncertainties, and Anaconda has attempted to fulfill its full share of this demand. The principal contributions that we have been able to make have been in the Western portions of the United States and in our great sister republic of Chile. The financial demands to meet this program have been great, and one of the most important factors in our ability to meet the financial requirements of our expanding programs, has been the friendly feeling of cooperation and understanding of our needs and problems which we have encountered.

"May I express my pride and happiness in having the privilege of responding to the Governor of this Treasure State of Montana, and may its star in the field of blue of our glorious flag shine forever bright."

The next speaker was Glover. After relating the negotiations with the Harvey Company which he had carried on to a successful conclusion, he said:

"When the matter of transferring the power contract and obtaining the appropriate governmental agreements and authorization was undertaken, it did not take long to discover that other forces were at work and that there were designs upon the use of the Hungry Horse power outside of the State of Montana. A political battle-royal ensued. We had become convinced that unless Anaconda, with its existing Montana organization, built the plant there would be no aluminum plant built in Montana and that the power generated from Hungry Horse would be utilized outside the state. Others were apparently likewise of this opinion and every effort was made and every possible political string was pulled, in an endeavor to prevent us from engaging in this enterprise.

"On the other hand, the issues were equally clearly understood in Montana and we found ourselves in the fortunate situation of not only having the complete backing of the Governor of the State but also of our entire Congressional delegation, including Senator Murray, and the man who was then Congressman from the Western District, Senator Mansfield. Not only did we have this support, but the people of the state, headed by various organizations in the Flathead Valley, battled vigorously in our behalf, with the result that finally the President himself intervened and directed that the development of this plant should be permitted to proceed.

"I have in my possession a letter from Harry S. Truman, as President of the United States, to John W. Bonner, as Governor of the State of Montana, assuring Governor Bonner that the project would be permitted to proceed. I am sure that all of you know the many physical difficulties and problems that are involved in the design and construction of a plant of this magnitude, but it is seldom that the final determination to proceed is accompanied by such complications and difficulties; and may I say to you that even with the active opposition of his former chief, and of the likewise active opposition of his then chief, the

Secretary of the Interior, Dr. Paul Raver, the then administrator of the Bonneville Power Administration, never for one moment wavered from his determination that the power generated from the Hungry Horse project must be utilized if at all possible within the State of Montana. He considered this to be the intent and meaning of the Act of Congress authorizing and directing the Hungry Horse project.

"It happened that I was fortunate enough to be the person in Montana who was called upon to carry out the directions of my superiors in connection with the early days of the development of this project.

"Long before, Anaconda had departed from its original concept as a copper mining company. In checking back into the history of this company we find that from the time he became its chief executive, and even before, Cornelius Francis Kelley had been looking forward to an ever-expanding program of development and diversification. From a little mining company with operations on the Butte Hill it has developed into a world-wide enterprise of mining, smelting, refining, fabricating and the marketing of the products of non-ferrous metals; and here I wish to distinguish between the terms, growth of a company, and development of a company.

"Many times a company will grow merely because of production from physical resources it already owns, just as it may deteriorate from the lack of the proper use of its resources. On the other hand, the development of a company, such as I have in mind, and as has occurred with Anaconda, means imaginative and aggressive management with an inquiring mind and with a determination to go into fields of endeavor that are compatible with its organization and the purposes for which it was incorporated.

"This is the type of leadership that has been furnished through the many years by Mr. Kelley. The ever-expanding development and diversification of Anaconda have been the direct result of his leadership and, contrary to the general concept of the tendencies of mankind, his later years have been the most productive. At no other time during the history of Anaconda has it developed at the pace that it has during the past ten years, and this has been the result of the aggressiveness, the background of rich experience and the restless spirit of its chief executive. The dedication services this afternoon are the direct result of the free exercise of those qualities.

"It was Mr. Kelley who made the decision that this plant would be built; and the tougher the going and the greater and more complex the problems, the more was his determination that Anaconda would do the job. I had the privilege of being closely associated with him in this undertaking and of being able to observe at first hand his clear concept of what was to be accomplished and his determination to succeed.

"At this time nothing could be more appropriate and nothing could give me greater pleasure than to present to you, Cornelius Francis Kelley, Chairman of the Executive Committee of The Anaconda Company and the dean of American industry."

Early in his speech Kelley said:

"Today is destined to become historic in the industrial development of Montana. It ushers in the beginning of a new industry, the future of which cannot today be visualized but which, in my opinion, will be expanded and become a potent factor in the economic development that is bound to come.

"I am happy and gratified that this auspicious beginning bears the name 'Anaconda.' That name, I am proud to say, is significant with the progress that has made dynamic achievement in the art of mining, reduction and manufacturing of non-ferrous metals since its beginning on Butte Hill to its present activities on this hemisphere and the marketing of its products throughout the world.

"There is something symbolic about the name 'Anaconda.' I am constrained to believe there must have been a hope in the mind of that Irish prospector, Michael Hickey, when eighty years ago, he staked a mining claim on Butte Hill and christened it with a name that came from the pen of the great editor, Horace Greeley, when he used it to describe the movement of a great army planning for a victorious accomplishment. It is a name symbolic of accomplishment, and as it has been wherever it has undertaken to venture, so it will be here where we are dedicating this magnificent plant today."

This was the conclusion of Kelley's speech:

"The genesis of this undertaking was the availability of power, so, therefore, it lies in the melting snows that cover yonder mountains and cascade down the ravines and gulches to the valley, where they flow into a channel that now has been obstructed by one of the greatest concrete dams built by man. Here, gathered over thousands of acre feet, the water is permitted to flow in a turbulent stream and expend its energy in the giant turbines of the latest manufacturing skill, where it is converted to a mammoth output of electric current, part of which is transmitted at 230,000 volts to the bank of transformers at the plant. Here it is reduced to a controllable voltage of 13,800 when it enters the plant to pass through rectifiers that convert it into direct current to be used at such amperage and voltage as may be required for the particular job to be done.

"This plant should be described simply as a vast assembling of materials of various kinds from many different geographic locations which are brought together for the purpose of being so mixed and blended in proper proportions that in the process of electrolyzing, various chemical reactions will occur that will result finally in a product of aluminum metal of exceptional purity. This metal will find its way into many channels of economic use.

"We trust those products will add to the comfort and convenience of mankind, that they will help improve the standard of living of all in a world of peace and prosperity. And should, and I trust that God will forbid, the plant's production be needed for the national defense, we consign it, every pound of it, for that purpose.

"And now, with construction practically finished and operations started, we dedicate this plant with, I am sure, what is the heartfelt wish of everyone here assembled, that it will have a long, successful life for the purposes for which it was conceived and built."

Altogether, it was a festive and memorable day in the history of Columbia Falls and the Flathead Valley. More than five thousand people, coming from near and far, inspected the plant and marvelled at its wonders.

For well over half a century Anaconda had been a household word in Montana. On that August day in 1955, the company added a new star to its crown of achievement within the confines of the state.

♠ 16

ANACONDA ON THE MARCH

THE PANORAMA of Anaconda, with its sequences of color, drama and adventure, has now passed in review. Its achievement could never have been possible without the stimulus of Free Enterprise which has provided the incentive for advance in American industry. The aftermath of political freedom, won from Bunker Hill to Yorktown, has spelled economic freedom as well. It has meant initiative, and the encouragement of initiative, with rewarded success and untrammeled opportunity, not for a privileged few or for the "vested interests" of the demagogue, but opportunity for all. Thus, Free Enterprise has become the American Economic Bill of Rights, an unwritten mandate for individual and corporate progress.

For more than sixty years the name "Anaconda" has been symbolic of copper, onetime Cinderella of mining. From being regarded as a nuisance in the early hectic days of the Butte camp, it has become the indispensable metal. Without copper, steel is an inert mass. The Machine Age developed through the utilization of these two vital metals, with copper making the era of electricity and wire communication possible. The Machine Age has reached its maximum development in the United States where, with

340

only 7 per cent of the world's population, there is consumed each year approximately 51 per cent of the world's copper production.

Copper per capita consumption in this country in 1955 was 16.24 pounds as compared with 5 pounds in 1900, 6.3 pounds in 1930 and 9.5 pounds in 1940. Consumption in the Free World countries is 2.4 pounds a person and 1.4 pounds in other countries. In these figures you have an illuminating commentary on the American way of life to which the red metal is such a contributory factor.

Based on a report by the Econometric Institute, world population is increasing at the rate of 1.4 per cent a year—1.7 per cent in the United States. Assuming that consumption continues at the same rate as in 1955 for the next ten years, there will be an increased demand for copper of 16.86 per cent over 1955.

With increasing consumption of copper in mind, the inevitable question arises—what is the future reserve of this all-important metal? Ten years ago alarmists were predicting that there remained only a twenty-five or thirty year reserve. With oil there is a safeguard against depletion of reserve because oil can be produced from coal for all commercial purposes. There can be no synthetic copper. In the final analysis, man has not yet found a substitute for it.

Despite copper's versatility it must meet the competition of aluminum in view of the recent advances in metallurgy. This competition, however, poses no serious threat. Although aluminum has, to some extent, encroached upon some of copper's traditional markets, there is no concern among copper producers because the markets for their products are not only growing but new uses are being found for the metal.

How, then, can the copper reserve be safeguarded? Anaconda is doing its full share to insure a future supply for its operations. In the vein mines at Butte there is constant effort on the part of management to keep reserves ahead of increasing production. Development procedure has long succeeded in replacing every ton of ore mined with a new ton, which means that the tonnage available for mining at the beginning of each year shows no decline.

The ton for ton procedure is only part of Anaconda's operations at Butte to insure an adequate future supply of copper ore. The Greater Butte Project and the development of adjacent areas, already described in this narrative, will make for a reserve of 180,000,000 tons of copper ore. Intensive diamond drilling and development work have disclosed an entirely new concept of the Butte District. The company can look forward to a larger and greater future even than for the period of the Hill's glorious history as a mineral producing field. The expanded producing area at Chuquicamata and the rich promise of El Salvador combine to increase the Anaconda reserve. Anaconda today has a larger ore reserve than at any time in its long history.

Anaconda is writing another insurance policy for its future supply of copper ore with the highly organized and efficient Geological Department. The evolution of this activity spans an interesting chapter in mining history and is rich in both promise and achievement.

Back in the time of Daly and Clark and, for that matter, decades previous to their entry upon the mining scene geology, so far as the location of ore deposits was concerned, was an unknown quantity. The prospector was the sole mine seeker. With his burro and grubstake he roamed the hills. He was the lone wolf of mining for he usually went on his own. He wanted no prying eyes to behold the long elusive pot of gold at the end of his rainbow if he were lucky enough to find it. The sky was his roof, the campfire his hearth, the vast solitude of nature his sole companion. Prototype of the "wildcatters," whose indomitable faith opened up empires of oil, the prospector contributed a picturesque chapter to the drama of what became a great industry. Oldtime prospectors found Anaconda, Cripple

Creek, Tombstone, Leadville, the Comstock Lode, Silver City and many of the other famous bonanzas.

The day of the prospector is now gone. No longer does he make his lonely forays into the stony places for the reason that external ground indications are practically picked clean. The search for ore is largely underground. With the passing of the prospector, romance departed from mining. Science, in the form of geological research and exploration, has taken its place. The geologist, equipped with an array of scientific apparatus, has superseded the prospector's hunch. Prospecting has become an art with a technique that would amaze the onetime delver who went on the hunt with pick, shovel and pan.

It remained for Reno H. Sales, then associated with Horace Winchell in Butte, to pioneer the way for the technique of accurate, detailed geologic mapping which has become standard practice today. In the hectic days of the Heinze legal battle it became imperative for Anaconda to refute the Heinze apex claims with detailed maps of underground workings. These maps formed part of Anaconda's arsenal of defense in the long-drawn litigation. On more than one occasion Sales risked his life to obtain the needful data. Such was the origin of scientific mapping which now plays such a potent part in Anaconda mine exploration.

Scientific mine exploration received an impetus following the depression. Alleged experts were publicizing the fact that the copper supply would be exhausted in twenty or thirty years. When Weed became Vice President in charge of mining operations he sensed the value of stimulated scientific exploration, sparked it with his vision and energy, and brought about an expansion of what had already become something of a program. At every stage Kelley stood behind it.

The Anaconda Geological Department conducts its exploration in both old and new areas. Due to its efforts Yerington, Darwin, Shoshone, El Salvador, part of The

Greater Butte Project and Grants were developed. At Grants, as you have seen in a previous chapter, aviation was, and remains, an important factor in exploration.

There is a geological unit in every going Anaconda mine operation, working in conjunction with the operating staff. It translates observations into accurate geological plans and cross-sections. From planning and mapping, the next step is drilling, shaft sinking and tunneling which locate the ore if it is present.

The close coordination of geological exploration and mine operation is responsible for the entry of new areas into the ken of Anaconda operation. This welding of interests became the means of developing and maintaining ore reserves for Potrerillos, Butte and other districts contributing to the Anaconda output. At Chuquicamata the coordinated effort of geology and mine operation has more accurately defined the great open pit ore body and aided materially in its exploitation.

Two phases of the work of perpetuating Anaconda's supply of raw materials will indicate the interlocking of geology and the mining and metallurgical functions. One is in a red brick building in the heart of the plant area in Anaconda. At casual glance the observer might merely regard it as just another plant structure. Yet, inside that building is being written another part of Anaconda's insurance policy for future ore supply.

The red brick structure is the Practical Research Laboratory housing Research Engineering. It was devised by Frederick F. Frick when he was Research Engineer Director. Frick, as was the case with so many of his Anaconda colleagues who rose to eminence in their profession, began as laborer in the then Anaconda Copper Mining Company after his graduation from the Colorado School of Mines. He then became a fireman in the Reverberatory Department. His advent into the Technical Staff gave him the first opportunity to utilize the talents that made him one of the metallurgical greats. It was here that he met Laist, then Chief Chemist, with whom he developed a close and enduring friendship. Together, they achieved what was little less than metallurgical miracles. One of Frick's conspicuous achievements, among the many operating processes which concerned him, was his association with the electrolytic zinc process, an epochal event in metallurgy. Frick became Research Engineer Director in 1915. Upon his retirement in 1955 he was succeeded by Francis L. Holderreid, who had been his able assistant.

The Practical Research Building contains a complete pilot plant which includes miniature working models of grinding mills, flotation, roasting furnace and equipment for what is called housekeeping work.

One vital operation makes for more economic processes in the extraction of low-grade ore considered valueless in many instances. Even a quarter of a century ago only higher grade ore was mined. Ore of less copper content was left in the mine. Summed up, one objective of research is to make the reject of today the ore of tomorrow.

The importance of the work in the Practical Research Laboratory cannot be overestimated. Part of its task is to anticipate future demands and increase output to meet the ever-expanding use of copper for air conditioning, radio, television, kitchen equipment, refrigerators and motor cars.

The second phase is in the so-called Moonlight Laboratory in Butte. Here are two procedures. One is basic geological research to obtain knowledge of ore mineralization and associated rocks. The other is to serve as a utility for mineralogical problems. Research scientists work in the laboratory on a variety of problems involving both the study of deposits owned and operated by The Anaconda Company and new prospects under consideration as possible sources for additional ore supply.

There is also a Geophysical Laboratory located at Tooele,

Utah, where advanced basic research is under way to discover new methods for the effective measurement of physical phenomena as a means of detecting the presence of hidden ore deposits. Application of new and established techniques in geophysics is directed from the Tooele Geophysical Center.

Mines are a wasting asset. Hence, the urgent need for new deposits if the supply of copper is to be maintained and, if possible, increased. The one formula for replenishment lies in what the Geological Department is achieving. Research, laboratory work on ideas and rocks, and the synthesis of mineral relationship, are being capitalized to create a new philosophy of ore finding. Mines must be found in the new scientific way. It involves statistical studies of old workings, district regional studies in South America, Canada and Mexico, exploration for new ore, improved extraction and the enlistment of substitutes in the shape of new metals such as aluminum to enhance the supply of basic raw materials. Under the aegis of The Anaconda Company (Canada), Limited, a wholly owned subsidiary, extensive geological exploration is being carried on in Canada under a Dominion Charter.

Directing the all-important Geological Department is Vincent D. Perry who has eminent qualifications. He received his Engineer's Degree at the College of Mining of the University of California. Upon graduation he wrote to Sales, then Chief Geologist, asking for a job, only to be turned down. He then went to work as mucker in the Melones mine at Angel Camp, California. Here one of his fellow muckers was Brinckerhoff. Both were destined to high place in the Anaconda organization.

Perry then went to the Department of Geology of Columbia University for his Master of Arts degree determined to be an oil geologist. During his final year Sales delivered an address at the university. Perry paid his respects to him whereupon Sales asked him what he intended to do. When Perry told him he expected to be an oil geologist, Sales said: "Nonsense. I will give you a job as a mining geologist." In this way Perry entered into the Anaconda service. He became, in time, Chief Geologist at Cananea. Later he was named Chief Geologist of the company upon the retirement of Sales from that post after long and distinguished service. Anaconda still avails itself of Sales's service since he remains as Consulting Geologist.

The Geological Department is an invaluable asset of The Anaconda Company. In purpose, technique and operation, it is a bulwark for tomorrow.

Anaconda's research is not confined to the open spaces. In Butte there is a highly organized research department whose objective is greater efficiency in mine operation, safety and reduction of costs. Efficiency means larger output. Here is another safeguard for the future.

The present Research Department at Butte had its beginning many years ago with the inauguration of experimental investigation in rock drills and detachable bits. It was first known as the Efficiency Department and, later, as the Rock Drill Department. In 1927, Hobbins, then President of the company, decided that work of an investigative nature should be coordinated in a department to be known as the Engineering Research Department. From a modest start the activities of the Department have extended to cover practically every form of equipment and underground methods in use not only at Butte, but in every operation under control of Anaconda in various parts of the United States and elsewhere.

At the start the Department was placed in charge of E. R. Borcherdt who has developed it to the present stage of high efficiency. Its innovations and economies touch practically every Anaconda operation. It was Borcherdt who initiated timber package and the increase in the size of ore cars. These comprise only a few of the improvements he has achieved. He is now Director of Mining Research of all Anaconda properties.

Early in its work the Research Department realized the great advantage in cost reduction brought about by standardization of equipment. The mine switch represents a case in point. Formerly mine switches were constructed in small lots at the blacksmith shops at each mine. Individual preferences dictated the use of several types with variations in the details of their construction. The Research Department set about to produce a standard switch in large quantities at one of the large shops where the use of dies could be substituted for hand work. In this way the economies of mass production were achieved. A high grade product was the result with a low unit cost. Another benefit was derived. When a man changed from one mine to another, it was not necessary for him to learn how to install a switch different from the one he was accustomed to install. It is typical of many other changes, all making for economy in operation.

In New York, Anaconda conducts the Industrial Research Department instigated by Kelley in 1943 for the purpose of making an intensive study of the effect of plastics competition on the markets for copper and brass products. Since that time the Department, which is under the direction of Clarence W. MacKay, has been used by company executives for long-range planning and policy making, as well as for problems that arise from day to day. The activities of the Department may be grouped in three broad categories—Special Reports, Annual Industry Comparison Reports and Information and Reference Service.

Before Anaconda undertook to spend over $100,000,000 for additional facilities in Chile, Kelley asked the Department to prepare a twenty-year forecast of the demand for copper in the United States. This was several years before the United States Government Paley Report made long-range forecasting a commonly accepted business practice.

Shortly after General George Marshall made his famous speech at Harvard University on economic aid to Europe as a means of checking the growth of communism, the Department undertook a study to determine how much copper would be required by the Marshall Plan. Later, when war broke out in Korea, the Department made a study of copper requirements of the National Defense Effort of 1950–52. Of special interest are the many aluminum surveys and reports made by the Department. Starting with the original light metals report of 1943, there were over a dozen comprehensive aluminum studies made prior to Anaconda's decision to enter the aluminum field.

One of the most important services rendered by the Department is the issuance of the *Daily News Letter*. This is compiled from newspapers, magazines and other literature received in the library. All news that is considered of interest or importance to more than sixty Anaconda executives is reviewed and condensed into short paragraphs. Sources of information are listed if more details are desired. One outstanding feature of the *Daily News Letter* is that the information is compiled and printed the morning it is received and is on the desks of the New York executives by noon each day. This is the only company news letter in the metal industry that is published and distributed so promptly.

All this Anaconda research, whether indoors or out, reflects the tendency of industry today. Prior to 1930 industrial research was regarded as highly speculative and was engaged in by comparatively few corporations. Anaconda was one of the first to appreciate and capitalize its advantages. In 1930, when the Federal Government started research to develop military material, the amount expended for industrial research never exceeded $500,000 a year. Since that time the growth of industrial research has been little short of phenomenal. It has become one of the nation's great activities. One-half of the outlay for it is spent by industry on civilian problems and the remainder for military research.

Amid the expansion of Anaconda, stretching as it does from the Great Divide to the Andes, Butte stands as the cradle of the company, a community unique in the story of copper. The fabulous Hill, "breast-rounded among the cragged Rockies" and still the richest hill on earth, remains not only as a repository of mineral wealth but also the setting of gallant mining adventure.

Few, if any, other cities have undergone such kaleidoscopic change as Butte. Where once the flannel-shirted miners dominated the turbulent scene, today a varied citizenry, alive with civic pride, comprise a population that has more than quadrupled since the fateful day when Daly took over the Anaconda mine. Modern apartments have risen on the sites of the tents of the rip-roaring days; department stores have been built where once the rough, board-front stores stood; stately churches have supplanted the frame meeting houses. Yet, with all its progress, Butte still retains something of the frontier touch. Greetings are hale and hearty; the Western broad-brimmed hat is the vogue; the silver dollar heavily burdens the pocket. Nor has Butte lost the setting so intimately associated with its growth. On the scarred Hill which looks down upon the city the forest of headframes point skyward; you walk on mines that underlie the streets while blasts shake the pavements upon which you stroll. By day you have a dust-colored mining community but at night there is "a horse-shoe of incandescence" sparkling amid the granite slopes of the Rockies, a picture of surpassing beauty.

Over all Butte there spreads the generous hand of Anaconda, not only as a source of nearly sixty-five per cent livelihood, but as almoner of the community as well. There is scarcely an activity, civic or philanthropic, that does not know a company benefaction without regard to race, creed or color. Company generosity built the Butte Community

Memorial Hospital and endows the St. James Hospital; it gave the city the beautiful Columbia Gardens, a happy playground for young and old.

Anaconda's solicitude for its workers is fittingly expressed in the Employees Club, housed in a five-story building in the heart of the city. Once the Thornton Hotel, it is now the popular rendezvous of the company employees in the Butte area. The wives or husbands of employees are associate members. Its membership of more than 10,000 makes it the largest social-recreational club west of the Mississippi River. Operation is on a "no dues" basis.

On the ground floor of the club is the main lounge, a snack bar, and a large assembly hall called the Crystal Room which has stage and screen facilities. The main lounge, with its high-beamed ceiling, numerous windows, comfortable furnishings and effective lighting, is adorned with oil paintings by Montana artists. There are also a pool-billiard room, a game room and bowling alleys.

The Employees Club at Butte is typical of the interest that Anaconda displays for its 46,707 workers which are spread over two continents. Wherever you find a company installation, whether mine or plant, you find the best possible working conditions and adequate recreational facilities.

Unlike some corporations, Anaconda has never recruited a top executive from another company. Anaconda's executives have all risen, not only from the ranks but in many instances have advanced from manual labor in, or about, mines. The list of onetime muckers, for example, who have attained high status includes Weed, Newlin, Caples, Mendelsohn, Sales, Brinckerhoff, McGlone, Perry, A. C. Bigley, Knaebel, Mitchell and Wardlaw. Dwyer started in the blacksmith shop at Anaconda; Mitchell and Frick began as laborers.

From its beginning as a corporate entity, the company has given its employees every opportunity for advance-

ment. Nor has advance ever created envy or jealousy.
Rather has it stimulated ambition for a larger dedication
to company accomplishment. Moreover, the humblest
worker can put forth his ideas, have them considered and,
in many cases, adopted. As Kelley once put it, "Where
else can you get the same knowledge, the same loyalty that
an organization like Anaconda develops? If you had super-
men, God-blessed, you could not get it without years of
training and experience."

Upon assuming the chairmanship Glover initiated a personnel and an industrial relations program, each of which
has been received in the organization with enthusiasm. The
purpose of the industrial relations program is to keep everyone in the organization informed as fully as possible of the
prospects and problems of the company. It is directed toward executive and laborer alike, and covers the entire
organization, domestic and foreign.

At a staff dinner in Butte, on May 16, 1956, Glover described the objectives of the program:

"If you tell employees what the score is, if you tell them what
we are trying to do, get it across to them. Let them understand
and, even more important, try to understand *their* problems. If you
do that, you will find you have a partner instead of an antagonist.
And that is what we want in our Anaconda organization.

"We are all working for the same objectives and we are engaged
in an industry than which there is nothing more important in this
material world, the production of non-ferrous metals. And that is
the real objective of our industrial relations program. We want
you men who are in positions of responsibility to be advised and
to insist that you have information. If there is anything that is
bothering you or that you would like to know, we want you to
freely ask and we will see that you obtain it, because there is not a
hidden page in our book, not one, and there is not one page of it of
which we are not proud.

"The other thing I would like to talk about is our personnel
program, which, as of the present time, is limited to our salaried
employees. You will probably be surprised to know that we have

ten thousand eight hundred and some of salaried employees in the Anaconda organization. That is quite a lot and we have not had much information about them beyond their immediate superiors. I had an example of that in our Research at Anaconda. Mr. Caples and Mr. Holderreid were looking over the outside field for men. They took a look at our personnel cards—it is only the domestic branches that are completed—and found over one hundred in our Anaconda organization who had metallurgical research background of one kind or another. Some of them were in such jobs that we could not hire them for research but, nevertheless, there they were.

"You may have wondered why we insisted on having each of those cards filled out by the individual instead of having a clerk or supervisor help you to fill it out. We wanted to get your concept of yourself. In setting up that program we had the benefit of research and work that has gone into personnel programs of great industrial organizations all over the United States and abroad. Ford Motor Company, for instance, had a team of men working for two years just preparing their code of classifications. It came the most nearly to being a code that would fit Anaconda. They said, 'Here, we like you people. Please take this with our compliments and adapt it to your needs.' We have had fine cooperation all through industry and we have examined personnel systems of the very best from the East to the West and from the North to the South in the United States and we have a system that I think fits Anaconda and our organization both here and abroad.

"The idea, fellows, is to knit it all together. We are a great big outfit. We are pretty small in individual units. Every card is classified as to the potential skill of the individual. There will be a complete file of the entire organization maintained in the New York office, and there again we have gone out to bring together the company knitted into one. We have a fellow from the Brass Company who has gone down to New York for our industrial relations organization, and to his great surprise we brought a fellow up from Antofagasta, Chile, and put him in charge of personnel in the New York office. The idea back of it is that whenever there is a job available we will look at our personnel cards in a division and see what is there. If we do not have somebody, we go to the central file and see whether there is somebody in Potrerillos, Grants, Butte, or Conda, Idaho, or anywhere else, that would have the qualifications to do that job. If there is a man hired from the outside there will have to be adequate reason shown why he was not available within our own organization.

"We want to feed the fellows in from the bottom. We want the fellows in this organization to start at the bottom and we want to bring them along. There is nothing mysterious in any of these jobs of ours, provided a man has the technical qualifications and good brains. We think we can follow this policy of bringing the men from the bottom and bringing them on up through the organization. That is the purpose and the objective of this personnel program. We do not want a man to feel that when he sits at a desk in an office in Butte he is limited to that particular job or department, but that he has a chance with everybody else for every job that comes along.

"We hope to arrange for an interview with every man at least once each year to talk over his situation with him, to discuss with him what progress he is making and what he is doing to improve himself for a better job, and to give him guidance and help. The result of the interview becomes part of his file. A man may have concluded that he wants to take a correspondence course in electrical engineering. He may be up at the warehouse. We find out what he is trying to do. Let us try to help him. We see what progress he is making and let us see if we can put him in a place where he can fulfill his objectives. Each one of you should constitute yourself a committee of one and organize it to the best that you can, to bring along fellows under you to guide them, to help them, to encourage them to get a good future for the fellow who will get down and work, plug into it intelligently and try to better himself."

Appraise the reasons for Anaconda's success and you find that Kelley's almost uncanny ability to foresee the possibilities of the future and to capitalize them, has been a dominant factor. Moreover, his understanding of the problems of his subordinates has achieved a unity of effort that has invariably accomplished results. In short, Anaconda personnel, far and near, has worked as a team, loyal to its chief.

On the mining and processing side, success has stemmed from faith and initiative to explore new fields, from progressive improvement in metallurgical methods, from large-scale conversion of low-grade ore into a profitable product, from research in every phase of company operations, from courage to expand in troubled economic times when the rest of industry was contracting and finally, from diversification of output to meet the needs of a changing world. Behind, and animating all this, has been the dynamic leadership of Kelley, a constant source of inspiration for both high and low in the service of the company.

One of the most striking developments in American industry over the past two decades has been the increase in the number of stockholders in large corporations. It betokens a rising interest in companies that serve their needs and make for a betterment of their way of life. These stockholders are the real owners of the concerns whose stock they own and are thus enabled to exercise a proprietary interest in them.

Many stockholders merely sign, or fail to sign, proxies automatically and let it go at that. The 115,848 holders of Anaconda stock who, at this writing account for 8,674,000 shares, are not automatic proxy signers. As a typical example, at the annual meeting held May 16, 1956, 79.32 per cent of the shares outstanding were present in person or represented by proxy. This was the largest stock representation that has ever been achieved at any annual meeting in the history of the company. Three hundred and thirty-five people attended the meeting. Every one of the forty-eight states is represented in the roster of Anaconda stockholders, the largest number being in New York, with Pennsylvania second and California third. Canada, United States possessions and Holland are included in the list.

The distribution of shares and the sex of individual owners reveal interesting figures. The number of female stockholders is 52,707 while males number 43,344. The remainder of the stock is distributed among fiduciaries, institutions, brokers and others. Another fact worthy of note is that by far the greatest number of holdings by an individual is in from 1 to 24 shares. That "little man," so to speak, is becoming a factor in corporate life as attested by the revelation that, as of the end of 1955, there were 8,630,000 stockholders in the nation's publicly held companies, a gain of 33 per cent in the preceding four years. Two-thirds of them earn less than $7,500 a year.

This, then, is the story of Anaconda, an industrial epic that is part of the larger epic of America. In the sixty-one years since its incorporation as The Anaconda Copper Mining Company which became The Anaconda Company of today, the most kaleidoscopic period in the march of civilization has been recorded. Empires have fallen, dynasties have tottered, the map of the world has undergone drastic alteration. Radical political ideologies have nurtured a super-state which is Russia; two global wars have ravaged the life and economy of over half the globe; the worst depression man has ever known took toll of capital and confidence; the miracles of the Oil, Steel and Motorcar Ages reached fruition. With the assembly line giving us industrial supremacy, the United States rose to financial and political leadership. It has been the most fabulous period of growth the universe has ever witnessed. Metals, copper in particular, have comprised one measure of that growth, for we live in a civilization made possible by metals.

Through those sometime fateful and troubled years, Anaconda rode the storms, advanced the frontiers of metals and reared a far-flung empire of production undeterred by economic retrogressions. It has contributed giants of metallurgy to the Mining Hall of Fame and written a saga of endeavor that is the biography of a Titan in metal output. Daly's dream of a great copper-producing entity has not only come true, but has far exceeded his imagination because he could not have envisioned the diversity of product that obtains today.

Thus, The Anaconda Company moves into another phase of its development prepared to make its contribution to a world of new needs and new ideas, a world where fresh challenges will be made and met and new goals realized. From its beginning in that small shaft on Butte Hill the company has expanded increasingly, and those who have participated in its growth, employees and shareholders alike, have benefited by their association with it. Down the years Anaconda has kept pace with the rapid changes in our economy, anticipating the needs of tomorrow and the demands made upon it. The metals it produces are essential to modern life.

Forward is the watchword. Anaconda is on the march.

INDEX

Sierra de Cobre mine, 255
Silesia, 6, 263
Silver, 1, 3, 7, 9, 13, 15, 19–32, 35, 37–39, 42–45, 50, 56, 57, 58, 90, 92, 134, 282, 289
Silver Bow Club, 106, 148
Silver Bow County, Montana, 66
Silver Bow Creek, 19, 20, 24, 76
Silver Bow mine, 24, 81
Silver Bow Town, 20, 27, 29
Silver Bow Water Company, 56
Silver Chief mine, 44
Silver City, 343
Silveropolis mine, 44
Single Tax mine, 81
Sister mine, 81
Skyrme, William, 61
Smith, Professor, 75
Smith, Robert B., 87
Smith Valley (Nevada), 266
"Smoke Case," 104–105
Snohomish mine, 124, 133
Snoozer mine, 133
Snow Bird mine, 124
Snowball mine, 81
Soda Springs, Idaho, 153
Sonora Hill mine, 265
South Dakota, 39
Southern California, University of, 210
Southern Pacific Railroad, 255, 269
Sowerwine, E. O., 262–264
Speculator mine, 81
Spencer, Aaron, 80
Spokane, Washington, 324, 325
Sprackling, W. E., 186
Spriggs, Lieutenant Governor, 87
Spring Creek, Montana, 55
Stahlman, Otto, 52
Standard Fire Brick Company, 88
Standard Oil Company, 93, 96, 116–117, 128
Steel, 340
Steele, Chester H., 269, 282, 328
Stewart mine, 140, 142
Stillman, James, 95
Stillwater County, Montana, 232, 233
Stivers, DeGay, 78
Storrs, Montana, 55
Stranahan, C. R., 316
Stripkill, Ltd., 247
Stuart, Granville, 16, 17
Stuart, James, 16
Sudden, Herman, 38
Sullivan, Julia, 68
Sullivan, Margaret, 68
Sullivan, Mrs. Margaret, 68
Sullivan, Nora, 68
Sulphuric acid, 91, 153, 233, 270, 285, 286, 288
Summit Valley District, 20
Superior mine, 259
Superphosphate, 7, 153, 154, 233, 286
Supreme Court of the United States, 113
Surracino, Willie, 301
Swan Lake, 103, 104
Swansea, Wales, 21–22, 47, 50, 253

Sycamore, Illinois, 186, 187, 249
Syndicate group, 57
Syracuse Standard, The, 63

Taussig, F. W., 156
Tecopa, California, 282, 291
Tempaloy, 181
Tennessee, 13
Tennessee Copper Company, The, 108
Terre Haute, Indiana, 176, 331
Territorial Enterprise, The, 43
Tevis, Lloyd, 33, 34, 35, 38, 50, 79, 88, 92
Texas, University of, 268
Texas Gulf Sulphur Company, 267
Thayer, Benjamin B., 101, 138, 144, 223–224, 258
Thomas, Henry ("Gold Tom"), 16
Thompson Falls Power Company, 146
Thornton, J. J. C., 258
Thornton, W. D., 258
Timber Butte Milling Company, 149
Tobin Bronze, 179
Toconce pipeline, 203, 204
Tocopilla, Chile, 199, 203, 209
Tombstone, 13, 65, 252, 253, 343
Tonopah, 108
Tooele, Utah, 143, 230, 291, 292, 345–346
Tooele Valley Railroad, 143
Toole, Joseph K., 128
Torrance, California, 327
Torrington, Connecticut, 171, 172, 174, 176, 182
Town Gulch, See Dublin Gulch
Town Site Company, 145
Trail, British Columbia, 121
Tramway mine, 124, 133, 277, 283
Travona mine, 23, 24, 81, 84, 232
Treasure City, 43
Treble-superphosphate, 7, 154, 288, 324
Tremblay, Joseph A., 103
Tremblay, Mary, See Kelley, Mrs. Cornelius (Mary)
Trenton Mining & Development Company, 95, 139
Treloar, Sam, 149
Truman, Harry S., 335
Tubular Woven Fabrics Company, 186
Tuolumne claim, 30, 81
Turquoise Gulch area, 216
Tuttle Manufacturing Company, 88
Twain, Mark, 43, 191
"Type ANW," 192
Type CB Cable, 192

Union Consolidated group, 57, 90
Union Pacific Railroad, 27, 43–44, 153
United Copper Company, The, 123, 134
United Metals Selling Company, 80, 114, 143, 193
United Press, 320
United States Bureau of Indian Affairs, 301
United States Bureau of Mines, 151, 237
United States Government Paley Report, 348

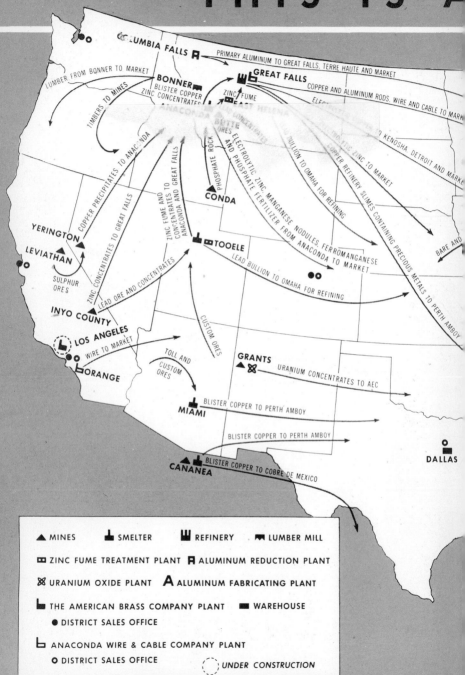

THIS IS A

LUMBER FROM BONNER TO MARKET

PRIMARY ALUMINUM TO GREAT FALLS, TERRE HAUTE AND MARKET

COLUMBIA FALLS

BONNER
BLISTER COPPER
ZINC CONCENTRATES

GREAT FALLS
ZINC FUME
EAST HELENA
ANACONDA
BUTTE
COPPER AND ALUMINUM RODS, WIRE AND CABLE TO MARKET

COPPER
ORES
CONCENTRATES

TIMBERS TO MINES

TO KENOSHA, DETROIT AND MARKET

COPPER PRECIPITATES TO ANACONDA

PHOSPHATE ROCK

CONDA

ELECTROLYTIC ZINC, MANGANESE NODULES, FERROMANGANESE
AND PHOSPHATE FERTILIZER FROM ANACONDA TO MARKET

BULLION TO OMAHA FOR REFINING

COPPER REFINERY SLIMES CONTAINING PRECIOUS METALS TO PERTH AMBOY

YERINGTON

LEVIATHAN

SULPHUR
ORES

ZINC CONCENTRATES TO GREAT FALLS

LEAD ORE AND CONCENTRATES

ZINC FUME AND
CONCENTRATES TO
ANACONDA AND GREAT FALLS

TOOELE

LEAD BULLION TO OMAHA FOR REFINING

BARE AND

INYO COUNTY

LOS ANGELES
WIRE TO MARKET

ORANGE

CUSTOM ORES

TOLL AND
CUSTOM
ORES

GRANTS

URANIUM CONCENTRATES TO AEC

MIAMI
BLISTER COPPER TO PERTH AMBOY

BLISTER COPPER TO PERTH AMBOY

DALLAS

CANANEA
BLISTER COPPER TO COBRE DE MEXICO

▲ MINES ⚒ SMELTER ⊞ REFINERY ⋈ LUMBER MILL

⊡ ZINC FUME TREATMENT PLANT ☐ ALUMINUM REDUCTION PLANT

✖ URANIUM OXIDE PLANT A ALUMINUM FABRICATING PLANT

⌐ THE AMERICAN BRASS COMPANY PLANT ▬ WAREHOUSE
● DISTRICT SALES OFFICE

⌐ ANACONDA WIRE & CABLE COMPANY PLANT
○ DISTRICT SALES OFFICE

⌐⌐⌐⌐ UNDER CONSTRUCTION